Confessions of a Left-Handed Man

sightline books

The Iowa Series in Literary Nonfiction

Patricia Hampl & Carl H. Klaus, series editors

Peter Selgin

Confessions of a Left-Handed Man

An Artist's Memoir

University of Iowa Press, Iowa City

University of Iowa Press, Iowa City 52242
Copyright © 2011 by University of Iowa Press
www.uiowapress.org
Printed in the United States of America
Text design by Richard Hendel

The University of Iowa Press is a member of Green
Press Initiative and is committed to preserving natural
resources.

Printed on acid-free paper

Library of Congress
Cataloging-in-Publication Data
Selgin, Peter.
Confessions of a left-handed man : an artist's memoir /
By Peter Selgin.
p.   cm.—(Sightline books: the Iowa series in literary
nonfiction)
ISBN: 978-1-60938-056-4, 1-60938-056-8 (pbk.)
ISBN: 978-1-60938-057-1, 1-60938-057-6 (e-book)
1. Selgin, Peter.   2. Authors, American—
21st century—Biography.   I. Title.
PS3619.E463Z46 2011   2011014174
813'.6—dc22
[B]

FOR OLIVER

"If the left side of your brain controls the right side of your body and the right side of your brain controls the left side of your body, then left-handed people must be the only ones in their right minds."
—W. C. FIELDS

"A work of art is a confession."
—ALBERT CAMUS

Contents

Acknowledgments

My thanks to Joe Parsons and Carl Klaus at University of Iowa Press for instigating this project and shepherding me through it.

Versions of some essays herein appeared in the following journals and are reprinted here by permission: "Dead to Rights: Confessions of a Caricaturist," *Colorado Review* (Spring 2008); "Dagos in Mayberry," *Our Roots Are Deep with Passion* (Other Press, 2006); "Black Words on Yellow Paper," *New Millennium Writings* (July 2005); "Straight Job," *Writers on the Job: Tales of Non-Writing* (Web Del Sol Press online version, February 2009); "Gjetost," *Alimentum* (Winter 2009); "To Die of Italy," *Ducts.org* (Winter 2001); "Keeping Up with the Days," originally published in *The Cincinnati Review* (Spring 2008), reprinted in *Writers and Their Notebooks* (University of South Carolina Press, 2010); "Estranged on a Train," *Salon.com* (2000); "Confessions of a Left-Handed Man," originally published in *The Literary Review* (Spring 2005), reprinted in *Best American Essays 2006* (Houghton Mifflin, 2006); "Restaurant," *Bellevue Literary Review* (Fall 2006); "My Locomotive God," *Tiferet* (Summer 2005); "The Man from Stanboul," *The Sun* (Spring 2007); "Alone: Two Types of Solitude," *Gulf Coast* (Spring 2010); "The Swimming Pool," *Fourth Genre* (Fall 2011).

Dead to Rights: Confessions of a Caricaturist

. . . and all the nice people will only
see the exaggeration as caricature.
—Vincent van Gogh

Early Influences

n kindergarten, when I presented her with crayon drawings of the *Queen Mary* and of the Empire State Building lit up like a Christmas tree at night, Mrs. Decker kissed my cheek, my first taste of artistic glory. By fifth grade already I was drawing faces. At the summer camp where my parents sent me (called Silver Lake, though on the map the same body of water went by "Mudge Pond"), I sat with a nineteen-cent Bic and notebook at a picnic table and "did" everyone, portraits the size of postage stamps. My likenesses may have been hit or miss, but I was a hit. Thanks to my drawing pen, for the first time I felt popular. Heather McGowan even agreed to go out on a canoe with me. The canoe tipped over. Still, I felt triumphant.

In high school I drew Mr. Schnabel, with his manatee nose and outrageous comb-over, and Mrs. Rigsdale, my French teacher, with her twisting Carvel cone of white hair. Those teachers with a sense of humor praised my talent; the rest sent me down to Mr. DeMillo's office. Since I was of Italian lineage, like him, Principal DeMillo found me *simpatico*. Seeing my latest artistic affront, he shook his bald-as-a-bowling-ball head, but could not contain a smile. "Pete," he said, "in choosing your subjects you need to exercise more discretion." On the other hand he had to admit that I'd gotten Mrs. Rigsdale "dead to rights."

To pin someone's likeness to a page in a few deft strokes, to snatch not only people's faces but their souls from thin air, to own them on paper, there was magic in it, something talismanic and even voodoo-like. In sketching them I distilled their essences, and could do with those essences what I pleased. Heady powers for a teenager.

My artistic gods were Vincent van Gogh and Mort Drucker. The first cut off an ear and painted burning cypresses under pinwheel skies at night. The second you would know if, like most late baby boomers, you grew up on *MAD* magazine. Drucker drew the movie satires, comic-book-style parodies of the latest movies. If van Gogh was the god of color, Drucker was the god of line. What that man couldn't do with a pen and ink. With the faintest thickening of stroke he'd render the shadow under a nose or a shirt cuff. No one, not even Al Hirschfeld—whose style I found too "arty"—could better Drucker's likenesses. His Paul Newman looked more like Paul Newman than Paul Newman. He got their gestures, down, too: Brando scratching his jaw in *The Godfather*, Burt Lancaster and Kirk Douglas each clenching three rows of teeth, Cary Grant always leaning slightly, like the Tower of Pisa, Katherine Ross ever on the verge of tears.

Through high school I taught myself to draw just like Drucker, carrying notebook and pen with me everywhere. When friends got sick of my drawing them, I worked from photos of movie stars. After graduating, not knowing what else to do with my life, I took a job as the helper on a furniture truck and kept my notebook with me as we rode to Wappinger's Falls to deliver a sofa bed, and to Great Barrington with someone's grandfather clock. The warehouse guys called me Leo, as in Leonardo da Vinci, and didn't mind my drawing them as long as I didn't make their beer bellies too big.

Going to art school felt more like a defeat than a decision. Drawing had been a personal, semi-intimate pleasure, with a tinge of naughtiness about it, like good sex. To expose it to pedagogy seemed a bad idea. My professors swiftly set to work to cure me of my bad habit, as if drawing caricatures were the equivalent not of sex but of something less productive, like nose or toenail picking. My protests—that Leonardo, Daumier, Monet, and Picasso, to name a few, had all been caricaturists—fell on deaf ears. An unrepentant sinner, I practiced my vice in secret, doodling likenesses of the model's face (we'd been instructed to ignore faces and genitals) on a corner of my newsprint pad, obliterating them with charcoal whenever the moderator came by. Telling me not to draw the model's face was like leading an alcoholic to an open bar with instructions to drink only ginger ale.

I tried to be good, I did, but always the impulse toward swift line and rude gesture rose up to defeat me. Blaustein, my painting professor, stepped up behind me one day in his studio and said, "You know what you are, Selgin? You're an artistic illiterate. Your paintings are all pat graphics and glib surface. They lack depth, struggle. You'll never be a fine artist."

Maybe Blaustein was right. Hell, I'd never even wanted to be a painter anyway. I hated the smell of turpentine and those little nubs in canvas that looked like plucked chicken flesh. I liked pens, ink, paper. I liked drawing; I liked to draw. For people like me, there wasn't even a decent name, nothing that carried the artistic panache of "painter." *Draughtsman? Drawer? Sketch artist?* Such was the prejudice of those who worked in pigment against those who expressed themselves by means of pure line, the dreg horses of the art world.

But even fine art *drawers* looked down upon caricaturists, just as they looked down on all those they lumped together as cartoonists: pen-wielding mercenaries, makers of comic strips and cartoons, frivolity for the hoi polloi. The closest thing to respect earned by such low enterprises came in the form of appropriation, with pop artists plagiarizing, blown up on canvas, the labors of unsung comic-book artists. If this was a form of flattery, it was booby-trapped. To accept it was to accept that the originals were anything but art. It took *real* artists to instill such works with a value beyond that of plebian amusement.

Around this time I met my hero, Mort Drucker. In despair of my low artistic status, I had written him a fan letter accompanied by a caricature of myself. He invited me to his home in a Long Island suburb, one of thousands of identical ranch houses clustered into a development, with water sprinklers spitting bows of water over half-acre lawns. Inside his house, in place of the bohemian wit, poetry, and irreverence I'd expected, I was met by the trappings of bourgeois conservatism, down to the framed Norman Rockwell prints on the wall. It was the home of a shoe salesman. In Mort's tidy studio, while I sipped a Coke on ice, he showed me the pens and paper he used, his kid-finish Bristol boards and Hunt crow quills. But by then my disenchantment was already complete. Superimposed over Drucker's voice I could hear Professor Blaustein sneering, *artistic illiterate!* Later, at the train station as we sat together in his station wagon waiting for my train, Drucker smoked an illicit cigarette and confessed to me how at times he still couldn't believe his fortune, that he could stay home drawing pictures while others toiled away at dull office jobs. Mort was a decent, modest, hard-working man, and talented, a superb technician, but not the person I had hoped he would be, someone to legitimize my artistic passions, and I rode the train home feeling betrayed.

A week later, after another dispiriting afternoon in Blaustein's class, I flicked on the portable TV in my room, and Richard Burton's acne-pocked face filled the screen. In his deep Welsh baritone, he murmured something about "bergin," "bergin and water." As he murmured on I kept watching, mesmerized. I watched the whole movie.

The next day at the Pratt Institute Library, among its glass-floored stacks, I found a copy of Edward Albee's *Who's Afraid of Virginia Woolf?* There, in black and white, was the "bergin" speech. I sat down on the glass floor and read the whole play. That a bunch of tiny black marks on a page had held me so in thrall astonished me. By the time I turned the last page, I'd made up my mind. I was going to be a writer.

I quit art school and hitchhiked around the country. I still carried a notebook and pen, only now instead of faces I filled the notebook with words. Where drawing had led me only to surfaces, words (I promised myself) would take me deeper.

First Commerce

Still, I had to eat. I was twenty-five and had worked all the usual shit jobs—waiting tables and washing dishes in restaurants, and driving trucks—when it occurred to me that I could live off my drawings of people. The bar down in Soho where I was washing dishes hired only struggling artists. It had an open kitchen and during slow periods, on the backs of yellow bar dupes, I'd sketch patrons as they sat at the bar. We taped the results to a wall next to the chalk menu. One day a customer asked one of the bar's owners who'd done the sketches. The boss pointed my way. The customer, a fashion designer, hired me to draw people at a party he was throwing. He paid me thirty dollars an hour, ten times my pearl-diving wage. I made a hundred bucks that night. A fluke, I thought then.

But then a few months later at a different job, this one at a copy shop, the same thing happened. Out of boredom I'd started drawing the other workers and our regular customers, putting their faces on display. It gave us all a laugh. The boss, Mr. Cheswick, didn't mind. He may have considered it good PR.

One day a woman came into the shop, pointed to a sketch of mine, and said, "How much?" I turned to Mr. Cheswick, who held up five fingers. "Five dollars." The woman nodded. I did her caricature, put it in a bag, and rang up the sale on the register. Soon the store was making good money on my caricatures, and I felt entitled to a raise. When Mr. Cheswick said no, I got huffy.

I put an ad in *New York* magazine's classified section, under "Entertainers": "THE GOOD, THE BAD, AND THE BEAUTIFUL: Fabulous Faces by Peter Selgin." With my ex-coworkers' help at the copy shop, and in Mr. Cheswick's absence, I created a brochure to mail to potential customers. Soon I got my first job, at a wedding reception in New Jersey. I had to rent a car and a tuxedo. After subtracting for them, the job netted me fifty dollars. I was launched.

Drawing an Income

For the next ten years I drew people at birthday parties, weddings, anniversaries, corporate events, and bar and bat mitzvahs. I worked at Sardi's, the Rainbow Room, the Four Seasons, 21, the Tavern on the Green, and Windows of the World. I was flown first-class to cities as far as Los Angeles, where, at a pool party in Beverly Hills, stars lined up for their likenesses. I drew my way across the Atlantic and back on the *QE2*, where I sketched the officers on duty on the bridge. When I sketched the captain standing in water up to his waist, he said, with a stiff British upper lip, "Hmm, I don't like the look of that." In gratitude the navigator flashed me the secret coordinates of the freshly discovered *Titanic* wreck.

I averaged fifty gigs a year, booked mostly between November and January first. In those weeks I would make enough money to carry me the whole year. I worked on yachts, trains, planes, and once on a private Learjet. I charged lawyers' fees, one hundred twenty-five dollars an hour, sometimes more, and insisted on being treated not as an entertainer, but as a special guest. Once, at a party thrown by a young Wall Street trader who'd just banked his first million, I arrived at the front door to be told by a butler that I had to use the servants' entrance.

"I'm not a servant," I informed him. "I'm a guest."

"All servants must use the servants' entrance," he repeated.

"In that case I hope you can draw," I replied and handed him my kit bag.

He let me in.

Five minutes, that's how long it took me to draw a caricature. Any longer would have been too slow. Like parts on an assembly line, the faces came and went. One face every five minutes, ten per hour, five hours per average gig, fifty caricatures per event. Times fifty events per year is twenty-five hundred faces; times ten years is twenty-five thousand—roughly the population of Aspen, Colorado, during high tourist season.

Some jobs were strange. Once my services were engaged by a guy who sought a novel way to propose to his girlfriend. Dressed up as a stereotypical French artist (striped shirt, beret) I sat, sketchpad in hand, on a bench in Central Park waiting for the couple to walk by. When they did, I all but assaulted the girl, saying, in my miserable French accent while framing her with my thumbs, "*Excuze-moi, mademoiselle*, but you have ze most *magnifique vision*. Please to allow me to draw it, *s'il vous plaît*." She demurred, but at her boyfriend's insistence she eventually gave in. What she didn't know was that the sketch had already been started and included a likeness of her beau genuflecting on the pavement in front of her. The image had scarcely registered when she turned to see the real man presenting her with a diamond ring as big as the Ritz. Since then I've often wondered, What if she had said no? What would I have done then? Given the money back?

Among the strangest events were what we called caricature "orgies," at which a dozen party caricaturists, the best in town, were herded into a ballroom at the Ritz-Carlton or the St. Regis. We'd set up individual workstations, then the floodgates would open and our subjects would pour in by the hundreds, Japanese businessmen, typically. They'd spend the entire party lining up and going from station to station to get their caricatures drawn, collecting as many as possible.

How to Draw a Caricature

To draw someone's caricature is to grasp their essence, a Zen-like undertaking, archery with a pen. People would ask me: What do you look for? Which parts do you emphasize? My answer: All, none. The whole, the gestalt, is what matters. As Max Beerbohm, who wrote as beautifully as he drew, said in his essay "The Spirit of Caricature": "The perfect caricature (be it of a handsome man or a hideous or an insipid) must be an exaggeration of the whole creature, from top to toe. Whatsoever is salient must be magnified, whatsoever is subordinate must be proportionately diminished. . . . The perfect caricature is bold in its execution, simple and ingenuous to its beholder as a wild flower."

With caricature there's no separating the parts from the whole, no chin except in relation to the jaw, no nose except in conjunction with lips and brow, no eyes without sockets, no hair without a skull grinning under the scalp. If someone sat before me with a jaw like an anvil, eyebrows like Lincoln's, or a nose like a toadstool, there would be that moment of isolated appreciation—as one admires a single character in a novel—but then one steps back to take in the story as a whole, the theme, if you will. No caricaturist worthy of the name draws parts and then, like Dr. Frankenstein, stitches them together; everything exists as a fraction of some total. A good caricature never exaggerates or distorts for distortion's sake but to get at the truth. Some of my subjects asked me to lie. "Leave out my freckles," they'd say, or "Give me more hair," or "Don't draw my double chin." Such requests I never honored. It was like asking a surgeon to amputate a perfectly healthy limb. I, too, was bound by an oath, one best expressed by Picasso: "Art is the lie that tells the truth."

How to draw a caricature? You start with mechanics, the basic forms: square, cone, cylinder, cube. Using these, you plot the basic features (using the eyes, or their positions, as guideposts: the double hubs of the wheel of the face), the head reduced to a set of geometric possibilities. From there you refine these basic shapes, ignoring superficialities like hair.

Then comes what I call *the moment*, and here no mechanical reductionism can penetrate. What happens then can be explained only by vague words like *magic* and *instinct*. As a horse knows its way back to its stable, the pen finds its way deep into the subject's soul. It does so through the eyes. At first the eyes are dead, without light, inert and dull as stones. But then, suddenly, if things go well, they flicker to life, and there on the page is someone looking at you. Meanwhile, the light has left the sitter's eyes—transposed, smuggled into the sketch.

As with the pianist who is only vaguely aware of his fingers, which seem to find the keys on their own, propelled by the notes that leap from the keyboard into his body—as if the piano were playing his fingers—so, too, with the caricaturist. Using the caricaturist's hand the subject's face "draws" its own likeness. All I had to do was find it on a sheet of paper with my pen, as Michelangelo found his *David* in a block of Carrara marble.

I'd start with a pencil—a mechanical one (no time for sharpening). In less than a minute I'd have the proportions roughed out. The next four minutes were given to inking, using smelly felt-tip markers with wet, flexible, V-shaped nibs, working swiftly but with a jeweler's precision; at this stage blowing a line would shatter the diamond. Done inking, I'd wipe away the traces of pencil with a kneaded eraser, an object of fascination to adults and children alike, who assumed it was a dead mouse or some sort of talisman with which I waved the pictures to life. (I never disenchanted them.)

Then I'd show them the result. This was my favorite part, seeing the faces I'd just drawn light up first with surprise and shock and then—hopefully—with a smile as they recognized and laughed at themselves. To see people laughing at themselves is to see them truly happy, free from the weight of self-importance that bears down on them through most of their days. One thing I learned from doing caricatures: *nobody really wants to be taken seriously*. In fact they yearn to be relieved of their seriousness. This lofty goal I helped my subjects achieve.

The Good, the Bad, and the Beautiful

The hardest faces to draw were the dead ones, the ones with no light in their eyes. I mean faces with no trace of wit, the kind that Hollywood and Madison Avenue churn out like widgets and that so many sixteen-year-olds crave, with the same bee-stung lips, the same high or sucked-in cheeks, the same stingy nostrils. When one of those faces sat down in front of me, I'd let out a silent groan, knowing I had my work cut out for me, and that the result was doomed to arouse only contempt and confusion in the wax figure whose insipid features I would soon replicate.

The best faces, on the other hand, belonged to old men. Old faces, with plenty of nooks and crannies for me to dig my pen nibs into—if only they would sit for me! But I rarely got to draw them. I'd see them out of the corner of my eye while sketching someone less inspiring. Sometimes I'd see someone so irresistible I'd chase after them, wanting to taste some cognac after guzzling gallons of tap-water bland faces.

Drawing beautiful women was a challenge and a luxury. What better excuse to look into their lovely eyes? They weren't easy to draw, true, but for all the right reasons. Not because their features were model "perfect" (read: symmetrical), but because their features were less easily pigeonholed into geometric shapes, and soft skin lends itself far less well to hard lines; it would rather be brushed or blurred. I had to coax the beautiful ones into smiling, they took their beauty so seriously, as though it were a religious calling or the cure for cancer. And though intrigued and aroused by some, I knew better than to ask for a date, since to them I existed only as a human drawing machine, a life support system for their likenesses.

I could tell much about people from drawing them. In five minutes, without their saying a word, I knew if they were happy or sad, content or frustrated, witty or dim, sensitive or numb, earnest or sarcastic. I knew them in ways their spouses and lovers might never know them. Their spouses and lovers had never drawn them.

Roots

The roots of caricature stretch back beyond written history, to the bovine drawings in the caves at Lascaux, drawings that certainly satisfy Baudelaire's definition of caricature as "a double thing; . . . both drawing and idea—the drawing violent, the idea caustic and veiled," and that anticipate Picasso's bull etchings by seventeen thousand years.

The walls of antiquity bristle with caricatures, the legacies of idle or confined men. In A.D. 79 a bored Roman soldier sketched a rudimentary but effective likeness of himself or a fellow soldier on the wall of his Pompeii barracks. On jars and vases the Greeks caricatured their gods with as much vinegar as some of the amphoras themselves held, turning Apollo into a quack doctor and Chiron into a blind old beggar struggling up a rickety ladder to be cured by him as nymphs survey the scene from Parnassian heights.

Long before the Greeks did so, Egyptian caricaturists depicted powerful men as beasts. One famous papyrus scroll shows a fox sitting on a throne, with a second fox waving a fan behind him, and a third presenting him with a bouquet of roses. Centuries later, in India, on the pages of the *Hindu Pantheon*, the god Krishna is presented as the jolly Bacchus, Don Juan of Indian deities, riding a palanquin formed by the bodies of his obliging female attendants.

The impulse toward caricature springs from our most primal urges. Give a child a crayon and the first thing she draws isn't the sun or a house or even a picture of her mother or father, but a caricature of these things, an image so conceptually laden it's more symbol than duplication or representation. The word "caricature" derives from the Latin *carricare*, meaning "to load." Children's art is almost always "loaded" with their emotional responses to things gained at the expense of what their eyes actually see. Picasso knew this, and dedicated his artistic life to recapturing and exploiting, often to shocking effect, the spiritedness of a child's loaded response to the physical world.

But long before Picasso, caricature informed the works of fine artists, from Leonardo da Vinci, whose improvised grotesque faces featured toothless lantern jaws and melting noses, to Hieronymus Bosch, whose surrounding figures in *Christ Carrying the Cross* echo Leonardo's grotesques. Near the close of the sixteenth century, Annibale Carracci applied Leonardo's exaggerations to true portraits, creating the first bona fide caricatures, inventing a new type of art to which he lent both his name and this bold defense: "*A good caricature, like every work of art, is more true to life than reality itself.*"

From Carracci, through Gian Lorenzo Bernini and others, the new art form reached Paris, where, in the mid-1800s, Daumier's indignant lithographs of pear-headed monarchs filled the pages of *Le Charivari*, a radical journal with a disgruntled bourgeoisie readership. Simultaneously caricature found its greatest exponent in Baudelaire, who, in his famous essay "On the Essence of Laughter," called caricature the common currency of an advanced society and praised it for revealing the essentially contradictory nature of men, who are both divine and grotesque: "The laughter caused by the grotesque has about it something profound, primitive and axiomatic, closer to the innocent life and absolute joy."

As I once emulated Mort Drucker, Claude Monet, long before he became the great painter of cathedrals, haystacks, and lily pads, emulated Nadar (Gaspard-Félix Tournachon) and Étienne Carjat—the best caricaturists of his day. From Monet the technique spread to the Expressionists, to Max Beckman and Edvard Munch, whose "The Scream" is by any definition a caricature. From Munch one moves swiftly through Picasso to Miguel Covarrubias, whose caricatures enlivened the *New Yorker* and *Vanity Fair* in the 1920s and 30s, and Al Hirschfeld, whose drawings of Broadway stars graced the theater pages of the *New York Times* for seven decades. From Hirschfeld an even swifter stroke of the caricaturist's pen leads us back to Mort Drucker and *MAD* magazine.

Fame

To make it as a party caricaturist you had to be not only accurate, but fast, *very* fast. Partygoers stood for hours waiting to be drawn by me. My popularity made me feel like a celebrity. And I dressed the part, in dazzling vests tailored from elaborate silk brocades, some costing more than a hundred dollars per yard, with buttons of ivory and gold, worn Tom Jones–like over a white shirt with the sleeves rolled up. You would have thought that I was a faith healer, or the pope, the lines stretched so long. And yet I had nothing to offer my supplicants but their own faces. When at the end of a long night I'd switch off my work lamp, the stragglers would beg me for "one more." They'd throw money at me, twenties and fifties, even (if the straggler was rich and drunk enough) an occasional hundred. "Please!" they would plead. Occasionally people grew belligerent. One guy grabbed me by the collar of my brocade vest, pulled me into his cigar-and-whisky-reeking face and said, "You gonna do me, or *what?*" Through constrained vocal cords I answered, "No, sorry." I thought he was going to hang one on me. But he let me go and, with a look of resignation so absolute I had to pity him, slumped away.

Such power over doctors and lawyers and Wall Street financiers. I remembered high school and how, with a few flicks of my Bic, I had so easily unhinged my less sanguine teachers. It was that same power I experienced now, but in reverse. Now my *unwillingness* to sketch people unhinged them. My drawings had evolved into a sought-after commodity. What Mrs. Decker had stolen for a kiss in kindergarten, these high rollers now begged me for.

Disillusionment, Dissolution, Disease

To all this glory, however, there was a dark underside. Bringing up the rear of those endless lines of people wanting to have their faces drawn was the rest of my life, with all its deficits and failures, including a file cabinet stuffed with rejection letters for four novels and dozens of short stories. Writing—that was my real vocation. The caricatures were but a gross means to that noble end. I drew people as other would-be novelists drove cabs, washed dishes, and taught middle school English classes, to pay the bills. The brocade vests would come off and with them all the sparkling frippery of some tuppenny music hall humbug. I hated being equated with gypsy palm and tarot readers, magicians, face-painters, balloon sculptors, and other so-called "party performers." I was a writer, damn it all, a serious artist. Only no one seemed to know it but me.

Drawing people at parties took a physical toll, too. Among the hazards of the caricaturist's life, in addition to eyestrain, deafening music (how I learned to hate djs), sore backs, performance anxiety, and spending hours in a cloud of other people's cigarette and cigar smoke, is the availability of free booze. I'd start with a glass of wine, a little something to thaw the ice on that first drawing, which was always a ball-buster, with the wait before my first subject equivalent to the actor's purgatory in the wings (though the wings of a stage don't come with an open bar), or a dentist's chair with the instruments all laid out and gleaming. And since I didn't work well with food in my gut, I'd restrict myself to a liquid diet, with wine giving way to gin and tonics, then to martinis, then to straight gin with a few olives plunked in, my only solid food. As the lines grew ever longer, or seemed to, I found myself drinking not only to loosen my drawing arm, but also to numb my senses against the endless parade of bodies whose souls it had fallen to me to capture.

I was up to my third martini one night when a silver-haired, elderly gentleman sat down in front of me.

"So," he asked me as I sketched, "when you're not doing this, what do you do?"

When I told him that I was a struggling writer, the man shook his head. "Oh, don't tell me. So was I. God—what misery! Do yourself a favor: give up now, while you still can!"

He took his caricature and left. But later, toward the end of the party, he returned, looking sheepish. "I take it back," he said. "Years from now, when you're my age, what would you rather say to your grandchildren? That you tried to write novels and failed, or that you were a stockbroker?" And he walked away as quietly as he'd come.

I drowned in my sense of failure, which I in turn tried to drown with free booze. I had reached the five-martini mark when my guts, already weakened by performance jitters, gave out on me. But it wasn't just my stomach. I had started waking in the middle of the night with headaches that had me squirming on the floor. My ears squealed—a sound like rushing water—so loud at times I couldn't hear myself in speaking to others. My vision swarmed with amoebic floaters. It was hard to read, let alone write. Still, I kept drawing.

I was diagnosed with a peptic ulcer, anemia, and several vitamin deficiencies. My bowel movements had turned mucoserous and bloody. A doctor ordered an MRI and a colonoscopy. The MRI was negative; the colonoscopy wasn't. Ulcerative colitis, a supposedly incurable disease of the large intestine, and a notorious precursor to bowel cancer.

I cut out the booze, but my symptoms persisted and multiplied. I suffered from panic attacks. As in the movies where the dramatic scenes are often accompanied by feverish violins, these attacks were accompanied by a little voice whispering to me, over the squeals and hissing of my ears, "*He took his life*"—not a bulletin, a suggestion. The gentle matter-of-factness with which my unconscious dispensed this advice, like a doctor prescribing a pill, was as upsetting to me as the prescription and the little voice itself, a voice that I grew to despise the way a rhinoceros must despise those pesky little birds that flit about its great head.

Xylene

During my last holiday season, at a party at the restaurant 21, one of my subjects suggested that something other than stress, booze, and cigarette smoke might be to blame for my deteriorating condition.

As I sketched her, she waved a polished hand in front of her face and said, "God, how can you stand it?"

"What?"

"The smell. It's so *strong!*"

At first I didn't know what she was talking about. Then I realized what she meant: the sweet, pungent aroma of xylene, a chemical solvent commonly used in felt-tip marker pens. I couldn't remember the last time I'd smelled it. For ten years I'd been soaking in a cloud of the stuff, filling the blood cells in my lungs with its highly toxic bouquet.

The next day I consulted a book called *Health Hazards Manual for Artists*, in which I read that xylene exposure, even for short periods, is known to cause headaches, dizziness, lack of muscle coordination, and confusion, and even to affect one's sense of balance. Short, concentrated periods of exposure can irritate the skin, eyes, nose, and throat, and can lead to respiratory problems, memory lapses, digestive ailments, and changes in liver and kidney function. Repeated, frequent exposure over a period of years can have drastic and permanent effects on the nervous system, with symptoms including but not limited to fatigue, poor coordination, difficulty concentrating, loss of memory, and personality changes (increased anxiety, nervousness, irritability). At high levels, xylene has even been known to lead to unconsciousness, coma, and death.

Perhaps not coincidentally, around this time the pens I'd been using were suddenly withdrawn from art store shelves, replaced by alcohol-based markers with similar felt nibs that dried up twice as fast and were less flexible and nowhere near as versatile. I couldn't draw with them. Before I'd read about xylene, and thinking that I was doing myself a favor, I bought as many of the discontinued markers as I could find, over a hundred of them. After discovering that they were poisonous, I wasn't sure what to do. I hated to waste them. But then it dawned on me that a good caricature may have been worth many things, but dying isn't one of them.

The Lie That Tells the Truth

It was an old woman who looked like Winston Churchill gone bad, not a chemical solvent with the name of a far-off galaxy, that finally made me throw in the towel. By God, was she ugly. Her face was baggy and bloated, with a wet rubbery lower lip and cheeks filigreed with capillaries, a thinning scalp, and rheumy, cataracted, crossed eyes. A wart sprouted from the tip of her nose, its hairs as white as corn silk. I loved old people's faces, so craggy and character-suffused, but this was too much of a good thing. For the first time in all my years of drawing people, I panicked. I didn't know what to do. Usually, I could find something redeeming in a face, some trace of warmth or joy or humor or wit or irony, something affirmative to lubricate my pen. But when someone's face simply repulsed me, my drawing arm would grow cold and stiff and my pen nib would run dry, or seem to.

In "Christian Morals," Thomas Browne writes, "When thou lookest upon the imperfections of others, allow one eye for what is laudable in them." As soon as this old woman sat down, I knew that I was done for. With a million eyes I'd have found nothing laudable in her looks. She was perfectly ugly.

There was only one thing to do, something I'd never done before. I had to violate the Caricaturist's Oath; I had to lie. I deflated that balloon-like lip, realigned those rheumy eyes, snipped the hairy wart off her nose, wiped away the web of capillaries staining her cheeks. I traded in my caricaturist's license for a set of diplomatic plates. Finished, I forced a smile and showed her the result.

The old woman's face, ugly to begin with, twisted itself up into something hideous. "That doesn't look one bit like me!" she snarled. And though I'd heard those words before, many times, this time was different: this time I knew they were true. My lie had only succeeded in exposing the truth: that I'd found this woman's face so repulsive I couldn't bring myself to be honest. She had seen this and been offended by it, rightly. For that reason alone I should have liked her; I should have begged her forgiveness. But it was too late. She refused her portrait and walked off, shaking her mangy head.

At the open bar I ordered a double martini, my first in two years. I was celebrating.

I'd drawn my last caricature.

The next day I threw all my markers, xylene- and alcohol-based alike, down the compactor chute. I folded my brocade vests into a trunk. I swore I'd never "do" another face. I took a job teaching creative writing at a Manhattan school known for its ubiquitous yellow plastic promotional kiosks. I went from earning lawyers' fees to earning a teacher's pay. Except for a doodle here and there, I've kept my vow.

On Never Forgetting a Face

Little evidence remains of my years as a caricaturist. The few drawings and brochures I've kept from them are tucked deep in dark closets and drawers. I never show them to anyone, nor do I speak of that career, not because I'm ashamed of it, but simply because it no longer feels like anything to do with me. Someone else wore those glitzy vests and sucked those heady marker fumes. The twenty-five thousand plus caricatures I did? Gone into cheap diploma frames or photo albums—or garbage pails. Or just plain gone, like Tibetan sand paintings, swept away.

I loved doing caricatures, but it was the kind of love slaves have been known to feel for their masters. As talents go I didn't own that one; it owned me. It was like some bright bird of exotic plumage that flew into my window and could be kept alive only by feeding it bite-sized chunks of myself, starting with my soul and ending with my liver.

Now and then I run into a past subject. Having drawn a face, you never forget it, any more than you forget the face of someone you've loved or been intimate with in some way. They don't forget me, either.

"I remember you!" they run up to me saying. "You drew my face once at a party, remember?" We shake hands, or hug, even.

I have no idea where or when the party was, or what the occasion, or what—if anything—we may have talked about. I have no idea, really, who these people are. But I remember their mouths, their noses, their ears, the angle of their cheekbones, the clefts in their chins, the slope of their foreheads, the curve of their eyebrows, the weight of their jowls, how their earlobes connect to their jaws . . . and their eyes.

Mostly, I remember their eyes.

Dagos in Mayberry . . . .

Columbus discovered no isle
or key so lonely as himself.
—Ralph Waldo Emerson

ne rainy evening in New York City not long ago I attended a reading and panel discussion featuring Italian American authors. I went because I'm a writer, and also because—though it's not something I'd given much thought to—I'm what some people call Italian American. And though I enjoyed the readings, the discussion afterward disturbed me. At some point in their lives each of the panelists had felt discriminated against as a direct consequence of his or her Italian background. As they told stories of jobs denied and promotions withheld, I listened with a mixture of unease, outrage, and bewilderment. It never occurred to me that I belonged to an oppressed minority, not one defined by geography, anyway.

In the small Connecticut town where we grew up, my brother and I were treated to all the customary names (Wop, Dago, Guinea) and boorish jokes (Q: Why is Italy shaped like a boot? A: They couldn't fit all that shit in a sneaker.). But to me those names and jokes weren't acts of discrimination, but part of being a boy among boys, as in *persecuted*. Had our ethnicity not furnished them with a convenient excuse for doing so, to be sure the neighborhood kids would have found other ways to torment us.

This, at least, was how I'd always looked at things. Now, sitting at that symposium hearing those speakers, I wondered if maybe all my life I had been naive—or worse, in denial. As the stories of anti-Italian discrimination mounted, I got so uncomfortable I took my umbrella and stormed out into the rain.

It had been pouring all day. As I lurched into the dark, wet street my anger toward the panelists rose to a fever pitch. What paranoia! What absurdity! They reminded me of a support group I once attended. As one by one the veterans introduced themselves and elucidated their ailments, I couldn't help noticing the relish with which they inventoried their symptoms and surgeries, displaying them like campaign medals and ribbons, dropping names of doctors and procedures like those of celebrities in a gossip column. This was no support group, I thought, it's a fan club. The rain fell harder, gathering in steaming black puddles at curbsides where the storm drains were clogged with litter. As I splashed my way toward the subway, I concluded that all these Italian Americans crying discrimination would likewise never be cured of whatever ailed them. They were too invested, too obsessed, too intoxicated by their grievance, too in love with being a persecuted minority.

Now I see how unfair this assessment was. But I was upset. Those panelists had disturbed what until then had been the equilibrium of a smoldering volcano. All your life, they said to me, you've had a disease and you never knew it. At forty, suddenly I was forced to confront something I'd never confronted before, namely my ethnicity. As I stood dripping wet on the subway platform I wondered, *What has being an Italian American meant to me? Has it been a source of pain, or pleasure? Has it helped or hurt me?*

The Connecticut town I grew up in is called Bethel. Think of Mayberry, television's version of Anytown, USA. There was a brick town hall with a public water fountain, and next door to it a greasy little diner called the Doughboy after the verdigris-covered statue overlooking the town square. There were two barbershops, Patsy's and Chris's, each with a revolving candy-striped pole. At Mulhaney's variety store, for a dime you could buy a Fudgsicle from the freezer case, which on hot summer days exhaled clouds of cooling mist. Add the dreary ruins of a dozen abandoned hat factories, and voila: my hometown.

When my parents moved there in the summer of '57, Bethel's population was still under 8,000. Though some of its residents commuted to Manhattan (a two-hour train journey), most worked in the local factories and businesses. My father did neither. He was an inventor, his laboratory a crumbling stucco shack at the bottom of our driveway.

My father's was no ordinary Italian immigrant's trajectory. He came here as a twenty-year-old in the early thirties, at the height of the Depression. He spoke perfect English, having learned it in England, where he'd spent his summers as a boy, and whose culture and language he preferred to his own. At Harvard he earned a graduate degree in physics, and soon went to work in Washington, D.C., for what is now the Department of Weights and Measures but was then the National Bureau of Standards. While vacationing back in Italy he met my future mother. A flurry of romantic letters crossed the Atlantic, culminating in an engagement that would result in a beautiful but very provincial girl's migration to a country brimming with fresh possibilities, uncertainties, enormous cars, milk shakes, and ham sandwiches.

When my mother married him, my father was division director of his department at the Bureau, earning $40,000 a year—a tidy sum back then. From that prestigious post he could easily have moved on to a cushy job with IBM or Westinghouse or any number of Fortune 500 companies. Instead, my father threw it all away to go it alone as an inventor. With his pregnant wife he set out in search of a property equidistant from New York and Boston, one with an outlying structure of some kind that could serve as his laboratory. In the waning Connecticut hat factory town he found a white Cape Cod on a hill with a sagging old farm building nearby. Within a year, with George and me only three months out of our mother's womb, he moved us to Bethel.

I've painted a picture of the town; now I'll try to paint one of my parents. For the purpose, another favorite 60s TV show will have to do. In *Green Acres*, white-haired Eddie Albert plays a corporate advertising executive turned gentleman farmer, with Slavic bombshell Eva Gabor cast as his dimwitted, spoiled rotten, Budapest-via-Park-Avenue wife. Accustomed to ordering in from New York restaurants, Eva's culinary skills extend no farther than what she with her thick Hungarian accent calls "hotcakes." One of the show's running gags has her forever inflicting this dubious culinary treat on her beleaguered husband.

My papa was no gentleman farmer, but technically he worked on—or in—a farm. In its previous incarnation the building that housed his laboratory had been a black market farm, selling poultry, eggs, butter, and other items heavily rationed during World War II. And though mother wasn't Hungarian (nor was she dimwitted or spoiled), her good looks made her every bit as stunning as Eva Gabor, and her accent was just as thick—as pungent as the Genoa salamis my father would bring home from his weekly trips to New York.

Like Eva Gabor, Mom was a fountain of glamour and flirtation, ever smiling for the paparazzi cameras in her head, instilling crushes in every male of the species who ventured into the bridal boutique where she worked. A sucker for glamour, she married my father (she told me one day) because he reminded her of Charles Boyer. But it turned out that this Charles Boyer wore the same ratty cardigan and stained pants day in and day out, his zipper yawning much of the time. My father was the least glamorous person in the world, as oblivious of his appearance as my mother was attentive to hers. Mentally she still lived in Italy, in the land of *bruta figura*, where appearances were, if not everything, close to everything.

In this respect as in so many others, she and my father were opposites, oil and water. Where Papa was pedantic and rational, Mom was dramatic, emotional, operatic. Mom was all instinct and innuendo; Papa all logic and intellect. That he was fifteen years older and twice divorced added to the disparity. In the midst of their colorful clashes, George and I would often turn to each other and mouth or say, "Hotcakes, dahling."

It took little to stand out in Bethel. That our parents were foreigners helped, but that was but one of their eccentricities. As I've said, our mother was ravishing, a combination of Sophia Loren and Heddy Lamar, with Loren's sculpted eyebrows and lips. Both sexes were drawn to her. To visit with her, UPS drivers shirked schedules and routes. Like sharks drawn to chum, my schoolmates formed a semicircle around her at her black Chambers stove, where, while stirring a batch of *Bolognese* sauce, she'd regale them with tales of Tripoli, Libya, where she grew up, and where, as a young girl, she plucked dates from a tree in her backyard, and tooled around on the back of Uncle Sergio's—her brother's—Lambretta, and had a pet monkey named Guerrina ("Little War"). She was by far the most exotic woman in town, which might have aroused envy and the malice that goes with it, had her foreignness not exempted her from Bethel's ceaselessly grinding rumor-mill. Thanks to her accent, Mom could get away with just about anything, including being glamorous in a place where glamour was as alien and suspect as a bottle of *Strega*, or an Alfa Romeo.

My friends found my father no less exotic. Every now and then he'd hire one of them to help me sort screws in his laboratory. We'd sit side by side, me and Lenny or Wesley or Victor, at a bench in the Building, picking screws out of a box and squinting at them, trying to determine if they were 6–32s or 8–32s. Meanwhile, my father's radio played, tuned perpetually to a station that broadcast nothing but static, however not loudly enough to mask Papa's dithering curses or his thunderous farts, to my friends' uncategorical delight. Apparently they'd never heard a strange man swear and break wind so often and extravagantly. To my father's farts and curses, to his explosive *fucks* and *shits* and *goddammits*, and to his trumpet-herald flatus, my friends' faces turned red and they wept with laughter. They loved Papa's inventions, too—his Color Coders, his mercury switches, his rotorless motors and thickness gauges. They couldn't get over the fact that he was an inventor. Like Henry Ford. Like Thomas Edison. Like Leonardo da Vinci. Like Dick van Dyke in *Chitty Chitty Bang Bang*.

I took for granted that my parents' eccentricities were part and parcel of their being Italian, and pitied other kids my age, whose fathers wore dull suits and worked at equally dull factory and office jobs; and whose mothers were anything but glamorous, who cooked ravioli from cans with winking chefs on the labels, who had to be persuaded that real Italian dressing was made from oil and vinegar and not something poured out of a pear-shaped bottle labeled Wish-Bone or Kraft. While George and I were being weaned on diluted *vino rosso*, they drank cow's milk and Kool-Aid with dinner, which they called "supper," and which would typically feature such ghastly bland items as cucumbers, and which they ate at an absurdly early hour. When it came to meals especially, I counted myself lucky for being the son of Italians. It broke my young heart to watch my friends' mothers opening tin cans of Dinty Moore and Campbell's (supper). Not that my brother and I minded that sort of fare; we got a kick out of it. But for us, beans and franks, creamed corn, and string bean casseroles were novelties; our friends had to eat such crap on a regular basis.

On the other hand, when they came over to our house they'd be treated to my mother's lasagna, which dripped mozzarella and oozed béchamel, and her *risotto ala Milanese* (thin-pounded veal cutlets dipped in flour and fried in olive oil, sprinkled with parsley, and served with sunny lemon wedges), and her chicken *cacciatore*. For dessert: *crostata marmalata*—jam pie—filigreed with buttery crust and served with a scoop of Mom's *tiramisu* or her *zabaglione*, soaked with enough rum or Marsala to besot a regiment—as if my mother's good looks weren't intoxicating enough.

And yet, the most intoxicating part of dinner was usually the conversation, if you could call it that, an endless barrage of anecdotes, jokes, opinions, tirades, pedantry, sophistry, and invective that swirled around the table, with no one, guests included, exempt or immune. Guests could join in the melee, or they could sit there and take it. While my mother held forth on her African childhood, our father specialized in bad jokes and worse puns, while George and I took charge of making fun of everyone. Was our dinner banter as much the product of Italy as Mom's tiramisu? If so, I thought, all the more reason to embrace my roots.

But there were other reasons, like growing up in a house full of books and paintings, the latter mostly my father's. Like Winston Churchhill, one of his heroes, my father was a dedicated Sunday painter. His slapdash oils covered every wall of our house. Those surfaces not covered by his paintings were taken up by bookcases sagging under volumes in French, German, Italian—all languages our polymath papa spoke fluently. He especially loved German, why I can't imagine. Just having all those books around made me feel worldly and sophisticated. Compared to most of my friends' homes, it was like growing up in a library or a museum. True, Lenny Polis's dad painted his bedroom ceiling with a *tromp-l'oeil* cloudy sky from which Mustangs, Spitfires, and Messerschmitts dangled on fishing lines in a permanent dogfight, and this had its charms. But it lacked the snob appeal of growing up in a house full of paintings and books.

And already by age ten or so I had become something of a snob. I believed that we Selgins had something special, something American families in Bethel lacked, something more than an antidote to canned food and bare walls. Nor was it simply that both my parents were Italians, exports of that boot-shaped land across the Atlantic; it was something bigger, broader, deeper, something with implications beyond the curly hair on my head, the brown color of my eyes, or the food that I ate. Somehow, for me, the world's boundaries were stretched wider. Our house on the hill was somehow closer than other houses—not just to Italy, but to the rest of the world.

Soon it would come to pass, though, that for every eccentricity of my parents that filled me with pride and delight, another caused me embarrassment and suffering. Example: my father owned a rusting Raleigh bicycle. Every day, winter and summer, until he was into his eighties, he pedaled his Raleigh to the post office and back. I can still see him now, dressed in his metal-stained shorts and black kneesocks, his calf muscles as boxy as toasters. Sometimes he wore his beret, a black one speckled with lint. Once a month or so, the school bus that George and I rode would overtake our father on his route; the bus's windows would fly open and a dozen heads would pop out, all of them shouting, "*Hey, Mr. Magoo!*" With a dreamy smile on his face my father would pedal on. I would personally witness none of this display; I'd be too busy cowering behind the seat in front of mine, waiting for the humiliation to pass. What self-respecting dad rode a bicycle, let alone a rusty one—and in *black kneesocks*?

Equally embarrassing were trips to the swim hole, the muddy one by the railroad trestle behind an abandoned hat factory, where Bethel dads brought their kids to fish and swim. Unlike all the other fathers in town, our father refused to plunge into the water. "I'm too old," he'd say. Instead he would wade in slowly, inch by inch, rubbing palmfuls of murky water over his sagging shoulders and his pale, sunken chest, wincing and making faces like a torture victim. George and I, having already jumped in, would yell, "*Jump, Papa, jump!*"

"Strictly out of the question," Papa would refrain. "I'm too old for such things." In time I came to equate *old* with Italian, and wished my father were American, as if that would have made him younger. Had Papa been American he'd have plunged—like Burt Lancaster in *From Here to Eternity*.

My father detested sports. This, too, I chalked up to his being Italian. I never once saw him handle a bat or a ball of any kind, let alone a Frisbee. He "loathed" (his word) baseball. He refused to watch us play the game, let alone join us, which goes some way toward explaining why my brother and I were so inept at that and other sports. Nor were we much good at defending ourselves. Except for what we learned from going at each other's throats, we knew nothing about fighting, whereas American boys, all of them, knew how to fight expertly. It was in their blood.

Such (as I began to see it) were the drawbacks of being an immigrant child. Still, I failed to see myself as the victim of any prejudice. If I didn't fit in, it was my own fault for having the wrong parents, or for being born in the wrong country. Rather than blame those who taunted and bloodied me, I envied them. I envied their fair, straight hair and pale, squinty eyes, their skill with a baseball bat or hockey stick, their ability to throw passes and dribble basketballs. I coveted the careless expertise with which they blew bubbles with their Bazooka gum, and whistled through their fingers, and shot gobs of spit through their teeth. The deeper my conviction grew that I *wasn't* one of them, the more I longed to be, to score their winning touchdowns, to hit their home runs, to shoot their hoops, and to blow those magnificent pink Bazooka bubbles. I yearned to be a *real* American, to cut off my European roots and plant myself firmly in U.S. soil, to trade Mom's *zabalione* for a slice of All-American apple pie.

My father didn't think of himself as Italian. Long ago he'd forsaken his homeland, leaving behind everything to do with it—its language, its religion, its accent—even his name, which he altered to Selgin, one of his less successful inventions.[1]

Among the very few things my father didn't leave behind in Italy was his mother, who lived with us in her own little apartment on the ground floor. Though Nonnie supposedly spoke twelve languages, English wasn't one of them. During my visits with her I had to speak Italian.

Nonnie's apartment was its own cramped museum of trinkets, doilies, and Japanese fans. It smelled of mothballs, lilac perfume, and fried foods. She would recite to us from an ancient leather-bound volume of Dante, its pages foxed and gilded, or from the *Aeneid*, the syllables falling from her papery lips, along with the dust from its pages. She taught me the legend of Romulus and Remus, the twins who, suckled by a she-wolf, went on to found the City of the Seven Hills. On her windowsill she kept a bronze miniature Capitoline wolf. She'd point to the twins under it one by one and say *"Questo e Giorgio, e quello li Pierino."* It amused me to know that my twin and I had founded Rome, the capital of Italy—a country to which, so far, my grandmother's apartment was as close as I'd come.

That would soon change. In 1968, aboard a Greek ocean liner, my mother, my brother, and I set sail for Italy. As far as I know, we were the first people from Bethel ever to set foot there. Since Mom was afraid to fly, we were forced—*forced*—to travel by boat. Before docking in Naples, the *Queen Anna Maria* stopped in Lisbon, where my mother parlayed her considerable charms to gain us an audience with Italy's deposed King, Umberto II, with whom we were photographed on his portico. On a busy Neopolitan street someone pinched my mother's behind (she yelped, but I think she got a kick out of it). From Naples we rode a fast train to Rome, and from there a much slower one to Milan, where Uncle Sergio, older and with no Lambretta, met us.

Uncle Sergio had all the advantages of an adult (including a gold pocket watch and a Kodak camera) and none of the drawbacks (including a sense of responsibility or shame). He wasted no time teaching George and me every Italian *parolacci*, including some we didn't already know. The three of us never stopped giggling. Uncle Sergio was sixty-two years old.

Everything about Italy thrilled us. The little cars that looked like toys; the coffee called *cappuccino* with a fun layer of foam on top; the ice cream called *gelato* that was far superior to American ice cream (especially *nocciola*—hazelnut). The soda called *Chinotto* was brown and bubbly and looked like Coca-Cola, but George and I found it superior; we found everything in Italy superior. Water was served in tall green bottles with fancy labels and carbonation, and beat all hell out of American water. The trains, the trees, even the birds, all struck me as being a cut above their New World equivalents. So did the clay tile rooftops, the old shutters in all the old windows, and the sounds the church bells made—heavenly enough to fill even a ten-year-old atheist with piety. Everywhere I turned I saw spewing fountains and naked statues, paintings and frescoes on stucco walls, sculptures, cloisters and *cortiles*—courtyards with cloudy willow trees like the ones running up our driveway.

From June to September we took in the major cities and sights, as far north as Bergamot on the Swiss border, where we went mushroom hunting, then back to Naples to catch the ship home, two Italian bicycles crammed into its cargo hold, George's cherry red, mine lemon-lime yellow. As the *Queen Anna Maria* pulled away from the dock both of us cried, something we hadn't done when sailing out of New York Harbor.

Those bicycles proved to be our downfall. They were the first ten-speeds ever to grace the streets and sidewalks of Bethel, making us the envy of the neighborhood, briefly. They came with stubby touring handlebars and leather toolkits. *Legnano*, said the decals on the frames. *Campagniola*, said the S-shaped appendages hanging from the rear hub sprockets (and named *derailleurs*, like an elite daredevil wing of the French Resistance). The neighborhood kids couldn't get over all those gears. "What are they all *for*?" they wondered, scratching their heads.

The bikes were too big for us; a year would pass before we reached the pedals. Meanwhile, appreciation turned to envy, envy to resentment, and resentment to mischief. One day I let Wesley Conklin "hop on" my bike "just for a sec." A mistake. Next thing I knew he was pumping away down Wooster Street with me on foot in hot pursuit. I chased him all the way to town, past Jerome's five-and-ten-cent store, past the Doughboy Diner, past the town hall, across the middle school parking lot, past the ruins of two hat factories. As dusk settled I sat down on the front stoop of Wesley's house, with raw eyes and sore legs, waiting for him and my *Legnano*. Seeing me there, his parents took pity on me and invited me in for supper: Campbell's cream of mushroom soup and a salad with Wish-Bone Italian dressing.

A week later it happened again. This time Sean Ziegeldorf took off with my bike. I called his parents and lodged a complaint. The next day Sean cornered me in the school lavatory and bloodied my nose.

By the time ninth grade started, George and I had had our bikes stolen no less than a dozen times, to where we finally gave up and bought Schwinn's, with chintzy chain guards and saddles with fat springs under them, bikes no one would bother stealing. Meanwhile, the *Legnanos* gathered cobwebs and rust in the garage. As I pedaled my piece-of-shit Schwinn around I felt the eyes of the town watching me, laughing at me the way those kids on the bus laughed at my father on his Raleigh. For the first time I tasted the alienation that would hound me for years to come: the sense that I didn't and would never fit in, that I was unique, all right, but also suspect, inferior, and incongruous. I convinced myself that my ostracism was born of envy, and took it as a backhanded compliment. But under that tough exterior of false pride my skin was raw, wounded, resentful, and full of defensive egotism, my scorn a substitute for dignity. I wore it like a crown of thorns, and refused, in spite of myself, to climb down off of my touring handlebarred, lemon-yellow, Italian import, ten-speed high horse.

Instead, like the survivor of a shipwreck clinging to a floating hatch cover, I clung to my "uniqueness." Since I liked to draw and had a knack for it, and since artists were known to be suffering misfits, I seized on that convenient identity for myself, and when it came time to pick a college I chose an art school in New York City, where brooding misfits like me were most likely to fit in. And if I didn't—well, no one would notice.

In time I'd write stories and plays and earn a living as an illustrator. When I could afford to, I traveled to Italy, where I pretended to feel at home. I married a woman of Italian descent who shared my love of wine and anchovies, and who is herself an artist. I had good friends and lived among paintings and books and felt, on the whole, pretty lucky. If I was marginalized, if I didn't fit in with average people, it was my own damn choice. And anyway isn't marginalization the ultimate, if not the only, condition for an artist?

Still, there's that familiar sense of displacement that follows me everywhere I go, along with an ache of loneliness, the kind that people feel when on a gray day they stand at the edge of a pier looking out to sea. Is it because of who I am? Or is who I am because of where my parents were born? Am I alienated by disposition, by circumstance, by blood—or by all of the above? If I never really managed to fit in, is it because, at bottom, I'm in the wrong place?

Whatever its cause, the fact is I no longer mind feeling unique, or marginalized, or whatever you want to call it. Maybe I've just gotten used to it. Maybe the only place I'll ever feel at home is that uncharted island halfway between here and Italy, a country the size of a hyphen.

But I'm not an Italian American any more than I'm American or Italian. What I am is this: the American-born son of two Italian immigrants, rife with their eccentric genes. When they look at me some people may see an Italian American. But I see what I see in us all: a mixture of where we've come from, what we've been through, and— most important—what we choose, or refuse, to be.

NOTE

1. "We're the only Selgins in the world," our mother would remind us. I found it hard to believe. How could there be no others? It was as hard as believing that in our whole stamp collection—two overflowing shoeboxes— there wasn't one one-cent magenta British Guiana stamp worth sixty thousand dollars. The 'g' in Selgin, though meant to be soft, as in "gin," is invariably hardened, as in Lord Elgin, and so the name is no less prone to mispronunciation than the original: Senigaglia.

Black Words on Yellow Paper

write this with a black Sharpie on yellow paper. Yellow is the color of lies. I had a friend named Victor who was a liar. Victor Szentgyorgyi, pronounced Saint George. He lived three houses down from us on Wooster Street, and he was fat, extremely fat, so fat (we used to say) his mom had to use the driveway to iron his pants. Fat enough to crush you in a snowball fight, or playing so-called touch football. He would come down on you and you'd be under him, screaming through flattened lungs, "Get off of me, you fat tub of shit!" This made Victor laugh. His fat flesh would jiggle its way deep into your suffocating heart. To be tackled by Victor Szentgyorgyi was to die a horrible if temporary death, like being buried alive under an avalanche of sweaty Jell-O.

Since Victor's parents were not especially fat, we speculated that his obesity was due to his drinking too much water. Wherever a source of drinking water presented itself, Victor would bend and slurp. Show him a mud puddle and Victor would bend. The town hall held the coldest, sweetest water fountain. Oasis, it said in stainless steel. On blistering days one waited in despair of Victor's relinquishing the town water supply. He would keep slurping until the chilly water was gone and only lukewarm dregs remained. I see him now, as I write these words, slaked and sodden, wiping a fat forearm across dripping glossy lips, the depraved gape in his eyes of a man who has just quaffed a bucket of blood.

Victor's lies were as big as Victor. There was nothing Victor wouldn't lie about, nothing his lies didn't touch. He couldn't part his lips without lying.

Most of Victor's lies had to do with his unemployed father, a former hat-factory worker. We grew up in a town of hat factories, dead and dying, their extinct smokestacks lording over the landscape, brick middle fingers up-thrust into the gray Connecticut sky. You could still read the names of the factories in faded paint on their ruddy shafts: MALLORY, LEE, KNOX, CROFUS & CORBET, HOWES VON-GAL, MOHAWK CAXTON-DUMONT . . . The nine chimneys rose taller than the town's tallest trees, taller than the junior high school cupola, taller than the steeples of the Lutheran, the Congregational, even the Catholic church. Once those smokestacks darkened the sky with soot and prosperity. But by the time I lived there, only their shadows still darkened things: black shadows stretching across parking lots and playgrounds, bending over rooftops, curving around car hoods and convertible bonnets, slithering down alleys, sliding onto porches, climbing into kitchen and bedroom windows, sweeping past the hours and minutes of each day like the hands of a gigantic gloomy clock.

Until it burned down in 1965, Victor's dad had worked in the so-called "back" or "wet" shop of the Mohawk Hat Works. The back shops were where the pelts of beavers and rabbits were processed into smooth, soft, malleable felt. The process was known as "carrot-ing" and involved harsh toxic chemicals—including mercury, until it was banned before World War II. The cemeteries of Bethel and Danbury next door bristle with the stones of factory workers who died of mercury poisoning, or hydragyria, known also as Mad Hatter's Disease—and, locally, as the Danbury Shakes. To this day the river sediments of my hometown are saturated with mercury.

According to Victor, his dad had:

  a. skippered a submarine in World War II
  b. skippered a PT boat in World War II
  c. killed a Nazi in a fox hole with his own dagger (and brought home his coal-scuttle helmet) in World War II
  d. helped build the bridge over the River Kwai (etc.)

In his bedroom, hanging above a closet door, dangled a machete with a long, curved, and deeply rusted blade. This object, along with the coal-scuttle helmet, Victor offered us as proof of his dad's heroics. The German helmet had a provocative dent in its left side. Touching it, you couldn't help imagining Mr. Szentgyorgyi leaping like Vic Mor-row in *Combat*, teeth gritted, nostrils flared, eyes bulging, plunging a bayonet once, twice, three times into an ice-cold, leathery Nazi heart.

Of his various acts of bravery we were told never to speak to Mr. Szentgyorgyi. "It might set off a flashback," Victor explained soberly by the campfire one evening. The woods behind the houses where we lived were strewn with improvised meeting places. Fort Copperhead, where two dilapidated stonewalls converged, was where we built our campfires. "You should hear how my dad screams in his sleep sometimes. One night he jumped out of bed and tore all the bedroom curtains down. I swear to God. He'd dreamed that he was on bivouac and the Nazis set his tent on fire." Our own campfire belched and roared; the flames painted Victor's face ruddy sunset colors. None of us had any idea what a "bivouac" was. Not that it mattered, since we knew Victor was lying.

But then Victor's lies were so much more engaging than our truths. They were collective lies. He lied for all of us, Victor did; he made heroes of *all* our fathers. Through Victor and his lies we climbed the Matterhorn; we ran with the bulls at Pamploma; we rode in the cockpit of Chuck Yeager's X-1 jet when it broke the sound barrier ("They wanted to test the effects of g-forces on a newborn, so they picked me").

Victor's lies embraced our deepest hopes and fears. Victor, bitten by a run-of-the-mill mosquito, caught malaria. The 110 degree fever raged for six days and nights; a priest was summoned to his bedside. Last rites were administered. "I saw the Virgin Mary at the foot of my bed," Victor confided in us as the campfire sizzled and snapped. "She wore a green plaid skirt just like the girls at St. Mary's. She waited for my mom and dad to leave the room and then—I swear to God—she bent down and gave me a blow job."

We listened, rapt. Like the rest of us back then Victor had fallen under the sway of Don Herbert, TV's Mr. Wizard, and his Saturday morning array of edifying stinks and bangs. In the name of scientific research, with something less than princely decorum, Victor claimed to have set his own asshole on fire. "I was conducting an experiment to determine whether farts really are ignitable," he explained. "First, I ate a whole can of Boston baked beans, cold. Then I went up to my bedroom with a whole box of Ohio Blue Tip safety matches. I let the first big fart accumulate, and then I let her rip into an empty Coke bottle. A half hour later when I finished farting I put a match to the opening of the bottle. Sure enough it produced this silent little blue puff of flame. There's even a technical term for it: pyroflatulance, also known as blue darting or fart ignition. No shit, I looked it up."

Still, Victor's empirical skepticism was not 100 percent satisfied. "So I waited for a brand new huge fart to come on and then I got down on my knees in front of the armoire mirror, and . . . " The rest of Victor's tale unfolded predictably, with Victor as *Hindenburg* exploding. *The lives, the humanity.* He was subsequently treated—not for second, or third, but for *fourth* degree burns, the likes of which even the seasoned nurses at New Haven Hospital's burn unit had never seen before.

"They had to peel all the burnt skin off my butt. A female surgeon did it using a pair of dermal forceps. It took her twenty-two hours. She looked just like Sophia Loren in *El Cid*, I swear to God. She told me how before going to med school she'd been an opera singer at La Scala. To prove it, while peeling off my skin, she sang Violetta's '*Ah no più*' from *La Traviata*. Then she bent down and gave me a blow job."

Those disasters and diseases that we most dreaded stout Victor endured for us. Through him, vicariously, we took the cure for rabies, an endless series of injections administered through the chest wall straight into the heart's right ventricle. "The damned needle was so long I swear it tickled the back of my throat," Victor informed us. The doctor, we were told, was the spit and shine of the perfidious Dr. Zachary Smith in the television show *Lost in Space*. "I swear, he smiled and snickered the whole time," Victor said. "Then he bent down and tried to give me a blow job, only I wouldn't let him."

When not gathered around the campfire, we would congregate at the Spitting Pole, the street signpost at the corners of Wooster and Keeler where we waited mornings for the school bus to growl 'round the bend, intent on hauling us off to the minimum security facility that was Bethel Middle School. The Spitting Pole earned its name on frosty winter mornings when, to amuse ourselves, Lenny, Victor, Wesley, and I would each hawk and spit onto its pitted green shaft, then stand back to watch our boogers make their ways—slowly, steamingly—down the pole, like mini wet locomotives, taking penny bets on whose oyster would reach the sidewalk first: may the slowest booger win. In time the Spitting Pole grew so encrusted with our combined DNA offerings that a fresh coat of green paint would have been redundant.

While hawking, spitting, and waiting for the bus we'd take in more of Victor's bright and shining fabulations. By then we were twelve years old. Sex had invaded our thoughts like a Special Forces Unit. He told us about the box of rubbers his father kept in the desk drawer of his home office, how he found them there one night while searching for a certain deck of playing cards. The box was as big as the drawer, almost, and squirmed with hundreds if not thousands of rubbers.

"He must have purchased 'em wholesale," Victor surmised. "He probably buys 'em by the pound."

Lest we doubted him, Victor showed us one. He whipped it out of his back pocket. It looked like an anemic balloon. We stood with jaws hanging, marveling at its exalted, if less-than-perfectly understood, purpose. Having snatched the specimen from Victor's grip, Wesley put it in his mouth and inflated it, which cracked us up, but not nearly as much as when Victor noted that the rubber had been used.

The playing cards Victor had been searching for were, it goes without saying, pornographic, with each card displaying, in a gritty sepia photograph, a scene heretofore unimaginable to us. According to Victor, the degree of obscenity of each card was commensurate with its face value, with aces high and the Ace of Spades highest of all. He flashed us one card per day, starting with the lowly two of hearts, then went on to describe in vivid hard-core detail what our eyes had barely glimpsed.

"Fifty-two cards," Victor reminded us each morning as the bus growled into view. Thus, for fifty-two days he held us spellbound, so eager to arrive at the Ace of Spades we nearly died in the waiting. When at last he had worked his way through all the face cards and every other ace, he gave notice that, alas, the cards had been stolen back from him.

"I guess my dad must've missed them," he said.

We never questioned Victor's lies. To have done so would have been as pointless as questioning the existence of Santa Claus, or the Loch Ness Monster. What for, when to believe gave so much pleasure?

But I have yet to tell the biggest of Big V's lies.

First, though, I must interrupt my story. I cap my black Sharpie and rest it on my yellow pad. I am distracted by sounds of men working on the bridge next to the window of my Bronx home, which hugs the steep shore at the confluence of the Harlem and Hudson rivers, the dark wall of the Palisades rising to the right of my view. It's late afternoon, that hour when the sun invades brazenly, so I have lowered the Venetian blinds. For four months now they've been painting the railroad bridge that spans the creek. In its infinite wisdom the Metropolitan Transportation Authority has elected to paint the bridge canary yellow, the same color as the paper I write these words on. The sandblasting sounds like a rocket ship blasting off all day long without ever leaving the launching pad. The bridge lies half-wrapped under canvas, like a fresh corpse or a forsaken Christo project. A quarter of its span remains blue, the rest already yellow. I light a cigarette, take up my Sharpie, go back to work.

As we grew up, Victor's lies grew also, becoming more subtle and modulated, while mostly still revolving—like the planets around the sun—around the exploits of Mr. Szentgyorgyi, who was once a champion prizefighter. Victor had a set of boxing gloves to prove it, the very gloves with which his welterweight dad once pounded Rocky Graziano (or was it Marciano?) into a ninth-round technical knockout. There they were, wedded by their laces, dangling from a nail pounded into a rafter in the Szentgyorgyi garage. Victor being too fat for ladders, I got the gloves down. The desiccated leather was like sandpaper. We put them on, Lenny Polis and I, one glove each, and sparred there among dust motes in the garage, with Victor as referee, our gloveless hands bent behind our backs, like fencers. The parched gloves drew blood from us that dried the same clay color as their parched leather. We jabbed above the waist, below the neck. Lenny—his fuse notoriously short—took a stray uppercut to his jaw. Off went the one glove, out came bare knuckles. While he beat me blue, Victor laughed; he thought it was a gas. *You fat tub of shit*, I thought, *you miserable lying blubbery tub.* Still dazed from my beating, I ran to the septic pond behind the Szentgyorgyi home, where we caught bullfrogs, and chucked the boxing gloves in. They floated like twin brown blobs of shit.

We were told never to mention his boxing career to Mr. Szentgyorgyi, who gave up the sport after pounding an adversary into a coma. "Dad never did get over that," Victor mused, shaking his fat head. Nor were we under any circumstances to invoke the XK-E Jaguar that Mr. Szentgyorgyi kept locked in a New Fairfield barn, and drove only on fair weekends, with the top down and a silk aviator's scarf around his neck. "It's got a twelve-cylinder, seven-hundred horsepower engine and can clock three hundred miles per hour. If Mom ever finds out he'll be in Dutch with her big-time," he told us. (Mr. Szentgyorgyi's regular car—the one parked in the driveway—was a Pepto Bismol pink Rambler American.)

And now, at last, we arrive at the mother of all of Victor's cock-and-bull stories, the one about his father's train museum. Somewhere between the time he abandoned professional boxing and went to work at the Mohawk hat factory, Mr. Szentgyorgyi had, according to Victor, been a railroad man, an engineer on the Hartford & New Haven line.

"Dad engineered the last of the steam locomotives," Victor said. "This was back in the late 1950s. The day his foreman told him diesel and electric would be replacing steam, my dad, he takes off his striped engineer's cap, spits on the ballast, and says, 'In that case I quit!'"

Before quitting, though, according to Victor, Mr. Szentgyorgyi made off with seven locomotives. One by one, with the help of a contingent of fellow disgruntled engineers, he absconded with them in the dark of night to a secret location far removed from the salvage blowtorch in the green hills of southern Vermont. Having learned of Mr. Szentgyorgyi's noble undertaking, other engineers from every part of the country slipped away with their death-sentenced locomotives, secreting them under cover of darkness to Mr. Szentgyorgyi's covert hiding place, where they and he would patiently wait out the statute of limitations, at which point Mr. Szentgyorgyi would unveil the greatest locomotive museum in the world. "Steamtown, USA, that's what he's planning to call it," Victor proclaimed with something like glee.

By the time Victor advanced this lie we were both sophomores in high school. We were standing side by side before a bank of urinals, draining ourselves between classes. The tiled wall in front of me said IF YOU CAN PISS ABOVE THIS LINE, THE BETHEL FIRE DEPT. WANTS YOU. I was no longer the gullible and easily persuaded person I had once been. I had entered a cynical phase, one that would survive into my mid-twenties and beyond. I no longer found Victor's lies appealing or engaging, let alone convincing.

"Tell me something, Victor," I interrupted him and his micturation. "What makes you such a goddamned liar?"

Through the corner of my eye I saw his fleshy face drop and turn red, and instantly I regretted my remark. I waited for him to say something, anything, to try and wriggle out of the lasso I'd swung around him, to lie to me some more and make me feel a little less callous, a little less cynical, a little less cruel. But Victor didn't say anything. He just stood there, looking down into the bowl, licking his lips, holding his dick. And there I left him.

The next day Lenny marched up to me.

"What did you say to Victor?"

"I called him a liar," I said.

"Why did you do that?" The way Lenny said it, it was as if I'd wiped out a sand castle we had spent years building.

"Because," I said, "it's time he grew up."

"You shouldn't have done that," said Lenny, and went on shaking his head as he walked away.

Soon afterward, Victor stopped coming to school. We learned that he and his family had moved to Vermont. As for Wesley and Lenny, by my junior year in high school our friendships had cooled to extinction. I made other friends not based on bus stops and spitting poles. Wesley Conklin (I assured myself) had always been a moron, while Lenny Polis was a pugnacious thug, and if I never saw or spoke with either of them again it hardly mattered, since meanwhile I had become an arrogant, cynical snob.

More than thirty years have passed since I graduated from Bethel High School. And though I never saw or heard from Wesley Conklin or Victor Szentgyorgyi again, I did hear from Lenny Polis, who lives near Cocoa Beach, Florida, and works for the National Aeronautics and Space Administration, where he is a "fuel technologies specialist," that is he pumps liquid hydrogen for the space shuttles. Soon our email exchanges turned to reminiscence, and we got around to the Spitting Pole, to Victor, and to his lies.

Lenny wrote:

On a recent visit to Disneyworld with my niece and her twin five-year-olds, I ran into Victor and his family. Like me, he has two boys, sixteen and twenty, though mine are tall and slim and Victor's are fat, as he is still. His mother died of complications from diabetes. But his dad lives on, and (according to Victor) continues to pursue his dream of a train museum in Vermont. Assuming that this has raised your eyebrow as it did mine, I attach a scan

of the map Victor drew for me on the spot, showing said museum's location.
When he gave it to me Victor said, "If you run into Selgin, give him this."

One weekend, having better things to do but not wanting to do them,
I drove up to Vermont, to a town called Bellows Falls. I took Victor's
map with me. Along the indicated stretch of state highway I parked
my Honda Civic, got out and stood there, seeing nothing but a stand
of scraggly pine trees along an embankment where, according to the
map, Mr. Szentgyorgyi's locomotive museum *should* have been. I was
prepared to accept that I'd been the victim of a well-conceived and
richly deserved practical joke, when I decided to have a look through
those trees.

Having scrambled down the stony embankment, I saw them, soaking in the bright sun of a midwinter day: five, six, nine, a dozen—
more!—broad-chested locomotives, cinnamon-dusted with rust.
Tripping over tracks and ties, as though in a dream, I drifted into a
Mesozoic landscape wherein the dinosaurs were cast in corroded iron.
Dazed, I made my way from locomotive to locomotive, until, jutting
out from under a set of iron wheels, I saw a pair of human legs.

Though he'd grown older, had shed most of his weight, and had a
gray, frizzled beard, still, I recognized Mr. Szentgyorgyi. He told me
how the museum's chief financial backer, a man named F. Nelson
Blount, the millionaire founder of a seafood corporation, died two
years ago when the small plane he'd been piloting crashed, so the museum had lost its funding and was in search of a new sponsor. "Meanwhile it's all I can do," he said, lofting his oilcan, "to keep these poor
babies from rusting solid."

I spent the rest of that day helping Mr. Szentgyorgyi oil his locomotives.

To doubt is to own that much less of the world and its miracles. Life is
a whopper, disbelief a form of death. To the extent that one puts faith
in them, lies are negotiable. I write this not in black ink on a yellow
pad, but on my computer. My window faces east, not south. The sun
hasn't shone for days. The bridge is a highway, not a railroad, bridge,
and it's sea-green, not yellow, and they finished painting it years ago.

Oh, and I don't smoke.

Like Huck Finn I've told the truth, mainly. I did grow up in a hat-factory town with a gang of boys including Victor, a liar whose last name was Szentgyorgyi. He *was* fat. The Spitting Pole, the boxing gloves, the coal-scuttle helmet with the provocative dent, the pornographic playing cards, and the lies about World War II and the Jaguar and the train museum—all, all true!

I leave you with this: if you should happen to go to Bellows Falls, Vermont, there's a place along Route 103 where, if you pull off the road and walk down the bank through the trees, you'll find a ghostly locomotive museum. It is there; I have seen it. Do not ask me how it got there. I met a man with an oiling can; I helped him oil the trains.

Was he Mr. Szentgyorgyi? I leave that to you.

The rest of this story, so help me God, is true.

Straight Job

Nowadays they call it the "gap year," the year between high school graduation and college, when kids go off to experience the so-called real world. My generation, too, had a name for it. We called it "fucking off."

After graduating from Bethel High, I didn't know what to do with myself. I was college material, but what should I study? Concerning the future I knew two things only: that I would be an artist, and that I'd be famous. I'd be a famous actor, like Marlon Brando, or a famous novelist, like James Jones or Nelson Algren. Or maybe a famous painter, like van Gogh. Unable to choose among an embarrassing surplus of glorious destinies, I decided meanwhile to drive a furniture truck.

I wasn't hired to drive. To drive a truck that size you needed a Class-B commercial license, meaning you had to be eighteen years old or older. I was seventeen. I was hired as "driver's helper." That was my official designation. I was the guy in the passenger seat next to The Driver—the one who helped load the truck in the morning and who was charged with reading off directions and locating streets in the road atlas. I helped carry couches and sofa beds and beds of all sizes and fake antique rolltop desks and dining room hutches and copper-lined dry sinks and arts-and-crafts bookcases and grandfather clocks and all sorts of overpriced and not very well-made furniture and accessories into homes, apartments, condominiums, and office buildings in four states: Connecticut, Massachusetts, New York, and New Jersey, with occasional forays into Pennsylvania, Vermont, New Hampshire, Rhode Island, and Maine.

That was my official job. The "official" driver was Al G. When Al and I first met he had a big droopy mustache and long, graying hair. He must have been at least forty, forty-five years old, I guessed.

He was twenty-eight. Back then everyone had to have their television character equivalent. I decided that Al was the guy Rob Reiner played in *All in the Family*, the pinko/peacenik known to his bigoted father-in-law, Archie Bunker, as Meathead.

Except for the long hair, Al was nothing like the Meathead, really. He lived in a rustic, cabin-like house set in the woods, had a wife and two sons, slaughtered and butchered his own meat, and was as rugged as the truck we both drove, but more reliable. On blizzard-strewn winter days he'd pick me up in his muffler-less Toyota Corolla hatchback and we'd splutter off to Newtown, to the Ethan Allen warehouse, located next to the town dump. Before work Al would always pull over there to check for "treasures." One morning he found an antique egg scale; another day he found an umbrella stand with just one broken crosspiece. He'd bring the stuff to the warehouse, where Bobby, the furniture repairman, would fix it up for him; then he'd take it home. Al's house was clogged with treasures rescued from the dump.

Al, Bobby, Stan (the warehouse manager—Stan the Man): they were the guys I worked with. They were married with kids and hairy arms and potbellies; they drank beer and swore. I thought, *This is the world of men.* They poked fun at me for being young and single, and because they knew I'd go to college, eventually, as they never had or would, which mixed their feelings for me. *Peter the egghead; pointy-headed Peter.* As a form of vengeance I made fun of their potbellies. "Wait till you're twenty-five," said Stan, pointing at my flat stomach. "You'll be way the hell out to here." He showed everyone where my stomach would end up. I smirked, but I didn't think it was funny. Before bed that night I did two hundred sit-ups.

Depending on how far and wide, the office scheduled between ten and fifteen deliveries a day. If we finished early, we were supposed to head back to the warehouse, where Stan would make us pack the truck for the next day, or help with inventory, or do some other work. Understandably, we preferred to burn up the saved time on the road. One glance at the "trip sheet," the list of stops and addresses, and we'd know precisely how much spare time would fall to us. We'd stop for breakfast and lunch, and make extra pit stops at Dunkin' Donuts, Doughnut Time, or Mr. Doughnut, my favorite, where Margie, the cute waitress, charged us each for one doughnut but gave us two.

On summer days we'd pull over alongside a cornfield. I'd run out and come back with a load of golden ears. With luck the corn would be juicy and sweet; without, it would be feed corn that we'd spit out along with our curses. All that summer long I had the runs from eating raw corn.

In weather of all temperatures, if we happened by an abandoned house we'd pull over. Al would get out his toolbox and in we'd go, like a swat team, having broken a ground floor window or pried away a plywood barrier. Once we broke into what had been a private convalescent home and made off with a cast-iron, ceiling-mounted, oval professional chef's rack. Another time we scored a mahogany spinet piano. Whoever saw it first got to keep whatever we found. Usually Al beat me to the draw, but that piano had my name on it. It took an hour to walk it to the tailgate. Bobby did a beautiful job refinishing it. When it got to my parents' house it didn't even need tuning.[1]

I'd been working for Ethan Allen for about three weeks when one day, after we'd stopped to get some gas at a highway station, while I waited in the cab for Al to use the toilet, suddenly the passenger door next to me opened. Al said, "I'm sick of driving. Slide over there, Pete." (Al called me Pete; no one else did. With him somehow it was okay.)

I knew how to drive a standard shift but had never driven any kind of truck before. And this was no small truck. This was a forty-five-foot truck, also known as a "straight job," since it had a single chassis (unlike a tractor-trailer). Since it was powered by an International Harvester Loadstar 1600 engine, we dubbed it the Cornpopper, a nickname it more than lived up to during our cornfield raids. I still remember that first moment behind the wheel, with Al sitting there next to me as I adjusted my mirrors and moved the seat to make up for the three inches he had over me. Though identical to the passenger seat in other respects—made of the same beat-up green vinyl upholstery—still, somehow the driver's seat felt different under me. It made me feel stronger, older, more mature. My shoulders seemed to spread wider, my arms bulged thicker, my chest swelled under my green uniform shirt. The knuckles, veins, and tendons of the hand that gripped the gearshift knob (likewise green and worn shiny) stood out more sharply than they had just a few moments before. It occurred to me then that I had lost my identity, that—had I not seen the contradiction in one of those mirrors—I would have sworn I was no longer Peter, but Al G.; that we had switched not just seats, but souls. The feeling was so strong I was tempted to grab Al's pack of cigarettes from the dashboard where he kept them and slap one out of the pack as I'd seen him do a thousand times, and light up with his lighter and blow the first fumes out the lowered window, as Al did always in deference to me, his young helper (though not always without resentment), since I didn't smoke and didn't like the smell. Now that I'd taken Al's place, though, a cigarette seemed natural and even mandatory. One could no more drive a truck without smoking a cigarette than one could drive without feet or eyes.

Even without a cigarette it didn't take me all that long to gain a sense of the mass and distance behind me, to feel as if those forty-five feet of chassis were an extension of the man who turned the wheel, who shifted the gears, who controlled gas, clutch, and brake. As many an SUV driver would discover only decades later, when you drive a truck you're literally riding high. You sit above most traffic, and in sitting above you also sit beyond the jostling fray, the madding, down-there-on-the-ground crowd. Lotus and Lamborghini drivers may prize their asphalt-gripping centers of gravity; but when it comes to superiority on the highway, their squat little cars have nothing over a forty-five-foot truck. "People see a truck coming, they don't argue," Al said. Trucks invite submission. They are great levelers.

They're also great enlargers. In sneakers I'm five-foot-nine, barely, average height at best, a hundred and sixty-five dripping-wet pounds. But sit me behind the wheel of even a modest, forty-five-foot truck and watch my dimensions swell like a sponge toy. Is this why men love driving trucks? Not so much to haul things as to extend themselves?

So I drove; I was a truck driver. That appealed to me; it appealed to me enormously, as did the image of myself behind the wheel, wearing my green Ethan Allen shirt with name stitched in yellow over the left pocket, as reflected back at me in the truck's exterior mirrors, one large, rectangular and flat, the other small, round and convex, such that it accommodated not only my handsome truck driver's mug but the whole truck sweeping back in bowed perspective, including the tailgate, all forty-five feet of "her" swirled into that little round mirror like a Carvel chocolate sundae in a cup.

We took turns behind the wheel, to where Al felt comfortable enough that he'd fall asleep with me driving. Nothing could have pleased me more. That he could trust me so much, that he could feel so relaxed, helped me relax, too. One day I relaxed so much I started nodding off at the wheel, and would have nodded us straight across the divider and into the opposite lane had Al not awakened and grabbed the wheel in a nick of time. "Pull over," he said. When I did, Al chewed me out royally, to the point of tears.

"What, are you *bawling*?" he said, for sure enough the macho trucker had suddenly turned back into a seventeen-year-old boy, a barely mature one at that. For nodding off at the wheel and almost killing us both Al soon forgave me. For crying—that would take a bit longer.

It took three weeks and a cracked bell housing. The cracked bell housing belonged not to the Cornpopper, but to a Penske rental truck we'd hired from Eddie's Sunoco Station, while Eddie—who we called Half-Faced Eddie, or just plain Half Face (the other half scorched away by an engine explosion)—did a ring and valve job on the International. We discovered it after making our last delivery of the day: two end tables, an ottoman, and a cuckoo clock to a lady in Somers. We were coming down a narrow, steep, ice-slick road. Aunt Hack's Lane, that was the name of the road. I still remember. The truck's brakes were about gone, too, and so were the windshield wipers. The same stubborn patches of ice clung there from morning till dusk. Because the brakes weren't worth shit, Al had been using the transmission for a brake. All day it worked fine. But for some reason as we careened down Aunt Hack's icy back, the transmission refused to downshift.

"Hold on, Pete," Al said and applied the emergency brake. Instead of slowing, the truck's wheels locked and we started skidding.

A good thing I wasn't driving; I wouldn't have known what to do. Al did. He released the emergency brake, forced the transmission into neutral, and then, with a nasty sound of metal gears grinding and tearing ("Grind me a pound!"), rammed it into second. The truck bucked and lurched, but our momentum was impeded. With a skillful combination of emergency brake and clutchless shifting, Al got us down off that hill, my heart in my throat the whole time.

Instead of returning to the warehouse, we drove back to Half Face and told him about the bell housing, that he had to give us another truck.

Half Face shook his disfigured head. The hair on the good side of his skull was shiny and blond; on the bad side it was crinkly and dull red. "No can do," Half Face said. "I'm booked out of trucks until the New Year. You'll have to take her to Bridgeport." Bridgeport was where the Penske truck depot was located, forty minutes away down Route 25, a sporadically lit, narrow, two-lane winding road, prone to fog. And it was very foggy that night. And dark.

From the Sunoco station office, Al phoned the showroom and told the acting manager, Stillman, about the rental truck. I stood outside. From where I stood I could barely make out the shapes of the gas pumps, the fog was so thick. Through the window I watched Al grow more and more agitated, his forehead darkening as it did when he got angry.

After a few minutes he came out.

"He wants you to go to Bridgeport," Al said. Emphasis on *you*.

"I can't. I don't have a Class-B license. Remember?"

Al shook his head. "He knows that, Pete. And he doesn't give a shit. He's got fifty customers threatening to cancel orders if they don't get their furniture by Christmas. If one of us doesn't go he'll fire both our asses. And I'm not going."

"You said I'd go?"

"I didn't say anything. You don't have to do squat as far as I'm concerned. As far as I'm concerned he can fire me. Go talk to him."

None of the people I worked with at Ethan Allen liked Ron Stillman. Even as a funeral parlor director, his previous job before coming there, he had apparently not been well liked, which says a lot. In the showroom he would hit on the saleswomen and receptionists, telling bawdy jokes and inviting them for rides in his Jaguar, making their lives impossible when they refused. He had his eye on the manager's job. Frank Trimborn was the manager. And though Frank drank too much and was over-generous with bonuses and free furniture ("That chair you want? I wouldn't let my neighbor's dog shit on that chair. Do me a favor, would you, and please, *please* take it away!"), Frank had a big heart. When not working at the showroom, he was president of the Bethel Theatrical Association, which staged revivals of Broadway musicals. I played Tony in *West Side Story*, and Lancelot in *Camelot*. Frank got me the driver's helper job. One day, after a glass of scotch too many, Frank walked through a glass door in his own house, putting Ron Stillman in charge.

I got on the phone and talked to Ron. I waited until we were back at the warehouse and called from there, while the rest of the guys stood around. For myself I didn't care, but I wasn't about to let Al, who had a wife and two kids to support, lose his job. As the others watched, I told Ron exactly what a huge pus-dripping dickwad I thought he was, but that I'd drive his goddamn truck for him anyway, not that he deserved it. "And Merry Fucking Christmas to you," I said, and slammed down the phone dramatically.

The others were impressed. They whistled. They nodded. They shook their heads. They patted me on the back. "Way to go, Pete," said Bobby. "Fuckin' A," said Stan the Man.

But I was already on my way to the truck thinking: fuck them, fuck everybody. Stillman wants his truck exchanged, I'll exchange his damn truck, sure, no problem, I'll exchange it. Prick. Cocksucker. I climbed into the cab, started the engine, grabbed Al's cigarettes from the dashboard, and lit one. Fuckers.

I took off. I slammed gears and hauled bass down that foggy, dark road, high beams on the whole way, the fog sucking up most of the light they threw off. I was livid, afraid, tears and cigarette smoke mingling in my eyes. I wanted to mash that truck into Stillman's face, but I also wanted love: the love and respect of other men, yeah, but more than that I wanted to love myself as a man, a fully grown man, to feel at last that I had not only arrived at but gone beyond the crux of manhood. This truck with cracked bell housing gave birth to a new me that night. It produced a better Peter, a Peter who could drive a crippled truck forty miles to Bridgeport in the fog and ice, with a set of bad brakes. It gave rise to that fiercely noble male specimen known as Peter Selgin, Man among Men.

I shifted gears; I played the radio; I lit another cigarette.

When I got to Bridgeport, a man met me in the Penske lot to give me the keys to the replacement truck. I had to pull the injured one into a slot between two other trucks. By then I was so tired I could barely think, let alone back a forty-five-foot truck into a space as tight and narrow as a walk-in closet. I didn't hear iron slicing aluminum as my tailgate did a *Titanic* against the truck to my right, a two-inch gash half the length of the box. Fuck them, I thought. By then, mentally I was already halfway home. I didn't care what I tore up along the way. Who says grown men aren't destructive?

A week later Stillman called me into his office to show me the Polaroids he'd been sent showing the damage. He'd have to take it out of my pay, he said. I said that would be difficult since I quit, and threw the keys on Stillman's[2] desk to which I gave a solid kick before leaving. As gestures go it might have won an Academy Award for hollowness, since by then it was January, and I had already been accepted for mid-term enrollment at the Pratt Institute in Brooklyn, where I'd decided to study art. School started in two weeks.

NOTES

1. So I discovered when Reidun, the AFS student from Norway, played Gershwin on it. See "Gjetost."

2. A few years later I'd order a hotdog from an umbrella cart parked by the sidewalk at Western Connecticut State University. The man working the cart was Ron Stillman. "Give me a footlong," I said. "With everything on it."

Gjetost

eidun initiated me. An AFS (American Field Service) student from Norway, she had a moon face framed with tight blond curls, with eyes so big and blue and forehead so high she looked like a giant beautiful baby. A concert pianist, she banged out Beethoven and Gershwin from memory, and played Rachmaninoff to raise the devil. We spread a picnic blanket in a grassy clearing in the woods behind my house. I had brought a bottle of Mr. Boston apricot brandy from my parents' liquor closet; Reidun brought the gjetost (pronounced: yay-toast).

Reidun was different from other girls. Not just because she came from Norway and played the piano. She wore long, white, crinoline skirts that swayed and billowed when she walked. That was one of the things I liked about her, that and her accent and her piano playing, and the fearless way she had of looking at and smiling at you. Along with a Swiss Army knife, she took the gjetost from her rucksack. The knife handle and the foil the cheese came wrapped in were both the same dark red. The cheese was a three-inch square cube, its shape suggestive of a gold ingot, of something dense and rare.

As I poured paper cups of Mr. Boston apricot brandy, Reidun cut thin slices of the pale brown cheese. It curled away from the blade like planed wood. This was her favorite food, she said. In Norway she ate it every morning for breakfast, sliced paper-thin on a metal cheese slicer and served on a hunk of Norwegian flatbread. As a child she had eaten it with glasses of cold milk in summer and mugs of hot milk or cocoa in winter.

She softly fed the first slice into my mouth, her small, pink, piano-playing fingers grazing my lips. At first it tasted, I thought, like a cross between peanut butter and caramel, but saltier, and with a hint of gaminess that burst into full-blown rankness as I chewed. I had never tasted goat cheese of any kind before. Its funkiness spread to every corner of my mouth and pervaded my sinuses. The sweetness made it both better and worse. The sticky cheese stuck to the roof of my mouth; I had to pry it loose with my finger. Reidun laughed. "Do you like it?" she asked. She had the best smile.

"Mmm, mmmm," I said.

She handed me her cup of apricot brandy, which she found too sweet: a bad choice to go with goat cheese. It was summer. The woods around us were besieged with gypsy moth caterpillars, their ghostly gray tents haunting every other tree, the air alive with the sound of their invisible droppings, which mimicked rain. I was seventeen years old and not even slightly sophisticated for my age. What I still had to learn about life ought to have shamed and amazed me. I never imagined, for instance, that a cheese could be both rank and sweet, or that a pretty girl from Norway who played *Rhapsody in Blue* from memory could carry buckets of lust in her heart, or that in a few months she would break mine worse than it had ever been broken before.

Reidun lived with the Wozniaks, her American family, over in Chimney Acres, a development by the high school. Her AFS brother, Rardy, older than me by two years, worked at the bicycle seat factory, or at his father's Sunoco station—or both; I wasn't sure. Rardy never shaved. He didn't have a beard, exactly, just stubble. He drove a Pontiac with little or no muffler, wore his greasy brown hair pulled back in a ponytail, and dressed eternally in ratty, tie-dyed "I don't give a shit about anything" T-shirts. Unsavory: that is the word which, had I thought of it back then, I'd have applied to him. Though I'd never gotten close enough to Rardy to smell him, I assumed that he smelled like an unshaven, greasy, unsavory goat.

When I first met Reidun at the AFS welcoming reception in the Knights of Columbus pavilion, she sat before an out-of-tune upright, heaving herself into Gershwin's *Rhapsody*, head bobbing, nostrils flared, breasts heaving, sweat dripping from her face. As she threw her whole body into every note, I leaned coolly against the wall, doing my best in the green Ethan Allen windbreaker that I wore fresh from work to look like James Dean. A crowd had gathered around to listen to her. It occurred to me, briefly, that "getting her" might not be as easy as I had thought. Since my parents were European, it had seemed to me logical that I'd have the edge with a girl from across the Atlantic. Also, a year older, I'd already graduated from high school. Who were my competition but pimply-faced seniors and football-headed, Boone's Farm apple-wine-drinking hicks, and guys like Rardy Wozniak that no sane woman could ever possibly want to have anything to do with?

Now, seeing the crowd gathered around her and the unbridled fervor with which she all but attacked that piano, I wondered if maybe my worldliness had met its match, and also if perhaps the green Ethan Allen uniform might have been a mistake, given that lovely pleated skirt that she wore, which draped itself to the buckled floorboards. In collaboration with a frilly white puffy-sleeved blouse and the round baby face the skirt made her look angelic—a sweaty, heaving, bobbing, Gershwin-pounding seraph. And there I was, the jerk in the Ethan Allen uniform pretending to be James Dean, my tongue turned into a wad of paper towel in my mouth. Something smarter than me inside myself already understood that she was out of my league: too mature, too worldly, too sophisticated, too something.

The golden brown gjetost was by turns musty and sweet, golden and goaty, delicious and disgusting. In its own way it was a lot like sex, that cheese, at least to this still categorically adolescent male, perfectly if precariously balanced between love and obscenity. Stretched out on a scratchy blanket in the woods, Reidun fed me slice upon slice, kissing me between slices—her kisses and her gjetost both washed down with apricot brandy. Soon those kisses turned to heavier things, including some that, though I had often framed them in my mind conceptually, I had never done with or to anyone, until everything started spinning and I reeled around to throw up on the leafy forest floor. Was it the gjetost? Reidun wanted to know. No, no, I assured her, shaking my dizzy head vehemently, as though anything short of a vehement denial would have made me some sort of gjetost prude: as if the ability to ingest that golden gaminess were the test of a strong and thorough masculinity.

The rest of that summer I hardly saw Reidun. I kept working for Ethan Allen, winding along Connecticut roads in a truck packed with dry sinks, oak dining room sets, and sofa beds. When I asked her out, Reidun made excuses, a birthday party here, a headache there.

I wasn't concerned. She was new to my country, after all, with things to get used to—as I'd had to get used to the taste of gjetost. "Give her time to settle down," I told my green reflection in the furniture truck's round side mirror.

From June to September I saw her twice. Once I took her to the movies. I believe we saw *Dog Day Afternoon*—or was it *One Flew Over the Cuckoo's Nest*? Whatever, it was a poor choice for a date, one of those films that climbs into your head and stays there for hours after you've left the theater, and just when you and your date should be furiously making out, instead you find yourselves thinking. In my beat-up, leaky MGB parked in the rain across the street from the Wozniak house, I kissed and fumblingly fondled her, but Reidun's mind was elsewhere. At last, and with a perfunctory peck on the cheek, she left me to watch her run in heels through the rain up the driveway to her adoptive home. There, a kitchen light went on, and I watched Rardy Wozniak's sleazy shadow slide past the window toward the front door.

After that she refused all further invitations. I insisted on some explanation—in person, preferably. At last she agreed to go for a walk in the orchard with me, among rows of gnarly trees bursting with apples so ripe they perfumed the air with their cider smell. There she told me the truth: that she had come to America to sin, that she wanted nothing to do with romantic love—mine or anyone else's. I asked her what made her think my love was "romantic"? Reidun shook her head. "It's not possible for boys to feel any other kind. And you're still a boy," she said. "Boys—they fall in love. But I don't want love; I want lust." I assured her, tried to, that I had plenty of lust to offer her. She humored me with her smile. "You don't even know what it is. Not pure lust. As a fantasy, maybe, but not really." She took my hand. "You're very sweet, Peter. Sweet and sentimental. I don't want sweetness. Find a sweet girl. That's what you need."

I saw her one more time after that. It was Halloween. I had gotten it into my head to dress up like a gangster. I wore a double-breasted, blue, Nathan Detroit-style suit, with exaggerated pinstripes, a wide, garish tie, a fake red geranium in my lapel button, and spats improvised out of white handkerchiefs from my father's dresser drawer. From Papa's closet I secured a tired old fedora, badly crumpled, that

I donned at a rakishly sharp angle so its brim cast my left eye in deep shadow. Then two final touches: a fat unlit stogie and, back when such things were still to be had, a full-sized and quite convincing plastic toy Thompson submachine gun.

Dressed thus, in my aggressively ungangsterly MGB convertible with four different-sized tires and rusted-out rocker panels, I drove to Chimney Acres, to the Wozniak's house, Halloween my perfect pretext for knocking on the door. In the time-honored tradition of Dillinger and Capone I would acquaint our exchange student with the true spirit of America, while also, with any luck, getting it through her thick Norwegian skull that I wasn't the cloyingly sweet innocent she imagined me to be: that I, too, had my salty, musty, lusty, goatish side. Did I think all this through consciously? Of course not. I just thought it would be cool to present myself as a hoodlum to the object of my romantic longings, to be seen as anything other than a naive and innocent seventeen-year-old kid.

Though Reidun herself answered my knock, she didn't remain for long. Seeing me standing there with spats and machine gun her round eyes bloomed twice as round. With her piano fingers raised to her lips she backed slowly into the house, then turned and ran off calling her host brother's name. Presently Rardy appeared. He wore a tie-dyed T-shirt. He hadn't shaved.

"What do you want?" he said.

"I came to see Reidun," I said, sounding not at all like a gangster. Here was a true convergence: the sweet kid done up as a thug and the real McCoy.

"You scared the shit out of her."

"It's Halloween," I explained.

"Halloween's tomorrow. Today's the thirtieth."

"No it's not."

Rardy Wozniak shook his greasy head. "Jerk," he said, and closed the door in my face.

I lied when I said I never saw her again. I did, but only at a remove and in hopeless contexts, arm-in-arm with her incestuous American Field Service brother. She had come to America in search of untempered lust, and found it in Rardy Wozniak. I meanwhile quit my Ethan Allen job and toured Europe—to broaden my horizons, sure, but also to help me forget about Reidun. There I sampled all kinds of exotic cheeses: runny and moldy, stinky and musty.

In time I would taste all kinds of desire, too, from piquant longing to salty lust; from pungent infatuation to tart jealousy; from sour envy to saccharine adulation. Yet never again would the sweetness of longing be so perfectly balanced with the musky, gamy saltiness of lust as it was that summer when Reidun first opened my eyes—and my tongue—to hard/soft, musty/sweet, heady/mild, cloying/rank, golden/smutty, delicate/obscene gjetost, that most paradoxical of cheeses. As paradoxical, in its way, as love.

To Die of Italy

*ie of love or of loathsome disease,* I wrote in my journal. *Die of too much wine or sun or sex. Die of syphilis or suicide or old age. But die in Italy.*

It was the summer of Chernobyl. I sat at a seaside bar, sipping a *digestivo,* looking out over the water, my reveries interrupted by the occasional loud splutterings of Vespas. I was twenty-three years old and in Italy, alone.

Well, not exactly alone. My Uncle Sergio slept in a hotel room less than three blocks away.

Or maybe he wasn't asleep. Maybe he was already up, standing in front of the window rubbing his big belly against the sill, his gray features sagging like an old washcloth, searching for signs of me along the seawall, smelling of dead farts, Ben-Gay and grappa, tears welling up in his rheumy blue eyes.

I am thinking, I kept writing, *of the novel I have yet to start writing, of Italian women in general, and of my second cousin, Bianca, a.k.a. the Lady in the Castle, in particular. And of my uncle, who is driving me crazy, and how to get rid of him, the stinking pervert.*

Until I was nine, when Lenny Polis explained it to me, I didn't even know what a relative was. I'd heard the word before, spoken usually in embarrassed whispers. We stood at the corner of Wooster and Keeler, Lenny and I, waiting for the school bus. According to Lenny, who spoke from experience, relatives were bizarre, often dangerous strangers usually encountered at equally bizarre and outrageous events called family reunions, who somehow (and here Lenny was vague) had something to do with oneself.

That day, it so happened, Lenny Polis was bound for such a reunion, and I could only feel sorry for him. Like any healthy nine-year-old, I preferred to think of myself as a protean entity smuggled in from some far away planet in another solar system, posing temporarily as the child of some extremely unintelligent and unsophisticated humanoids. Parents were embarrassing enough, but relatives? I felt very lucky. My parents were from Italy; my relatives, assuming I had a few, were tucked safely away across a vast and mighty ocean, and might as well have been dead.

So I thought then. But less than a year later, as my father waved goodbye from a New York City pier, my mother and I set sail on an ocean liner across that vast and mighty ocean to the land of relatives.

I remember my first glimpse of Uncle Sergio. He met us on the gritty platform of the Milan train station. His head was oversized and stubbled, red and raw where it wasn't pale, his eyes small, sunken, wet, and blue. He cried, his whole fat body jerking with sobs. He wore brown pants belted high over his belly, with a mismatched brown suit jacket and a gray vest—everything brown and gray. Aside from the gold chain of his antique pocket watch, the Kodak Instamatic dangling from his neck, and the tears running down his stubbled face, he looked as if he needed dusting.

Cara mia! Mia sorrella! Mio nipote! Oh, cara mia!

Because Sergio earned his living as a hotel porter he insisted on carrying all of our bags. He walked with a limp, the bags bumping into his legs with every step. Once outside the train station he stopped, drew a handkerchief that looked more like a rag from one of his pockets, and swept it quickly across his whole face, which dripped sweat. Seeing me watch him, he looked me straight in the eye and, smiling, touched the top button of my shirt. "What's this?" he asked in Italian. I looked down, his finger went up.

I thought: this is going to be a long vacation.

Sergio lived in a *pensione* for poor people. His was a ten-by-ten-foot room with a sink and a hot plate. To shower you had to walk all the way around a veranda to the other side of the courtyard, to a small red door with a sign that said "W. C." You had to squat.

"How can anyone live like this?" said my mother, who checked us into a hotel immediately.

Three summers later Uncle Sergio came to the United States for the first and last time. I'd just turned twelve and was in the midst of discovering new and shockingly delightful aspects of my own body, a process I was in no great hurry to complete. Uncle Sergio's jokes, too, had grown more sexual. He still did the joke with his finger, only now he touched a different spot on my body. One afternoon we were cutting back shrubs along the driveway when, reaching over to pick up a pair of hedge shears lying between us, he made a grab for my crotch. I cried out; Sergio drew back, red-faced, indignant. He yelled at me. How, he demanded to know, in the space of two short years, had I managed to become such a sourpuss?

"For the love of God!" he said in Italian.

That summer of Chernobyl, I stayed with other relatives.

They lived less than an hour's drive south of Milan, in the valley of the River Trebbia, divided among two villas.

Bianca, one of a half-dozen second cousins, had just turned twenty-six, and was beautiful. Her brother, Ricardo, was my age. The Villa Bianca, as I called it, looked like a smallish castle, with a turret and crenellated battlements. It featured a separate picnic house, acres of vineyards, a pool graced by marble statues, and a full-time grounds-keeper who lived in his own adjacent cottage. A family of gazelles grazed on the nearby hilltop, with hay stored for them in a red stucco shack. But of all the villa's features the gate was my favorite. A long driveway of white pebbles led from the main road to the villa. At its entrance stood the tall and ornate cast-iron gate, which would open automatically, as if manned by ghosts, whenever I approached.

The Villa Gabbi—my name for the other villa—was an altogether different story. Cousin Gabbi was the mother of Paola, Stephania, and Giovanna—also my cousins, who were respectively eighteen, seventeen, and sixteen. With her wild eyes, black hair, and big bones Gabbi looked like Anna Magnani and made me think of a gypsy carnival roustabout. The stormy evening of my arrival I found her dressed in a yellow raincoat on the roof of her house, single-handedly spreading huge sheets of tarpaper.

In contrast, Gabbi's husband, Franco, was a bony, soft-spoken, and timid little man who owned a drafting supply store and wanted little more than to be able to watch television in peace. "Look at me, Peter," he said the night of my arrival after a lengthy supper as all three of his daughters clamored to dress for the discotheque. "I have three children—all of them girls." He stretched his arms out. "I am Jesus Christ."

The Villa Gabbi also had a gate, but it was small, plain, and rusty and left open all the time. There were some grapevines, but no gazelles, no picnic house, no marble statues, no pool, no turret. And the roof leaked. Gabbi insisted I stay there. "You will not like the other place," she told me in Italian (she spoke not a word of English). "They have a pool, yes, but they have no heart! They have marble statues—but they will treat you badly! Here is where you belong!" So saying she threw on her yellow raincoat and hurried back up onto the roof.

It wasn't long before I realized that my presence had rekindled a feud that had been dormant for many years. In the coming days each of the two villa families broke their backs in an effort to outdo each other for hospitality: more food, more wine, more entertainment and games. But once I made it known that what I really wanted was some peace and quiet in which to get my novel started, it became a contest between villas to see which could offer me more of each.

"While it is true," said Gabbi in Italian (none of my cousins, save Bianca and Ricardo, spoke English), "that we have no turret to offer you, what do you need a turret for? Here you have a beautiful room!" (It was true: they had given me a nice clean room all my own.) "All yours! And a lovely typewriter—Olivetti! Look—!" With two fingers she typed the word Olivetti. "You see? And though it is true that my girls come home late at night and they make much noise, we shall put a stop to that! From now on, no more discotheque! We have a writer in the house! An American writer! *Una scrittore!* I shall hang a sign: *QUESTO L'AMERICANO!* ('This is the American!'); I shall paint it in great letters on the roof! What more can you ask?"

I took the turret.

From my room I had an unobstructed view of the valley, with its green sloping hills and poplar trees, a butter-colored *factoria* (farmhouse) in the near distance, and the Trebbia River slithering like a green snake through the landscape. At night, with the windows wide open, the wind would rush through making whistling sounds.

Bianca's bedroom was two flights below mine. In the middle of the night, wearing nothing but a towel, I'd tiptoe ever so soundlessly across the game room's icy marble floor, then down two flights of stairs praying for them not to creak, then gently turn the brass handle on her unlocked door. She'd be lying there, stretched out in a sheer robe under her bed's ghostly canopy, the wind messing up her hair.

Two weeks had passed and, Olivetti or no Olivetti, I'd gotten no-where on my novel. Instead I sunbathed and swam in the marble-statued pool and took walks back and forth between the two villas, past the butter-colored *factoria* where a red dog would run out barking and snarling, and I'd curse it in ripe English. In the evenings there would be large gatherings down at the picnic house. We would eat hand-rolled *gnocci* and drink local wine from big green bottles. The wine stained our tongues purple.

One night, with our bellies full and our tongues stained, Bianca and I decided to go for a walk. Already I was in love with her, or something like that. "You—you are such a boy," she said in English. "You are not even a boy, you are Peter Pan!" We walked down the dark and unpaved road treacherous with big stones, past the yellow *factoria* where, mercifully, the red dog slept. The moon that night was the same butter yellow as the farmhouse.

As we walked, Bianca leaned her head on my shoulder. She was *ubriaco*, which means drunk. She told me all about the man she loved, a young count named Roberto who lived in the castle down the street. I smiled. "You cannot understand," she said. "You are an American. Americans do not have these problems." I couldn't have agreed more.

She leaned in closer. I could smell her hair; it smelled of the night before. She explained to me that in Italy things had not changed in over five hundred years. "Here," she explained, "women are all slaves. You cannot fall in love. If you fall in love, you are lost. Confess your love for a man, he will laugh at you. I want so to tell Roberto that I am in love with him. But if I do I will seal my fate. He will think that I am a whore." She pronounced it *whoor*.

I listened to her, but not really. I was distracted. In a few days I was to accompany my uncle Sergio on a weekend excursion to Chiavari, on the sea. I didn't want to go. I wanted to stay here, with my cous-ins, with Bianca and my novel. My heart cringed with resentment. We had arrived near the rusty and always open gate of the Villa Gabbi. I stroked and kissed Bianca's hair. An owl hooted in a nearby tree. The river, bloated with rain, rushed. The stars were clear.

"My cousins, they all look up to me," said Bianca looking toward the burning lights of the Villa Gabbi, where at this hour, no doubt, the three girls would be getting ready for the discotheque. "They think that my life is perfect. If only they knew how very lonesome I am." She sighed.

I looked into her eyes. She was beyond me.

"You are so lucky to be American," said Bianca. "In America it is easy to be in love." She hiccupped. "In America it is possible to be in love without making a fool of yourself. But that is only because all Americans are already fools."

"Two days," my cousin Ricardo warned me the day before I was to leave for Chiavari via Milan. "That is the maximum time limit." He referred to the time I would be spending with my uncle. "After that you risk permanent brain damage."

I wondered if Sergio would still be the same, with his Kodak Instamatic and his arthritic legs. Was it possible? Could time have stood that still? Would he touch the top button of my shirt—or some other part of me—and say, "What's this?"

"He cares so much for you," my mother's voice traveled through a telephone line across the vast and mighty ocean. "And besides, he has so little to look forward to: a pension that barely keeps him alive, and that horrible little room! Please," she pleaded. "Just two days. It will mean so much to him."

The next day, Saturday, Ricardo drove me to Milan. It was a hot day. By mid-morning the temperature had already reached ninety. We were to meet my uncle on a street corner near his favorite restaurant. He was late. We waited close to an hour, and I was about to say, "Oh, well," when Ricardo said, "Look at him there!" I turned and there was Sergio, looking almost exactly as he had looked ten years before. Aside from a walking stick and a bigger belly, nothing had changed. He still wore an unmatched, three-piece suit; the antique gold watch chain still hung from his vest pocket; the Kodak Instamatic still dangled from his neck; his face still had that raw, red, unshaven look; and his small blue eyes were still wet with tears—as if he'd never stopped crying. "For the love of God!" he said in Italian. "How big you have grown!"

He threw his arms around me. He still smelled the same, too. A ripe blend of grappa and old man.

He took Ricardo and me to lunch. At his favorite restaurant he guzzled glass after glass of red wine diluted with mineral water, covered his portion of the tablecloth with crumbs, slurped his *minestra*, and once farted so loudly that everyone within a radius of ten meters turned their heads, prompting him to excuse himself even more loudly, and then to explain to those at the closest table, who were in the middle of their meal, that he suffered from a rare and complex bowel disorder—which he took great pains to elucidate—and was, he concluded regretfully, therefore unable to prevent certain spontaneous bodily occurrences.

Ricardo laughed hysterically.

"It's easy for you to laugh," I said. "You don't have to spend the weekend with him!" Which made him laugh all the harder.

As our waitress bent over to wipe the table, Sergio pointed with his fork to her breasts, noting their size and softness and asking me would I not like to rest my head there and take a nap?

"For godsake, Uncle, quit embarrassing me!"

"Uncle? Uncle? What is this 'uncle' nonsense? Do I have such a big stick up my ass? Call me Sergio, for the love of God! And have some more wine! Here—put some mineral water in it! What's the matter, you don't like mineral water? It does the heart good they say. Makes you fart, too!"

Ricardo was in stitches. Through the meal, even with his mouth full, Uncle Sergio never stopped talking—except to suck on his teeth.

"How is your mother, my darling, my beautiful sister! The flower of my heart! When I am alone, I think of her and I am happy! I have thousands of photographs—all of my sister and my *nipote* and your father, my American family! And the dog! What is the dog's name? Pal! How is my little Pal?"

"Pal is dead."

"What a shame. Such a lovely dog—it makes me want to cry! Come closer. Why do you sit so far away, you mischievous devil, you bandit, you! Here, now, give your uncle a kiss, why don't you?"

"Cut it out!"

"Right you are, you're much too big for that sort of thing now. What muscles you have, for the love of God! May I squeeze them? Oh, I forgot. You don't like to be touched. My *nipote*—the Greek god! Do you know about the Greeks?"

Ricardo buckled over with laughter.

That night, I slept in Sergio's tiny apartment, on the floor next to his trundle bed. It was the same ten-by-ten-foot room, but now it seemed even smaller. Under his bed he kept pornographic magazines, stacks of them, along with photo albums brimming with Kodak snapshots taken during his trip to America a decade ago: our house, our garden, my mother, my father, me, Pal, my mother's car, my father's car, and Lenny Polis, who once, a long, long time ago, explained to me, or tried to, what a relative was.

He is so fucking lonely and alone, I wrote in my journal the following evening. *Even when with me he talks to himself — or to any stranger coming down the street. This morning, as we walked to the train station, he must have stopped at least a half-dozen people — magazine vendors, bartenders, taxi drivers, hotel clerks, merchants, prostitutes. He introduced me to every one of them, saying, "Good morning, may I present to you my American nephew!" I swear none of them had any idea who he was.*

According to my mother, Sergio once looked like Paul Newman. Tall, thin, with a head of tight blond curls, zooming around town in a white suit on a Lambretta. Now he kept his dentures in a jar and rubbed arthritic joints with grappa every night. I felt sorry for him. In the hotel room in Chiavari his snoring and farting kept me wide awake. I jammed wet wads of toilet paper in my ears; I buried my face in my pillow; I switched on the bedside lamp and wrote in my journal. *"He is so damned pitiful and disgusting,"* I wrote, *"that when he finally drinks himself to death on vino rosso and mineral water it will be an act of mercy."* I wasn't feeling charitable. This was the same uncle I'd loved as a child, who made me and George and all our friends laugh like crazy when we were ten, who was like having a grown-up friend.

With the lamp still burning I fell asleep, only to be awakened by a loud, smacking sound accompanied by my uncle's heavy breathing.

I got up, dressed, packed my bag in the dark, and closed the door gently behind me.

The next train for Milan left at nine-thirty. It was not even eight o'clock. Having checked my bag at the station, I walked along the seawall, imagining myself to be as insubstantial as fog, shadowed by vague feelings of remorse and uncertainty. Uncle Sergio was already up by then, wondering where I'd gone, stinking already of grappa. Someday, I wondered, will I be as old and wretched? As alone?

In a heap of jagged concrete forms the seawall came to an abrupt end. I stood there, watching a ship in the distance as the waves tore themselves to bits against the bulkhead. In the closer distance a trio of fishing boats bobbed like orange rinds. I imagined a great sign spanning the horizon—"The Search for Romance Ends Here."

At a quarter to nine I went back to the train station where, having claimed my bag, I stood in line for my ticket. Uncle Sergio was there, gripping his suitcase and his walking stick, his eyes red from crying.

"Forgive me, *nipote*! I am a dirty old man. Go on—give your uncle a slap, I deserve it!"

A loudspeaker announced the arrival of our train. I inched forward in the ticket line.

"I've already bought them!" said Sergio, waving two tickets in the air.

Uncle Sergio insisted on "escorting" me back to my cousins. At every station along the way he would jump up from his seat yelling, *Piacenza! Piacenza! Siamo arrivate!* ("Piacenza! Piacenza! We have arrived!"), causing other passengers to leap from their sound sleep, grab their bags, and rush to the door.

The passengers said, *Cosa credi che stai facendo?* ("What do you think you're doing?")

Uncle Sergio said, *Voleve solo aiutare!* ("I was only trying to help!")

I hung my head in embarrassment.

Neither the Villa Gabbi nor the Villa Bianca wanted anything to do with Sergio. Like a hot potato, they handed him back and forth saying, "But you would be so much more comfortable there."

For his part Sergio didn't seem to mind. He made himself at home in both villas. Where no one invited him, he invited himself. Otherwise he would go off into a corner and cry, until finally he would get his way. We called him "the beast" and "the burden."

Partly to get away from Sergio and his antics, Ricardo and I spent a day horseback riding. We drove to the stable in Ricardo's Renault with the gearshift sticking out of the dashboard. Once there, Ricardo ordered one *Inglese* and one *Americano*, assuming that I, being from the States, preferred to ride Western. We sauntered up steep, muddy trails, trotted down paved roads, cantered through fields. We were galloping through an apple orchard when I lost my balance and found myself hanging from one stirrup over the side. Unable to get the horse to stop, I let myself fall, which at that speed and angle didn't exactly feel like an act of volition. I fell headfirst and heard my bones crack against the red earth.

Ricardo sidled up beside me. "I'm okay," I said, wiping a wedge of red clay off my riding helmet. *Non c'e paura.* I was dazed; my head spun. "I'm fine, fine."

I got back on my horse.

On the way home the *nebbia* (fog) was so thick Ricardo had to turn on the windshield wipers. Bianca met us at the gate. Her face looked white. She told us to change out of our clothes—instantly!—and come quickly into the house. Inside, a dozen or more people, including Uncle Sergio, were gathered in the parlor in front of the television set, where an anchorperson spoke so swiftly that I could barely understand a word. They showed an aerial photograph of a steaming tower, and men in strange white suits. Gradually I understood. A nuclear reactor in Chernobyl, Ukraine, had blown up. It had taken several days for the news, along with a dense cloud of radioactive fallout, to reach northern Italy. Some experts claimed the radiation was one thousand times normal levels. Others insisted that the amounts were negligible, like having a half-dozen chest x-rays.

Non c'e paura, one expert kept saying. Still, fresh milk was banned, as were all fruits and vegetables. And babies were to be kept indoors.

That evening, in the picnic house, we ate pasta, played card games, and—having decided that we had about ten years left to live—got very drunk. We played a game called *sette domandi,* consisting of seven questions, each of which was filled in to make up a story: Who is he? Who is she? What are they doing? Where are they doing it? What does he say? What does she say? What do the people say? In almost every instance "he" turned out to be my Uncle Sergio.

That same night a party was held at the castle of the count who lived just down the road. Alone with Roberto, having fortified her courage with a great deal of local wine, Bianca attested to the full measure of her undying love. I found her at dawn, sprawled among grapevines, her lovely white dress edged with vomit.

"I am so disgusting," she said as I helped her to her feet. "I am so disgusting—and so are you."

"Why am I disgusting?" I asked.

"You are disgusting because you are my cousin and I hate you."

"I'm your second cousin," I reminded her.

"Yes," said Bianca. "And I am *your* second cousin, too. We are both second cousins. We are second cousins and we are both disgusting."

I held her. We stood in the middle of the road.

"Go on, go back to America!" she said.

"Why?"

"Because you are an American, and all Americans are disgusting!"

"And you're full of shit," I said, then I bent my head down and tried to kiss her. She smelled of vomit. She jumped away.

"*O dio*! What time is it? I have to make breakfast! *O—la miseria!*"

She ran down the road.

In the days that followed, various scientific findings relating to the accident at Chernobyl were released. According to one study, as many as twelve thousand people were likely to die of cancer as a result of radiation. Most of the victims would be people who were in Germany and parts of northern Italy during the days immediately following the blast.

Bianca dipped her big toe in the pool but decided it was too cool to swim. Having decided also that the sun was too hot, she turned her chair into the shade. It was never Bianca's way to be satisfied.

"Peter, help me," she said, like a child, sipping a *pompelmo* (grapefruit soda), her dark eyes hidden under even darker sunglasses. "I cannot go on living like this. I am a prisoner here. I live the life of a dog."

"So why don't you leave?" I suggested. "Pack your things, get in a car, and drive away."

She laughed. I asked her what was so funny.

"I can't drive!" she said, laughing.

"I'm serious."

"You are not serious! You are Peter Pan! In two days you will go home! You don't know anything!"

Five weeks in Italy and no novel. Who to blame more, Uncle Sergio or Bianca? Or myself?

It made no difference. In a few years I would be dead. We would all be dead. I had come to Italy to see my family and write my novel and now I was going to die and there would be no novel, not mine nor anyone else's, since the world was going to end.

My cousins took me to the airport. At the security check the officer in charge found a last-minute surprise parting gift from Uncle Sergio: one of his porno magazines spread open there in my suitcase, displaying what looked like a giant redwood rising up into the cloud forest of a woman's pudendum.

I said, *Non e mio!* ("It's not mine!")

Bianca said, *Sporcaccione!* ("You horrible pig!")

The people said, *Cento di questi giorni!* ("Many happy returns!")

Keeping Up with the Days . . . .

> *There is no doubt in my mind that a demon*
> *has been living in me since birth.*
> —*David Berkowitz ("Son of Sam") in his diary*

 pparently, I could be quite a show-off. Once, at a college dorm party, I engaged the guests by dangling by one arm from the terrace railing. The dorm was in a high-rise building, the party on the fifteenth floor. Another time, in the parking lot of an abbey in northern Germany, a similar desperate bid for attention had me jumping backward, or trying to, over a two-foot-tall post chain barrier. Apparently I was wearing cowboy boots; apparently the back of a heel caught; apparently I was out cold for two minutes. When I came to, I couldn't feel or move from the neck down. My first (apparent) words to my traveling companions: "Guys, I think I just ruined our summer vacation."

My nervous system recovered, but my memory didn't. If I say "apparently" it's because I don't recall either scenario. If not for the testimonies of multiple eyewitnesses, I'd dismiss both stories as apocryphal. I wish, too, that I could blame my memory lapses on alcohol or mind-bending drugs. But I've never been much of a drinker, and drugs played no role in my behavior or my memory loss.

If I don't remember either incident, it's because I didn't make a record of them on paper. For a period of about ten years, starting when I was a senior in high school, I was a compulsive journal keeper, you might even say *addict*. Wherever I went, I carried a notebook with me, and filled it with the flotsam and jetsam of my days. In the beginning the journals were oversized (twelve-by-sixteen-inch, some even larger), plain paper notebooks designed more for sketching than for scribbling, with spiral bindings that came unwound and caught on girls' sweaters and in their hair. In my journals I recorded observations, experiences, snatches of conversations, lush descriptions of landscapes and rooms, of people I met, places I visited. When at a loss for words I threw in some sketches, too. But mostly I wrote. In fact that's just about all I did. For ten years I was a machine whose primary purpose was to turn life into words and feed them to my ravenous notebooks, like a mother bird feeding worms to her chicks.

To give you an idea of just how bad my habit was, when dining among friends I'd keep my damned notebook open next to my place setting, between salad bowl and bread-and-butter dish, and scribble away between bites of food and sips of coffee or wine. (The few notebooks I've kept from those addicted days all bear ketchup, soy sauce, coffee, and wine stains to prove it.)

At first even my most indulgent friends balked at being shadowed by this recording angel, this stenographer escaped from the courtroom, this dime-store Frere Goncourt. Those who didn't like it had a choice: they could grin and bear it, or they could stop being my friends. I lost a lot of friends.

The ones I didn't lose got used to it, or they resigned themselves, I guess. I can't be sure. Honestly, their feelings weren't of that much concern to me. When it comes to an addict and his addictions, the feelings of others don't often count for very much. And like all addicts, I rationalized my behavior and its morality. After all, was not my habit as much a part of me as my arms and legs? Did my true friends—those capable of understanding me at all—not understand that to ask me to put my notebook away would have been like asking me to saw off my nose and slip it into my pocket? We were inseparable, my notebooks and I, like John and Yoko.

People think of diary keeping as a positive thing, a source of therapy and enlightenment, not to mention self-amusement. All over the country "journaling" workshops are the rage, with participants encouraged to unleash and unburden themselves daily in writing, to get to know themselves and tend their psychic and spiritual gardens. In the United States alone, five million diaries or so-called "blank books" are sold every year (it wouldn't surprise me to learn that the number exceeds that of annual first novel sales). In *Writing Down the Bones*, writing guru Natalie Goldberg instructs her disciples to "finish a notebook a month . . . Simply fill it. That is the practice." That is also a lot of notebooks. Julia Cameron's *The Artist's Way*, a twelve-step program for creative self-fulfillment (that, among other things, encourages its adherents to "journal" every morning), has been an international bestseller for years. Diary keeping, a once utterly private and even (with its faintly onanistic undertones) distasteful act, has grown into a vastly popular pastime and a multi-million-dollar industry.

But is diary keeping good for you?

In my case, it wasn't. But then I may have gone too far. I didn't just keep a diary; I kept it to an unhealthy extreme. My diary became not the place where I kept track of my existence, but where I lost it in a flurry of words, my spiritual garden choked with verbal weeds. My habit made me rude, terribly rude. I had no idea how rude I could be.

Well, I had some idea. One evening, on a double date in the East Village, I was given my comeuppance. My date was a Turkish conceptual artist named Gülsen (pronounced Goo-shen). We were sitting around her coffee table, drinking wine and eating caviar-stuffed eggs, when I got out my notebook and started writing. Gülsen, whose pencil drawings typically consisted of a single fine line drawn vertically down a sheet of tracing paper (a line so delicate you had to stand within centimeters to see it), and who could be as blunt in person as her drawings were subtle, put down her glass of wine and said, "Why don't you count the flowers in my vase, Peter, and write down the number? Or better still, why not take off all your clothes, count your pubic hairs, and tell your notebook how many there are?" It worked. I blushed and put the notebook away. But Gülsen's lesson was short-lived: you can't shame an addict into quitting. The next day I was at it again, and the day after that, scribbling away, trying as hard as ever to keep up with the days.

For that was what my compulsion was based on: the notion that one could somehow hold on to one's life by putting it down in words: that in recording my experiences I was saving them, keeping them from being ground to smithereens in time's garbage disposal. With each tick of the clock another moment was gone, forgotten. My sense of loss was great, or would have been, but I had the cure: I would hoard and preserve my experiences, vacuum-pack them away like peaches and pears in Mason jars, trap them like flies in amber. I would rescue my past from oblivion.

Little did I know that by so "rescuing" my life I would sacrifice it. Not only would I relinquish the past like everyone else, I would lose my memories of those days. I'd trade them in for a tangled web of useless, mildewy words.

My diary-keeping addiction didn't spring forth full-grown and in armor like Athena from the skull of Zeus. Its origins go far back. Though I wouldn't become a full-fledged addict until my twenties, I had my first taste of the wicked drug when I had just turned seven. For my birthday my mother gave me a diary: a four-by-five-inch book bound in synthetic white leather (which has since badly cracked), the words EVERY DAY DIARY stamped on the front cover over a cartoon basket of pink and red flowers. The pages inside were gilt-edged, ruled, and ticked-off with the days of the month. At the top of each page the words MY DIARY in vehement all-caps reinforced my already ironclad conviction that the little book had been manufactured for me alone.

The first entry is dated February 20, five days after my birthday. I quote it in full: *I went to the movie. The movie was all Western. I called it crap for babies.*

You see here in embryo the critic I would become in my later years, as well as the full extent of my literary skills, which, over the next decade, would not improve considerably. I remember how possessively I clutched that little diary to my seven-year-old bosom, like a BaMbuti tribeswoman suckling her newborn. I kept the diary in a carved wooden box behind my bed, locked away from my twin brother's probing fingers (which I threatened to break if he ever touched it). Unlike everything else in our lives—our sweaters, our friends, the games we played—this small book with its hideous floral cover was one thing I was not required to share, a sign that said, "I'm me— you're not!" With each word I entered into its gilt-edged pages, my sense of my own uniqueness increased.

But while part of me guarded my words as if they were gold bricks in Fort Knox, another, more hidden part longed to disperse them— like barbs from a porcupine's back. In addition to the days of the week, on the bottom corner of each right-hand page there were spaces set aside for Special Events. Under one such heading I wrote: *George Selgin stinks like the sewer he lives in. SUPER SECRET.* [underscored twice]— evidence that my "secret" diary wasn't so secret after all, that some part of me not only expected it to be read, but hoped, longed for it, as a hunter longs for the quarry to spring his trap. (Come to think of it, isn't every diary a kind of booby trap to be sprung long after its keeper has set it and fled? A bomb with a very long fuse?)

The entries in my EVERY DAY DIARY were sustained through Thanksgiving, when "we ate turky [sic] stuffing, peas, and an artichoke." Shortly afterward, my brother and I started a neighborhood club called U.N.C.L.E ("Unqualified Nazi Criminals Laundry Enamas [sic]"). Dues: 5¢. Objective: "But [sic] into peoples games and try to convince them you're one of the players." Eight more entries follow, listing names of club members with dues paid or owed. Then the pages go blank and stay that way.

Six years passed before I kept my next notebook, this one assigned by my eighth-grade English teacher, Mr. Prudhomme, and referred to not as a "diary" but a "journal"—a prophylactic distinction designed to forestall visions of Ann Margaret scrawling in bathrobe and bunny slippers. It was the early 1970s, and mood rings, powder-blue leisure suits, and creative self-indulgence were all popular. Ira Progoff would soon start flogging his Intensive Journal Workshops, but Prudhomme was a step ahead of him. He had us write in our journals every day, spurred on by e. e. cummings's words, sprawled in purple-blue ink down a mimeograph sheet:

> to be
>
> nobody but
> your-
> self
>
> in a world
> which
> is doing its best
> night and day
> to make you
> everybody
> else

I took the words to heart. I tried as hard as I could to be nobody but myself. It wasn't easy, with everyone around me trying equally hard and using the same means. Still, it felt good getting up early every morning and writing in my journal, over a mug of hot tea (not my father's bagged Lipton floorsweepings, but loose Formosa oolong, as Prudhomme and I had drunk it together, squatting at the Japanese-style table in the one-room apartment he rented at the edge of town). Scribbling in my journal made me feel mature, worldly—even a bit holy. I was thirteen years old.

Under Prudhomme's tutelage we did more than keep journals. We launched our school's first underground newspaper (knocked off on the same ditto-master), wore love beads, and staged sit-ins against the Vietnam War. Two months before the school year's official end Prudhomme left in a cloud of controversy.

With Prudhomme's departure, again my notebook keeping entered a long hibernation from which it didn't emerge until senior year, high school, with drawings—brazen caricatures of classmates and teachers—replacing words. These notebooks were practically community property, their pages greasy with the thumbprints of the curious, who passed them around as if they were oracles to be consulted in times of strife.

As senior year gave way to summer, and summer to backpacking in Europe, and Europe to art school in New York City, words crept back into my notebooks until—like kudzu strangling a forest—they took over again. Though I had no great command over them, something about words made them irresistible to me, possibly the fact that they weren't totally in my control. And so I wrestled with them, pinning them to page after page, not realizing that the words had me pinned, that my notebooks were writing me, displacing my life, consuming and ruining it.

Being an addict I saw none of this—or maybe I did see it, but I excused it, telling myself it was for a good cause, for Art with a capital A. I was an artist, burdened with an artist's dreams. One of those dreams was to produce a work unlike any other in its scale, rawness, honesty and originality: a direct transcription of experience that would spare no one and hold nothing back. This work, which I titled *Pure Flux*, would have no discernable plot, no theme, no consistent characters. It would be a work of chaos to match the chaos of life and would, in its own unique way, advance down that road well trodden by Miller, Céline, Kerouac, and Alexander Trocchi (whose *Cain's Book*, a novel in journal entries about a heroin junkie living on a gravel scow in New York Harbor, was the Holy Grail of my journal-keeping days) and a half-dozen other inveterate documentarians of their own dissolutions. Was I not preordained to produce a work to rival, if not surpass, theirs? Did I not have—as both a warning and a blessing—the words of Ralph Waldo Emerson, quoted in the epigraph of *Tropic of Cancer*, to guide and inspire me: "These novels will give way, by and by, to diaries or autobiographies—captivating books, if only a man knew how to choose among what he calls his experience that which is really his experience, and how to record truth truly."

If only! But I would know how to choose; I'd be one of those rare exceptions that prove rules—the rule in this case being that life, whatever else it may or may not be, is not a work of art. *Bullshit!* And so I scribbled on frantically, furiously, piling up notebooks like a bag person piling up magazines and newspapers, sure that all this piling on would add up to artistic triumph. To have confronted me then with the distinction between literature and graphomania would have been as pointless as telling a bag person that his bundles of newspaper don't amount to shit, much less salvation.

Having started down this path, I couldn't stop; I had to keep going. Even if they all but choked me out of my real life, still, I believed in my notebooks. This is the diarist's dire fate, and why—taking Anais Nin to task for her own incurable habit—Henry Miller cautioned, "You will never keep up with the days. It will be like a big web which will strangle you."

Miller wasn't alone in condemning diaries. Immanuel Kant, among many others, warned his readers to avoid the practice, which, he said, paved the way to "lies, extravagance, distortion of perspective, perhaps even to madness itself." Ironically, some of the most convincing arguments against keeping a diary are made by diarists in their diaries. Of the futility of the enterprise, the playwright Ionesco had this to say:

> Literature is powerless. I can communicate this catastrophe to no one, not even to my wife. The unendurable thing dwells within us, shut in. Our dead remain in us. And why am I writing this journal? What am I hoping for? Whom can these pages interest? Is my unhappiness, my distress, communicable? Who would take on that burden? It would have no significance for anyone.

Ionesco joins hands with Sartre, who famously described all literature as a form of neurosis. "Where there is no neurosis," said Sartre, "there is no literature, either." If all literature is neurotic, diary keeping is literature in its purest form. See the diarist locked up and scribbling away, generating enough morbid self-involvement to power a small eastern seaboard city. *I scribble, therefore I am:* such is the diarist's credo. No use explaining to him or her that a diary is to experience roughly what Cheez Whiz is to a cow. Or, to put it another way: just because you muck the stable doesn't mean you know how to ride a horse.

But diarists aren't just neurotic, they're also liars and cheaters. Of her own diary keeping Anais Nin admitted "an incentive to make your life interesting, so that your diary will not be dull"—a statement that betrays her willingness to stack the deck of existence. When Oscar Wilde quipped, "I never travel without my diary. One should always have something sensational to read on the train," he blurs the distinction between diary and novel. But that distinction will always be blurry, with diarists conflating transcription and embroidery. At the very least, a diary is selective experience. Intentionally or not, it lies through omission.

But then isn't the whole enterprise of diary keeping disingenuous, if not downright spurious? On the one hand, the diarist calls her pursuit intensely private; on the other, there's a record being made—for whom? Is there not, in the back of every diary keeper's mind, the desire—somewhere, someday, somehow—to be read?

In *A Book of One's Own*, Thomas Mallon's deft survey of diarists and their diaries, he writes, "Whether or not they admit it, I think all the purchasers of [diaries] have a 'you' in mind. . . . Perhaps in the back of their minds, or hidden in the subconscious strata, but there." Mallon goes on to say, "In fact I don't believe one can write to oneself for many more words than get used in a note tacked to the refrigerator, saying, 'Buy Bread.'" A diary with no audience is like the proverbial tree that falls with no one there to hear it: that it exists at all no one can prove.

Now, it seems that diary keepers are plagued with more than just the neurosis of their habit. A recent psychiatric study conducted in Great Britain showed that people who keep diaries are more likely to suffer from headaches, sleeplessness, digestive disorders, and social awkwardness. The study upsets long-cherished views of diary keeping as therapeutic. In fact, among test subjects who'd undergone traumatic events, the diarists fared worst of all. According to psychiatrist

Elaine Duncan of Glasgow Caledonian University, because diarists "continually churn over their misfortunes," they are less likely ever to get over them. So much for tending one's psychic garden.

By my twenty-eighth birthday I had filled over forty notebooks. But I didn't think of myself as a "diarist," or of my notebooks as "diaries." Nor did I view them, as many artists and writers see their notebooks, as the rough-and-tumble means to some perfected end, as scullery maids—rags on which to wipe their creative thoughts. As ever I looked to the exceptions, to works of art that began as notebooks and ended as masterpieces. No one would ever call Auden's *A Certain World* or Cyril Connolly's *The Unquiet Grave* scullery maids. Yet, both works more than qualify in style and content as notebooks.

But compared to what I had in mind those were shapely, tidy volumes. My own notebooks would culminate in something far more grandiose and exhaustive, a work of gargantuan ambitions and proportions to shame *Remembrance of Things Past* or *Ulysses*: *Pure Flux*, the notebook to end all notebooks!

During those ten years I seldom kept one address for more than a few months. Not wanting to carry all those notebooks around I'd ship them home to my mother, who stored them in the cellar of the house I grew up in on a Connecticut hill, and where a set of particleboard shelves groaned under their ever-increasing weight. Whenever I'd visit home, I'd pull one down off the shelf, blow the furnace dust from its pages, sit on the guest bed, and read. Like Oscar Wilde before me, I found my own notebook entries highly amusing. There was the element of surprise, compounded with the joy of not recognizing oneself. To read those notebooks was to encounter this odd person who had been me, and whose thoughts in ways paralleled but did not entirely match my own. What a curious fellow, I'd think, flipping pages scented with mildew, reeking of a past all but forgotten, as if I'd never lived it. Over time, with repeated readings, the entries took on the quality of myths, replacing the past they were meant to preserve. Meanwhile, my real past receded—like the lower layer of words in a palimpsest—growing fainter and fainter, until it disappeared entirely.

Not so long ago one friend reminded me of that episode in front of the abbey in Germany. More recently another friend told me of the time I dangled from that terrace. When I said I had no memory of these things, neither friend believed me. "How could you have forgotten?" Yet I had. Those episodes had escaped my notebooks; perhaps because they had been so embarrassing, I had "neglected" to record them. Therefore, they never happened; they didn't exist. Written words had crowded out genuine memories; diary had replaced memory. Where others had a cerebral cortex, medium temporal lobes, and a hippocampus, I had a bunch of fusty old notebooks.

I'm not sure what made me stop. Maybe the fact that I began writing fiction and publishing it. My dream of *Pure Flux* dissolved, replaced by more humble ambitions. After that, the few notebooks I kept were simply that, notebooks, places to jot down titles and ideas, to work out a paragraph, to take down the name of a book recommended by a friend. Whenever the temptation to record my days crept up on me, I'd swat it away.

I'm not the only one to give up the habit. These days more and more would-be diarists have taken to the Internet. What would have been diaries a decade ago are blogs today. The supposedly "private" act of recording one's feelings has torn off its hypocritical mask and gone totally public, turning into a flagrant spectacle of self-indulgence at the computer keyboard. In the old days writers drank in public and wrote in private. Now, at last, private vice and public performance have merged seamlessly. Booze gave us Hemingway, Fitzgerald, Joyce, Wolfe, Lowry, Faulkner . . . what will blogs give us?

A few years ago my father passed away. My mother sold the big house on the hill and moved to a condominium. She no longer had room for my notebooks. At the time, my wife and I were renting a one-bedroom in Manhattan. We worked at home, with little room to spare. Still, for a while I kept the notebooks there: they were like a bunch of old friends who came to visit with no intention of leaving. The few times I'd take one down from the closet to dip into it, I started sneezing; I couldn't stop. Was it the dust and mildew or the words themselves that made me sneeze? Anyway, I'd grown allergic to them.

One night I carried a notebook out to the compactor room, pulled the oven-like door, took a deep breath, and, feeling as Abraham must have felt, braced myself. Then I let go (I should have recycled, I know, but that would have meant putting it in the blue plastic recycling bin from which I might have retrieved it). As the notebook thumped its way down the chute I waited to feel either horror or relief. I felt nothing. Not a thing. So I did it again. I threw a second notebook down the chute, and a third, a fourth, a fifth . . .

It was past midnight. The rest of the building, including my wife, slept. I felt like a criminal. One by one the notebooks went down the chute, taking chunks of my ersatz past with them. In a sense, it was my youth going down that chute. I'd been holding on to it, thinking I might need it again someday.

With all but four notebooks gone I crawled back into bed next to my sleeping wife and lay there, staring up at the dark ceiling, feeling not a sense of relief, exactly, but one of quiet accomplishment.

That was five years ago. I've not had one regret about throwing those notebooks away. They were the first very rough draft of a life that has since taken on some meaningful structure and shape, and which has, if not a plot, at least a theme, and some good characters. Like all rough drafts, it was a means to an end, something I had to go through to get where I am. And for that I'm glad. But no, I don't miss a word of it. Why should I? After all, I still have my memories.

Estranged on a Train . . . .

With SNCF anything is possible.
—*French railway promotion*

E ver since I was thirteen, when I first saw Cary Grant and Eva Marie Saint in *North by Northwest*, I'd fantasized about having an affair aboard a train. So when, seven years later, I found myself alone in the sleeping car on the night train from Paris to Toulouse with a beautiful, sophisticated Parisian woman (Michelle: ash-blond hair, green eyes, no makeup), I was beside myself with anticipation. When the conductor came by to check our tickets and told her she was in the wrong wagon, my heart fell. However, the conductor went on to say that she might as well stay where she was, since we two had practically the entire train to ourselves.

"But what about the signs?" asked Michelle, referring to the little white cards marked "reserve" posted beside every couchette.

The conductor smiled and shrugged as if to say, "With SNCF (*Systéme Nationale de Chemin de Fers Français*), anything is possible." So went the publicity slogan of the French National Railway System. In any event, Michelle and I were left alone.

We spoke. About books mostly, and Henry Miller in particular, since he turned out to be Michelle's favorite American author, *Sexus* being her favorite of his books. A good sign, I thought. She asked me, "*Qu'est-ce que tu aimes?*" meaning "What do you like?" I could have told her many things, such as how I liked leaning against an open train window at night with Europe whizzing by and the wind whipping my hair, and an attractive woman who likes Henry Miller by my side. Instead I said, "I like Nelson Algren." Being French, she knew who Nelson Algren was; already I'd discovered that the French know our writers better than we do. But Michelle had actually read Algren—both *The Man with the Golden Arm* and *A Walk on the Wild Side.* I'd struck gold—French gold in an empty sleeping car at night!

Since sleep under strange circumstances never came easily for me, I had my trusty Valium supply on hand: four tiny canary-yellow pills in a prescription vial my mother had given me and that I kept in my pocket. But now I had second—and third, and even fourth— thoughts about taking any. Alone in the dark sleeping car, the French countryside rolling by under a veil of stars, our forearm hairs commingled as we stood side by side with the humid night air blowing past our faces. . . . I thought of the last scene in *North by Northwest*, where Cary Grant hoists Eva Marie Saint up into his couchette and the train plunges into a dark tunnel . . .

We spoke in hushed voices for several hours, sharing my bottle of water, Michelle having forgotten hers at the station. And she wasn't tired; I got the feeling she could talk all night. If only she'd come right out and proposition me, pull me into her couchette with her. She was Parisian, she was sophisticated. Eva Marie Saint would have done no less. Besides, I was too shy to make a move. Finally I said I was going to my couchette, that I'd be lying down there, adding that I wasn't *really* tired and, if she wanted to, if she felt like it, she could take the couchette next to mine and we could continue our conversation.

Michelle gave me a look. The look was half-sly, half-annoyed.

"Is that all right?" I asked.

"*Oui.*" She gave a toss of her limp bangs, then refocused her gaze back out the window, into darkness.

"You're not afraid to sleep in the same compartment with me, are you?" I asked.

She smiled. "No," she said. "I'm not afraid. I've slept with many strange men in many trains before." The ambiguity was, I felt certain, intentional. "But I'm not tired. I'll be here for a while."

"Will you join me—I mean, when you get tired?"

"*Tu ne veux pas me draguer?*"

Draguer is an interesting French verb. It means literally to drag up or to dredge, what a minesweeper does. In this context, however, it meant "pick me up," as in seduce, though by the sound of the word you'd think something more like rape was implied.

"No, no," I lied. "Of course not. Whatever gave you that idea?"

She smiled, seeing right through me. "Yes, I'll join you. In a while. I promise." She gave me another smile, this one positively conspiratorial.

"*Bonne nuit*," she said.

"*A bientôt*," I corrected and limped into my compartment.

The compartment held six beds—bunks, really, with leather pads and blankets and a mysterious piece of thin white linen, open at one end and sealed like a tube at the other, with a long sleeve or tongue about a foot wide extending from the slit-like opening.

At first I thought it was some sort of disposable night-robe, in which case it would have to have been the night-robe of someone with no arms and one leg, and that leg without a foot. In fact, this was my bedsheet—a cross between a sleeping bag and a combination top-and-bottom fitted sheet, except that it didn't seem to fit either the bed or me. Having spent the greater part of fifteen minutes trying to manipulate the thing into some useful configuration, I discovered two things: one, that I'd left the air-conditioning on, so the compartment was now freezing, and two, that my blanket was somewhere down there on the floor. Undoing all my manipulations I climbed down from the bunk, returned with blanket in hand, and started the process all over again, only to find this time around that I'd left the light on, and that the switch was over my head on the other side of the compartment.

This pattern repeated itself with minor variations two or three times more, until I was literally hopping crazed in my one-legged white potato sack of an SNCF ("With SNCF anything is possible") bedsheet, sweating from my efforts in spite of the air-conditioning, which somehow froze my sweat without keeping me cool.

At last I heaved away the blue SNCF blanket and lay there, in my undershorts, staring at the bottom of the bunk overhead, wondering: Where was Michelle? Was she coming, or not? Should I take a Valium, or shouldn't I? She had said she was coming, and she seemed so straightforward and . . . sincere! Was it conceivable that, on a French night train with no one else aboard other than me and this beautiful French woman, whose favorite book was *Sexus* and who'd read Nelson Algren and who had casually agreed to sleep with (or at least in the same compartment as) me—was it possible, was it indeed probable, that she wasn't coming? That she had, in fact, stood me up? With SNCF anything is possible. And so, having once again climbed down from my meticulously orchestrated bunk, and climbed into my wrinkled clothes, and patted down my matted curls, and double-checked my zipper, and rubbed the sleep from my face, I slid open the compartment door, and poked my head out into the windy aisle and . . . and . . .

Michelle wasn't there. She had gone to sleep, in her own empty compartment next to mine. We'd been strangers on a train, and now—before we'd even gotten to "know" each other a little—we were estranged strangers. Eva Marie Saint she wasn't; nor was I Cary Grant.

It was 3 A.M. I still hadn't taken my Valium. To complicate matters Michelle had absconded with my water bottle, meaning I'd have to dry-swallow the pills, which I did. Two of them. The second pill lodged in my throat, adding its bitter taste to that of unrequited sleeping-compartment lust.

It was clear now that the only other ride I'd be taking on this train, besides the one I'd bought a French Rail Pass for, would be the Valium Express, due to depart in approximately ten minutes. Knowing this I hurried back into my freezing/sweltering compartment, out of my sultry clothes, back onto my Hershey-bar mattress and into my "unisheet," where I lay, motionless listening to the gentle *thunk-whunk, thunk-whunk* of SNCF rails slipping by underneath me, *thunk-whunk, thunk-whunk* . . . sweeping away with them earth, trees, farms, homes, villages, cities—whole slumbering ways of life—desires, daydreams, memories, regrets (*thunk-whunk, thunk-whunk*), ambitions, emotions, fantasies, lusts (*thunk-whunk*), intellect, judgment, libido (*thunk-whunk, thunk-whunk, thunk-whunk*) . . . I entered that netherworld in which dreams cloud consciousness like milk poured into a cup of black coffee, and all was fine with the world, wherever it was.

Meanwhile, oxen in teams pulled a medieval cart along an ancient thoroughfare, past columns (Doric, Ionic, Corinthian) falling and splitting, as henna-haired women in scant dress and chained by the ankles popped dates and other delicacies into my mouth. Though it fell and I was its slave, the Holy Roman Empire was mine at last.

Sleep is good; sleep is kind: next to gravity one of the most useful things on the planet. Bless you, dear sweet Prince Valium, my lord, my liege . . .

Then the compartment door opened.

Michelle. She'd come after all!

With SNCF, it is said, anything is possible.

But not on 20 milligrams of Valium.

Damian (The Green Jacket)

He hadn't had sex in two years, he said. Except for a run around the park now and then, he never exercised. Two weeks out of every month he lived on fruit juice and macadamia nuts, and that's when not fasting. The rest of the time he ate avocados, bananas, and other fruits. He had wanted to be an actor since he was five years old, when he saw James Cagney in *White Heat* on TV. He would practice with a toy gun in front of a mirror. *You slap me in a dream, you'd better wake up and apologize.* He was twenty four.

We met at the Pratt Institute in Brooklyn. We were both undergraduates. I was a freshman still; I think Damian was a junior. I was there mainly to study painting and illustration, though I had no idea, really, what I wanted to do. I'd done some acting in high school, and Pratt had a theater department. I had yet to totally abandon my dream of becoming a movie star, so I signed up for an acting class. That's where I first saw Damian.

He wore a waist-cut shiny green (it must have been satin or rayon) bombardier jacket with a furry collar over a red T-shirt. The teacher, Nancy, had us doing improvisational exercises. In one exercise we were supposed to be trapped with people in a stuck elevator. I watched Damian and three other classmates do the exercise first. They got into the elevator and acted normally, facing the front, not speaking. Then Nancy said, "Stop," meaning the elevator had stopped. Everyone reacted in different ways. One student cried, another panicked, a third cracked jokes. Damian's improv stole the scene. He started convulsing. We couldn't tell if Damian's character was having an epileptic seizure or a heart attack. Whatever it was, it was very convincing, so convincing Nancy broke in and cut the scene. But Damian kept convulsing. A thin stream of vomit bubbled out of his mouth and down the front of his red T-shirt. Nancy yelled for someone to go call emergency. That's when Damian finally broke character, facing us with a toothy grin. It was all part of the act, the vomit and everything. I'd heard of actors crying on cue. Damian could *throw up* on cue, that's how good an actor he was.

I could have been Damian's slave, he was so good-looking, like a Puerto Rican young Brando, but with dark brown skin (I was a big Brando fan and considered Marlon the epitome of male beauty). Damian had Brando's forehead, the same heavy sculpted jaw, the same flat brows, the same thick neck and broad shoulders. He knew he was beautiful, you could tell by the way he walked. Damian didn't walk; he strutted. I asked him did he ever work out? "Nevah." He said it just like that, "Nevah," with a kind of mid-Atlantic accent and a whiff of disgust. "I don't believe in exercise."

If he didn't exercise, how did he keep in such good shape?

"I was born this way," he said. "And I eat well." He flashed me his smile. He had a beautiful smile lit up by a set of bright, large teeth like a bulb illuminating a dark closet. Speaking of things he had been born with, I wondered if his parents named him "Damian," or had that been his invention? Was he named after the eponymous hero of Hesse's novel? "Oh, no, no, no, no," he said, but refused to elaborate or discuss the matter further.

He invited me to his home. He lived in Manhattan, on the Upper West Side, in a high-rise apartment building on Amsterdam Avenue. I remember walking into a brightly lit lobby with a security guard and linoleum and waiting a while for the elevator, which had graffiti all over it, and pennies jammed into the round holes drilled into a cover on the porthole window, which had been smashed. Damian lived in a studio on a high floor. Sounds of at least five radios leaked out into the hallway, but once I entered Damian's sanctuary and he closed the door those noises were left behind, replaced by a woman's voice crooning some old American standard.

"Who's that singing?" I asked as Damian took my coat.

"You don't know?"

I shook my head.

"Judy," he said.

I had no idea who Judy was. Judy who? Which Judy?

Damian took my coat and put it on a hanger in his closet, next to his green satin jacket. I was impressed. I'd yet to meet anyone with an apartment of their own, let alone one in Manhattan, let alone one with a sliding closet door. He showed me the view from his window. If you looked hard over roofs and past the buildings and trees you could see gleaming white patches of the Hudson River. It was winter; the streets were full of snow. The sky was a bleary gray watercolor, wet on wet. Damian showed me around his apartment, the first genuine bachelor pad I ever saw. Things were very neat, very tidy. There was only one room, really, shaped like an L, with the bedroom occupying the bottom of the L, and a galley kitchen just off to the side of it through a curtain. Over the bed he had draped sheer yellow fabric, forming the impression of a Mongolian ger or Ali Baba's cave there in his apartment. A stick of incense burned. The walls were adorned with his paintings, macabre works featuring memento mori skulls and funereal flower arrangements on crackled black backgrounds. To the center of one painting, a small, coffin-shaped box had been affixed. "Go on," Damian said. "Open it." I did. Inside was a small dead bird. It gave off a sharp putrid whiff of decay. I closed the box.

"Death intrigues me," Damian said.

"Why?"

"I'm not sure. Because it's everywhere, I suppose. It's part of life. It doesn't depress me. It's just part of the natural order of things. One thing dies, another is born. You can't have life without death, can you?"

I nodded. Of course you couldn't.

That afternoon we went for a jog in the park. Although philosophically opposed to strenuous exercise, Damian didn't mind jogging. It relaxed him, he said. He had an extra jogging suit that he lent me, tan with brown stripes. By late in the day the sun had melted the snow so the streets were full of slush. We jogged around Central Park. The same hills that had me gasping, Damian broached effortlessly, without exertion. "All you all right?" he asked, jogging in place as I caught up with him. "Fine," I said, panting. We had gone once around the park—a distance of over six miles—when he waited for me again and said, "Are you sure you're not getting tired?" I shook my head. "Good," he said, and started around a second time.

That same night, as I lay sore and exhausted on his couch, Damian prepared dinner. He made a dish called "baccalà," with salt cod, tomatoes, and avocado, and sat watching me eat as he sipped from a large plastic bottle. "Aren't you eating?" I asked. Damian shook his head. "I'm in my fast," he asked. He fasted for three weeks at a time. Nothing but water with a dash of honey and lemon juice. He did it four times a year. "You should try it with me sometime," he said.

So I did. We fasted together. We started in November. Three days of fruit and leafy vegetables, three days of juice, six days of water (flavored with lemon juice and a few drops of honey "to sweeten the intestines"), and then the reverse. Through the course of the fast I'd want to do at least three enemas, Damian informed me. "Otherwise nothing moves."

When doing a fast like that, you're not supposed to overtax yourself. No strenuous exercise, so said Damian. I didn't listen. After two weeks, once I got past the hunger and headaches, I felt so light and full of energy I wanted to go out and run ten miles, and so I did. I ran all the way from Clinton Hill, Brooklyn, where I was living, to Damian's apartment building on the Upper West Side, a distance of over ten miles. It felt great, my body like a feather on air. I felt I could run forever. Damian scolded me. "You shouldn't have done that. You could have passed out in the middle of Broadway," he said. "You could have died."

"Death intrigues me," I said.

The watery part of the fast fell on Thanksgiving Day. I was invited to a Thanksgiving party at my friend Crystal's apartment in the Village. I remember standing among the guests holding my little bottle of lemon-and-honey-flavored water and sipping from it as they ate turkey, stuffing, candied yams, the works. I didn't mind. The only thing that bothered me was that every other word people spoke seemed to be about food. That's all anyone talked about. What they'd eaten the day before, what they were going to eat the next day. This meal, that meal. This restaurant, that restaurant. This recipe, that recipe. It amazed me how obsessed everyone was with food, with the very thing I was doing without. "Have you ever eaten at . . ." "Have you tried the pad thai at . . ." Twenty days earlier, under Jimmy Carter's watch, a group of militant Islamists had raided the American Embassy in Tehran and taken fifty-three hostages. We were going to war, I was sure of it. And here were all these people stuffing their faces with turkey and mashed potatoes and pearl onions in cream sauce and talking nothing but food, food, food. I left the party in disgust. How could people waste their time with such trivialities? I decided that eating was in and of itself disgusting, a decadent enterprise. I'll never do it again, I said to myself, sipping from my bottle of lemon-and-honey-flavored water. I'll fast for the rest of my life.

When I next saw Damian I had broken my fast and was eating normally like everyone else. He asked me to describe my experience.

"Strange," I said. "At first it felt great, but then I couldn't get along with anyone any more."

"That's exactly what happens. You have no patience or respect for eaters. The first few times I fasted, meat eaters seem particularly reprehensible to me. Of course, if you fast more regularly your feelings won't be so strong. Instead of judging them, when you see other people eating, you feel like an anthropologist coming upon some unknown, cannibalistic tribe."

But I never fasted again.

I think it was on my third or fourth visit with Damian that I slept over. We shared his bed, the one under the yellow drapes. I remember feeling a strange combination of comfort and fear as I lay next to him, feeling the magnetic pull of this beautiful dark body next to mine, both of us in our underwear. It wasn't so much that I wanted to touch him (I was never that way), only that I knew how nice it would feel if I did. But I didn't. We slept like brothers. He was like a brother to me, Damian. My Puerto Rican brother. He said so himself once. His white brother. No, he didn't say brother; he said "twin," "my white twin." I remember how proud it made me feel to hear him call me that. As if having one twin wasn't good enough; I needed two. I needed a Puerto Rican twin who looked like a dark Marlon Brando.

We went to the Dominican Republic together. It was Damian's idea. He went there regularly. We booked a hotel in Santo Domingo and rode a packed bus to the beach called Boca Chica—"Sweet Mouth." Our first afternoon on the crowded beach, Damian rubbed a concoction of baby oil and Mercurochrome on his brown skin. Then he told me to wade out into the surf about two dozen yards and look back at the shore. "Just watch," he said.

I did as ordered. I waded out twenty meters or so and then I turned and faced the shore in time to see all the heads there turning in sync as Damian paraded his mahogany limbs down the beach. Men, women, children, dogs—no one could take their eyes off him, so magnificent was he. For the rest of that long day strangers of all sexes threw themselves at him, inviting him point-blank to sleep and do all kinds of other things with them. I saw it firsthand. Damian showed absolutely no interest. He waved them away like flies. He told me he had no interest in sex, none at all, that he was asexual, that he'd been that way for a while. I asked him why. "Oh, Peter," he said, "I am so *thoroughly* bored with all of that. I've had enough sex to last me the rest of my life." He sighed. In fact, I remember thinking that Damian didn't need anyone else to make love with. He had himself. And anyway who else could compare?

"But don't you ever get horny?"

"Not at all."

"But you must get lonely, don't you?"

He shook his head. "Me? Lonely? *Nevah!*"

For many years we were very close friends. He really was like a brother to me, like my second twin. Then suddenly Damian stopped returning my calls. I still remember my last visit to his apartment. I remember it because of an odd thing that happened. That green jacket he used to wear? It had been a long time since I'd seen him wearing it, so I asked, "Whatever happened to your green jacket?"

"What green jacket?"

"You know—the one you always used to wear? The satin one with the fur collar?"

"Oh, that horrible thing! I burned it!"

"Burned it?"

"Yes—I burned it! I couldn't stand to look at it any more." He made like to shiver.

"Why burn it?" I said. "Why not give it away? Hell, I'd have liked it!"

"You don't understand, Peter" (the way Damian said my name,

with his faux mid-Atlantic accent, it came out *Pee-tah*)—"if I had given it to you I'd have had to look at it whenever you would come to visit me. And I couldn't have borne that! No, I couldn't have!"

"What about Goodwill—or the Salvation Army?"

"It would be the same problem, don't you see? One day I'll be walking down the street and—boom!—there would be that awful green jacket following me around like some sort of curse! No, I wouldn't have it. And so I burned it. I *always* burn my old clothes!"

The reason I remember my last time in Damian's apartment is because, while he was showering, I just happened to look in one of his closets—not the one where he would always hang my things, another one. There, hidden deep behind some other clothes, was the green satin jacket. I reached a hand in to caress the fur collar. As I did so, I heard my name and turned. Damian stood there, dripping with a towel around his waist. Gently, with a disapproving look, he slid the closet door shut.

That was my last visit there. After that, I called and called and always he made excuses, until at last I got fed up and stopped calling.

By then I was living with my wife on the Upper West Side, less than ten blocks from the apartment building where Damian still lived. It bugged me whenever I thought about it, to know he was that close and we never saw each other, that he had so completely lost his interest in our friendship. Why? Because I was married? Because he hadn't become a great actor? He'd played a street-gang leader in a low-budget cop movie, and had a small role in a play that ran for only two weeks on Broadway. Those were his biggest roles. Okay. So what? I hadn't been so successful myself. Life is like that. New York is a tough town. Who cares? We'd known each other—what? Over ten years. And now he no longer returned my calls. Fuck him! It made me bitter.

Then one day—around 1990—I'm walking alone down Broadway when I see a man in a plaid shirt selling posters. I recognize one of the poster images. It's a lithograph of one of Damian's paintings, the one with the dead bird inside a coffin, but since it's a lithograph the coffin isn't three-D. I turn to the man in the plaid shirt. "I know this artist," I say. The man looks at me. When he does, I realize: the man is Damian. Only it isn't Damian. He's too short, too slim, too old and insubstantial to be Damian. This man has gray hair. His shoulders are bony. Dark red, scabby blotches cover his face. His teeth are small and clogged with tartar (Damian had big, beautiful teeth). This, I tell myself, is Damian, yes, but in another dimension, in the Dimension of Death. This is Damian dying. Or is it just more theater, another example of his tour-de-force method acting, Damian playing dead?

"Damian?" I said and instinctively, without thinking, reached out to touch one of the ugly scars.

"Don't!" he said, and pushed my arm away.

"Damian—how are you?" But of course I knew the answer: he was dying. He had AIDS. How did he get it, without having had sex? I asked myself, but didn't really wonder.

"I'm fine," he lied. But his eyes said something very different. Black and hollow, like windows with the glass missing. They looked deeply, fiercely into mine and said, *Keep walking, go away. Forget you have ever seen me like this.* If he was trying to act friendly, it was one performance of his that failed to convince.

I forget what exactly was said then. Somehow we parted—awkwardly. I left him there on a corner of whatever and Broadway selling his posters, dying. And that was how it ended. I never saw him again.

For years afterward I tried to learn more about Damian, what the rest of his life, the part I knew nothing about, had been like, who his other close friends had been, if he had family, what they might tell me about him. I interviewed doormen, fruit stand and bodega owners, but learned nothing. It occurred to me that I had no photographs, no letters, nothing at all dating back to our days together to prove that Damian had been a part of my life.

It was as if our friendship had been a performance, a limited engagement run starring Damian Colon, produced just for me. In the end, I couldn't even verify his death. Though I searched every known public database, I found no record of anyone in New York City by that name, living or dead.

Restaurant

The game couldn't have been easier for Papa to play. All he did—all he had to do—was sit in his lawn chair with his *New York Times* and put in his order. I'd bring back steaks (rocks), beans (pebbles wet with the garden hose), frank-furters (bulrushes), fish (milkweed innards), and salads (assorted leaves), arranged on a paper plate and served with a proud "Voila!"

To say the least the game was one-sided. My father, a solitary inventor and genius, never pretended to eat or in any way enjoy the food I so proudly served to him. He'd bestow a perfunctory nod of his gray, balding head, and, with the paper plate balanced precariously on one knee, go back to reading the paper. Sometimes I'd try to spur him on. "Papa!" I'd whine. "You're not playing!" But most of the time I kept my mouth shut, knowing if I pestered him too much he would get up and walk down the hill to what we all called the Building, his laboratory, and then I'd have to play alone (or worse, with my twin brother, whom I despised).

When I was in my thirties my father suffered the first of a series of strokes that would leave him brain-damaged and ultimately kill him. I happened to be visiting my parents at the time. Suddenly I heard a strange wailing noise coming from outside. It was morning. I'd been sitting in the breakfast nook, sipping a cup of my father's favorite tea, eating a slice of his toast with his beloved orange marmalade, reading one of his books when I heard the sound, and so went out to explore. In the closed, dark garage, my father sat in the back seat of his Subaru.

"Ah, there you are, Peter, my boy," he said. "Perhaps you can enlighten me? Where the hell is the bloody steering wheel?" (Though born in Italy, my father learned English in England, and he liberally salted and peppered his speech with "bloodies.") "I can't seem to find the bloody thing!"

In his car, I drove him to the Danbury Hospital emergency room, where my mother met us and where she and I paced the corridor as they scanned my father's brain. The test results indicated a "transitory ischemic attack," or a TIA—an invisibly small stroke brought on, most likely, by a mild case of late-onset diabetes or an elevated cholesterol count, or both. Too much orange marmalade on his toast, too many soft-boiled eggs.

My father recovered. But then, a few weeks later, it happened again. We had gone for a hike on one of those very mild Indian summer days toward the end of September. A wet, mossy smell filled the air. A rainstorm the night before had rinsed all the colors of the world, leaving everything clear and crisp and looking as though it might shatter like glass. The hike was my father's idea; he loved to walk in the woods. We drove to an abandoned railway bed that we'd explored when I was a child, where a pair of tunnels carved through the granite passed over and under each other, and where I was once bitten by a hornet.

This time, though, we didn't go through either of the tunnels. Instead, we walked the opposite way down the tracks, to where the abandoned rail bed curved through a stand of willow trees like the ones lining our dirt driveway. Next to them, at the base of the embankment, there was a small pond, its surface covered with demure yellow leaves blown off the willow tree's branches. The sun felt warm on my arms and my neck. An ardent swimmer, I couldn't resist. I sat down and untied my shoes.

My father said, "What are you doing?"

"I'm going for a dip."

"Are you daft? It's much too cold!"

"Rubbish!" I said.

I wasted no time and plunged straight in off the gently sloped embankment. At my urging, my father sat on a rock and took off his clothes. Soon he was up to his knees, massaging handfuls of water over his sagging chest and potbelly, his ancient penis casting its drooping shadow as I treaded water nearby, floating via the merest butterfly movements of my fingers.

"I don't suppose there's any way I can get you to jump in?" I said.

"Strictly out of the question, my boy," my father said.

"Oh, but it would mean so much to me, Papa."

"I can't, dear boy, I simply can't! I'm too old!"

"Sure you can, Papa. Just close your eyes and think of England."

It worked. To my great pleasure and surprise, with his eyes closed and with a prolonged "Yeeeeeee!" my father didn't plunge so much as let himself fall, like a chopped-down tree. We swam across the pond several times, me freestyle, my father doing his trademark sidestroke/scissorkick, our bodies cutting twin black paths through the gold carpet of leaves.

We were headed back to my father's car when suddenly he could no longer remember the word for "forest." He said "wood," "arms" "*alberi*" (Italian for "trees"). As he continued to speak, familiar words gave way like a collapsing rope bridge, leaving him stranded at the edge of a chasm. As he kept trying to speak, his face turned red, until I made him stop, afraid he'd give himself another, even worse stroke. This time, by the time we got to the hospital he couldn't remember his own name, or mine, or say who he was. The verbal world was a closet full of suitcases, all without handles. He couldn't grasp anything.

Over the next few days, in his over-bright hospital room, my father and I evolved our own private language, a language of *isms* and *tions* and *nesses* that eschewed all concrete nouns and active verbs in favor of blurry abstractions, to the dismay of my poor Italian mother who, with her bare grasp of English, sat uncomprehendingly nearby. Hour after hour Papa and I jabbered on about "proportions" and "essences" ("Yes, yes," he and I agreed with respect to the view through the hospital room window, "there is a certain clear, positive quality, a quality of lightness, a luminance, or *luminessence*—yes, that's it, a luminessence, a dreamy vernal effect")—sounding like a pair of Mensa Club Martians. Slowly, one by one, like a flock of lost birds, the missing words flew back to my father. He made a nearly full recovery.

But then, not very long afterwards, he had another stroke, and two months later another. And over time he was reduced to sitting in his living room chair staring off into space, or, if the weather was good, outdoors, in the backyard, in the same spot where he used to sit and play—or not play—Restaurant with me when I was a boy. Back then he would read his paper. Now, after his strokes, he could no longer read, or watch television, or do much of anything other than listen to the radio, and none of us could be sure what he made of that.

But he could eat. In fact, aside from sleeping, eating remained the only thing he was still able to do. And the only thing left that I could do for him was feed him. Every time I visited him, I'd try to feed my father, supposedly to give my mother and the visiting nurse a break—but really to still be in some meaningful way close to him.

I sliced up his chicken and his carrots, stirred one-percent milk and Sweet'n Low into his tea, made sure nothing was too cold or too hot, too salty or too sweet. And then I fed him, one sip or spoonful at a time, wiping his chin every now and then, trying to intuit, as best I could, which order or combination of foods he'd prefer. Should I feed him some boiled chicken first, and then some carrots? Or the other way around? Or a mixture? Maybe he'd like a sip of cranberry juice in between? Or a combination of juice and tea?

There are no strict rules, of course. Standard dining protocols did not apply. After all, a nursing home isn't the Four Seasons, or Lutèce. My father might even like a spoonful of dessert mixed in with his main course, some strawberry ice cream served a la mode with his institutionally boiled peas, a dab of chocolate pudding with his broccoli.

But as time went by, confronted with a spoonful of whatever, my father was more apt to shake his head violently and refuse to open his mouth. He was losing his appetite, a bad sign for someone his age, especially someone in his condition. Never a fussy eater, as each week progressed my father grew more and more finicky, and feeding him became more of a challenge.

And a mathematical riddle. For with each passing day it seemed that he wanted to eat only when things were given to him in very specific quantities, and in cryptic combinations. An alimentary safecracker, it was my job to unlock his appetite, to decipher its secret sequences. And like a safecracker I worked carefully, remembering those summer afternoons spent trying to get him to play Restaurant with me. I was still playing Restaurant, only now the stakes were much, much higher. Now the food was real and, unless I could get my father to eat it, he'd die sooner rather than later.

"Papa, you're not playing!" I want to shout at him every time he shakes his head and refuses me his mouth, sideswiping the spoon that scrapes his stubbled chin. But I don't, knowing the next time my papa gets up and goes to the Building, it will be for good.

After the Planet Uranus

Ourania was her name, Pronounced: *ooh-ray-née-yah.* Greek. Named after Uranus, third largest planet and seventh from the sun. An "ice giant," having the coldest atmosphere of any planet in the solar system, its interior composed mainly of ice and rocks. Slow in its orbit, and, for a large planet, remarkably dim.

In fact she was small, dark, petite. She walked into the snack bar at Western Connecticut State College where I was an undergraduate. I had transferred out of two other schools. At twenty-three I was older than nearly all my fellow undergraduates. I considered this and my jaundiced attitude toward a college education marks of distinction. I'd been "out there" in the "real world," "proving myself." I was in the habit back then of identifying certain characteristics of mine as positive distinctions when in fact they were deficits.

Everything about Ourania was oval—her eyes, her cheeks, her lips, the overall shape of her head. She looked like a collection of eggs from an assortment of birds. Attractive in an exotic way. I sat there, at one of the tables, plucking the humpbacked Spanish guitar someone gave me in exchange for a charcoal nude I'd done at the first of my three alma maters.

She introduced herself. "We should get to know each other," she said.

I said, "Really? What for?" I'd yet to fully emerge from my Brando-as-Kowalski phase, wherein I wore chest-tight undershirts and practiced random acts of harshness on the opposite sex.

Later that same afternoon, Ourania pulled uninvited up the driveway to my parents' house where I'd resumed living. She drove an American Motors Pacer, a car that looked like a steel egg on wheels, like something hatched rather than built. I remember saying to myself: okay, if that's the way she wants it.

It was winter. There were still a few inches of snow left on the ground from a storm days earlier. My parents were away, gone off on separate vacations, my father to Europe, my mother to Mexico. They never traveled together, my parents. They slept in separate beds in separate rooms. I'd never seen them kiss or hug. My father kept a spare bedroom in the laboratory where he invented things, to retreat to in times of domestic strife. Once, as the climax to one of their fights, my mother grabbed a black grease pencil from a kitchen drawer and scrawled all over the living room walls that she had painted purple less than a week before. The argument had been over that color. When my mother asked him what color she should paint the living room, my father responded, "Paint it purple, why don't you?" He had been joking. He was quite the joker, my father. My mother didn't know he was joking. She painted the living room purple. It took two gallons, four coats, two days. Mom was terribly proud of the result. It was like living inside a grape. When my father let her in on the joke, that's when the fireworks went off. Papa slept in the Building that night, among his inventions.

When Ourania paid her visit, my twin brother, George, was away, too, at Drew University in New Jersey—or was it Duke in North Carolina? I never could get my brother's colleges straight. I had the house all to myself. The day before the storm I was lying on the sofa in the purple living room when I heard a scratching noise coming from the fireplace, the one that we never used. Rodents were known to get stuck in there. I jiggled the flue. Something flopped to the floor, then sailed in a brown blur across the room into the wall and fell to the floor again, where it lay stunned. Then it fluttered back to life and flew into the dining room, where I found it perched on the hutch: a screech owl. For the next twenty hours that owl was my constant companion. I sat with my humpbacked guitar serenading it while it stared at me with those yellow eyes, so big they took up two-thirds of its face. Ours was a relationship not based on mutual trust. Having failed to get the owl to eat a piece of raw hamburger, I caught it and threw it outdoors. I was both sad and relieved to see it fly away.

Though the house was unoccupied and we'd have been far more comfortable in it, Ourania—who grew up on a barren island in the Cyclades—insisted that we go up into the woods (the same woods where I'd taken Reidun, a Norwegian AFS student, some years earlier). We carried two blankets and a thermos bottle full of hot tea, our boots crunching through glazed snow and cracking twigs. I remember, while we walked, seeing through the layer of snow broken remnants of childhood toys that my brother and I had played with, shards of plastic tanks and hand grenades. While our parents fought we played war, our games turning into the real thing, with rocks secreted into dirt bombs instigating sudden trips to Dr. Randolph and the emergency room. The woods hadn't changed, I thought.

We climbed up to a grassy clearing, stretched the blankets over a patch of snow, and set about doing what we had come there to do.

A week later Ourania found me in the snack bar again. "I'm leaving my husband," she announced. I hadn't known that she was married. I said, "Why tell me?"

"I just thought you'd want to know, that's all."

I nodded. "Okay," I said.

After that I kept my distance, or tried to. I made it clear that I wasn't interested, that we'd had a fling and that was that. But she kept pursuing me. I tried to be reasonable, at first, but when that didn't work I took to being rude. "Look," I said. "How do you say 'no' in Greek?" I even teased her about it. "Christ, you never give up, do you?" Nothing seemed to dissuade her. Finally, when school ended, I moved back to New York City. I assumed that would put an end to it. It didn't. Ourania wrote letters, made phone calls. At last I said to her, "What's *wrong* with you? Haven't you gotten the message? Do I have to spell it out for you?" But the letters kept coming, handwritten ones on pastel blue paper. So did the phone calls. I'd hang up; she'd call right back. I had to change my phone number, it got so bad.

I'd been in New York about six months, struggling with a friend to make it as a musician, playing gigs in seedy, mostly empty dives, living in a ratty tenement by the Holland Tunnel, with grease fumes from the diner downstairs, and traffic noise and flashing tunnel entrance lights ransacking my sleep. Gruesome days, those were. To pay the rent my friend and I worked in a photocopying shop, sucking toner fumes and putting up with customers who complained when their copies weren't perfectly straight or were too dark or not dark enough. An accident that winter cost me the use of my left hand (I'm left-handed). The copy shop boss fired me. My musical partner took off for the West Coast where, he insisted, life was easier. I moved into a single-room-occupancy hotel off Gramercy Park. There was a sink in my room but no toilet. The toilet was down the hall. My second week there I broke my leg coming down the stairs. I was unemployed and unemployable.

Around that time a pastel-blue letter arrived from Ourania. How she got my address I don't know. She was living in New York, working at a Midtown advertising agency. "I'm director of typography," her letter went on to say. "I hire freelancers." She could pay me twenty-five dollars an hour, good money back then. "You can learn on the job," she said. "I will train you." She gave me her phone number.

The next day I called her. What choice did I have? I was in no position to turn down favors. The following Saturday morning we met at her ad agency. We spent the whole day there, me with my left hand still bandaged, learning computerized typesetting code. Afterward we ate in a posh restaurant, her treat. Over our meal I asked her why she was being so nice to me.

She shrugged. "No reason," she said.

"It's not like I deserve it," I had to admit.

"Why don't you let me decide that?"

Three weeks later, when I'd learned how to set type and was already freelancing for her, Ourania asked if I cared to move in with her. Again I asked her why.

"Because—I would like you to," she said.

"I know," I said. "But *why?*"

"You need a place to stay. And I have room."

"Are those good enough reasons?"

"For me they are. I know what I'm doing. Look, there's no need to make a decision just now. Why don't you think about it and let me know what you decide?"

I thought about it. I was sick of living in that rotten hotel, with its cockroaches and rats and a room so small I could barely squeeze be-

tween the bed and the dresser. And I knew I couldn't afford a place of
my own. Three days later I phoned her.

"No strings attached?" I asked.

"No strings attached."

So I accepted. To be honest, I was so grateful to her for having
bailed me out of my nose-diving life that I'd have agreed to just about
anything. I might even have married her, I was so hard up. But I was
also genuinely touched by her generosity.

So I broke my lease with the hotel, packed up my stuff, and went
to Astoria, where Ourania lived at the second-to-last stop on what
was then the Double-R elevated line, in a neighborhood of low, flat-
roofed buildings sprinkled with Greek-style cafes, orthodox churches,
and motley fruit stands. Today I take it that Astoria has some panache,
but back then it was just dreary. Even the fruits and vegetables at the
corner stands looked forsaken. The railway bridge, roaring over that
neighborhood on massive, Roman aqueduct-like stone pylons, cast its
gloomy shadow over a park where children and adults relaxed, played,
and scattered their litter, and which, though grassy and full of trees,
oppressed me with its squalor no less than everything else in that
neighborhood. It was as if Seurat's *Grande Jatte* had been piled onto a
garbage barge and tugged straight to hell.

As for Ourania's apartment, it was a one-bedroom over someone's
garage. Of it I remember little beyond that every piece of furniture in
it was sealed with covers of thick protective polyurethane, or poly-
styrene—some such substance with an alarming chemical pedigree.
Dining table, sofa, chairs, pillows . . . aside from the coffee table, everything was swathed in this stuff that might have been used to manu-
facture clear body bags, and that made the apartment's already funereal
cheap reproduction Louis XIV furnishings look positively embalmed.
Imagine Liberace's apartment after he'd died but before the coroner
arrived. In point of fact a formaldehyde-like odor suffused its rooms.
This may have been from the plastic coverings, or it may have been
from the fixative that I used to protect the pastel drawings I'd started
making around that time, mostly of the three derelicts living in an
abandoned playground nearby. Or it may have been the odor of the
solvent Ourania used to remove the polish she wore on her fake nails,
or the Adorn with which she sculpted her hair into an outré 6os bee-
hive. Whatever its source, the smell invested itself into every fiber of

that apartment, in every sip of beverage I drank and every bite of food I ate there. It gave me headaches. I'd no sooner open the apartment door than my head would start throbbing.

In the apartment's modest dining alcove Ourania had installed a massive oak dining table meant to seat twelve, such that it was hard to get around. One had to push all the chairs against the wall, and even then the table was as much of a challenge to circumnavigate as Magellan's globe. We had our first big battle over that table, Ourania and I. I wanted her to remove just one leaf. But no, she apparently operated under the delusion that we constantly entertained vast numbers of guests, though in truth we never had anyone visit, ever. Who the hell wanted to come to Astoria? Yet, here was this table big enough to accommodate the Last Supper, and that you couldn't walk around.

The dining table wasn't the only thing we fought about. We did lots of fighting back then, in and out of the apartment. Like cat and dog, we fought. As small as she was, with fists I could fit inside my own, Ourania could pack a punch. I'd wake up the next day with bruises on my forearms and chest. She threw things, too, just as my mother had. Along with its cheesy Louis XIV furnishings, her apartment bristled with louche ornamental vases and other decorative objects, mostly of Greek derivation. These were what she threw when she got angry, to where I had to wonder if that was what she'd bought them for in the first place.

To get away from Ourania's vases and our fights, I'd take my pastels to the abandoned playground and sketch the three bums living there. I remember their names: Red, Jimmy, Tex. All day long they passed a pint of "hootch" in its brown paper bag. Their clothes, their gestures, the way they talked, all suggested another place and time, as if they had been beamed onto that playground in Astoria from Missoula, circa 1932. I found them picturesque, but it may be just as true that some part of me identified with them. Wasn't I a bum, too, after all, despite having a job and a roof over my head? What is a bum, if not someone with little or no self-respect? Here I was, shacking up with this woman I didn't love, or even respect, being kept by her, more or less (I contributed to the rent, but still . . .). Having failed to take proper care of myself, I'd taken advantage of her. I stunk. A moocher, that's what I was. A tramp. Pass the hooch!

It got to where I dreaded going "home." I dreaded the fights, but

I also dreaded the lovemaking that followed them as surely as mushrooms follow a spring rain, and that was the only sure way out of the fights: lovemaking that, for me, was as obligatory as washing the dishes or hauling ashes from a cold furnace. Who am I kidding? We weren't making "love." If anything we were in the hate manufacturing business. I hated Ourania. I hated her for making it possible for me to become so dependent on her, for aiding and abetting my total loss of self-reliance, self-confidence, and self-respect—for, in few words, making me hate *myself*. My inability to love her despite all efforts only added to my sense of failure.

Yes, I tried to love her, I did. I *wanted* to love her. It would have solved so many of our problems, hers and mine. And I had come to feel that she *deserved* my love, that she had earned it, that I *owed* it to her, that it was my duty.

And Ourania wasn't without her good qualities. She was extremely good at her job. She treated freelancers kindly and knew how to balance the demands of nervous clients with those of egotistical bosses. She was artistic, too. She did watercolors, not very good ones, but then she wasn't ambitious, like me; she painted strictly for her own pleasure. She smelled good, too, and kept a neat, clean house, albeit one sealed in formaldehyde. True, her tastes could have stood some improvement. She read mostly potboilers by women with hard-sounding names and relentless facelifts. Her love of art didn't extend beyond Monet and his lily pads. Her sentimental streak was as wide as her temper was short and brutal. But then the same sentimental streak delivered me from destitution. My point here being that I did appreciate her; I just didn't *love* her. I couldn't. And this made me hate us both.

Ourania's cooking became the focal point of my hatred. Like many Greek Americans, Ourania's father was a professional short-order cook, yet his daughter inherited none of his culinary skills. She would bake spaghetti, as Greeks are known to do, but she'd either burn it or drown it in grease. She did the same with meat. I'd come home to thick acrid clouds and hunks of lamb burned beyond recognition, and be forced to sit at that plasticized dining room table chiseling away at my dinner like a starved Michelangelo. If I offered to cook, my offers were received as rebukes—which of course they were. She'd burst into tears and/or throw something, and the fight would begin.

One time, she took a pot of stew she'd burned and threw it at the kitchen wall. I was put in mind of my mother and that grease pencil. Come to think of it, Ourania looked like my mother. Ourania was smaller, rounder, but with the same high forehead, long nose, and fiery eyes. My mother likewise took up with a man who failed to love her properly, who criticized her as I criticized Ourania, and who'd cheated on her to boot, something I had yet to do to Ourania.

Her name was Marcia. She was a cartoonist. She lived in a building on the other side of Ditmars Boulevard, where the rents were higher. I'd stop by there in the afternoons before heading home. We'd have tea, talk. It was all innocent at first. We sat at her kitchen table, the bedroom two rooms away. She had a yellow stove that the ruddy, low-angled light through her kitchen window played off. I was twenty-four and still clinging to the illusion that I would not turn out to be my father. We were having tea, that's all.

Meanwhile, my fights with Ourania got worse. One muggy August evening, she, having turned the shish kebabs into charcoal briquettes, responded to my suggestion that we dine out by grabbing the carving knife and—holding the plate of scorched lamb with her free hand—offering to disembowel herself. I stood there, not quite knowing what to do or say, wondering if this was some sort of theatrical joke. But her tears were as real as the knife that trembled in her fist. (I was put in mind of the time when my brother, George, threw a steak knife at me, how it stuck in the roll of flesh at my waist and quivered there, like a cartoon.)

"Calm down, calm down," I said, and having disarmed her eased her out of the smoke-filled kitchen and into the bedroom, where we made love on the slip-covered bed, our sweaty bodies making sucking and squeaking sounds against the plastic.

By the time winter rolled around, our apartment having grown too small to contain them, our fights spread out into the rest of the world. In restaurants, in cafes, on the streets, on the subway, we fought.

People are frightened of screaming couples, with good reason. The high-octane rage generated by embittered lovers is enough to scare off even seasoned gang members and hardened criminals. When Ourania and I fought, chain-wielding thugs with arms as big as barrels got out of our way. Where fighting alone with each other only made us feel sad and desperate, our public fighting imbued us with a sense of power and authority that we otherwise lacked. Having it out among spectators in broad daylight made us formidable. It turned us into a blend of street performer and terrorist. It got to where fighting at home didn't do it for us anymore. Our hearts just weren't in it. We had to take it out into the streets; we needed the railroad train; we needed witnesses, just as my parents had needed George and me to witness *their* fights. From Vernon-Jackson to Newtown and 29th, from Queens Plaza to Hunter's Point, from 23rd and Ely to Ditmars Boulevard, we'd scream bloody murder at each other, our curdled voices rising to tangle among the elevated's sooty girders, as bystanders scattered.

It ended when she found out about Marcia. Ours was no great affair, and I wonder now if its unstated purpose had been to drive a definitive wedge between Ourania and me, to end what I lacked the guts to bring to an end myself. I thought Ourania would murder me, or try to. What else could she do to me? She couldn't divorce me, or threaten to, as my mother had so often threatened our father. By then she had already broken all the vases. As for scrawling all over the walls, the apartment was due for a paint job anyway.

Instead she packed and moved, leaving me to myself among her plasticized furnishings and the lingering perfume of charred lamb. She even left me the cat that we'd rescued from the ASPCA and named Odysseus, after the homesick Greek war hero, and that both she and I had hoped would bring some dignity back into our lives. Day after day I waited, expecting her to come back for the cat, for her clothes, for her books, for her drafting table, for the dining table, for her slipcovers, but she didn't. A month later, when I left the place myself, I left all her stuff there.

In her essay "On Self-Respect," Joan Didion writes: "To live without self-respect is to lie awake some night, beyond the reach of warm milk, phenobarbital, and the sleeping hand on the coverlet, counting up the sins of commission and omission, the trusts betrayed, the promises subtly broken, the gifts irrevocably wasted through sloth or cowardice or carelessness. However long we postpone it, we eventually lie down alone in that notoriously uncomfortable bed, the one we make ourselves."

I try to forget those terrible days in Astoria. When I remember them they remind me of a terrible night's sleep in a rumpled, sweaty bed. The bed was made by four people: me, Ourania, and my parents, who sowed in their son the desire to be happier in love than they, while also sowing the seeds of his own downfall. But I'm not writing this essay to blame my parents or anyone else for what Ourania and I did to each other. To do so would be to deny my responsibility, and I'm not twenty-three any more. It was lack of responsibility that drove me to live in Astoria with a woman I didn't love to begin with, lack of responsibility that divided me from my own self-respect. As Didion goes on to say, ". . . the willingness to accept responsibility for one's own life—is the source from which self-respect springs."

I never saw Ourania again, have no idea where she ended up, or how she has done, or whether she even still lives or not. Is she married? Does she have children? Has life been good or bad to her? Most of all I wonder: has she forgiven me? Has she forgiven *herself*?

Now at least I've committed my memory of those days to paper. It's all I can do. However belatedly, I've taken that much responsibility. I've made this bed in which to lay those unhappy days to rest.

May they do so in peace.

Confessions of a Left-Handed Man

The dog that mauled me was a black Labrador retriever belonging to a woman I'll call Miss Leachman, who owned a condominium in Westchester. In exchange for using her apartment, from which we commuted to New York City, my songwriting partner Mark (his surname shared with a twenty-mule-team soap product) and I agreed to water Miss Leachman's plants, forward her mail, and take care of Gus, her dog, a stray she had taken in from the street. Mark and I were both in our early twenties, and broke.

We'd been there for less than a week when, one night when I got up to go to the bathroom, Gus sat in the hallway blocking my way, baring his teeth and growling. Miss Leachman had instructed us—in case Gus should "get out of hand"—to wave his choke collar at him. The choke collar hung from a hook in the kitchen pantry; to get to it I had to get past Gus. I made my move. Gus lunged. His jaws went straight for my wrist, the left one.

Luckily Mark was there to hear to my cries. He threw a dining room chair at Gus, who let go and whimpered away. My torn, bleeding wrist wrapped in a towel, I rode with Mark in his rusting VW Squareback to the emergency room.

It was a few weeks before Christmas. I remember passing under strung colored lights and thinking to myself what pretty colors, that they should string colored lights like that everywhere, always.

I'm left-handed. I write with my left hand. I draw with my left hand. I tend to pick up things with my left hand. Like most left-handers I have trouble telling my left from my right, and tend to flip through magazines backward. The tasks that most define me I've always done with my left hand.

There are many myths about left-handedness, myths that tell me, for instance, that I'm eccentric and artistic, that I'm more accident-prone, more subject to autoimmune diseases, more likely to suffer depression and/or to commit suicide, and statistically liable to die sooner than my right-handed counterparts. And though most if not all of these myths have little scientific basis, I have a hard time arguing with some of them, since I am an artist; I am accident-prone (case in point: getting mauled by a black Labrador); I have suffered from at least one autoimmune disease (a bout of ulcerative colitis in my thirties); and I've been, if not suicidal, suicidally depressed.

Coincidences, I'm sure.

My fraternal twin brother is right-handed. And though George and I aren't identical, until we were sixteen people couldn't tell us apart. Up to a certain age our existence was harmonious. I mean that literally. We used to sit in the back of the school bus, bus number nine, driven by obese, aptly named (since the town where we lived was known for its hat factories) Mrs. Hatt,[1] harmonizing on Beatles songs, belting out *Help!*, *You're Gonna Lose That Girl*, and *A Hard Day's Night*. No one minded; in fact everyone on the bus dug our singing—including Mrs. Hatt, whose hefty head bobbed to the rhythms of our singing; the whole bus rocked and swayed in sympathy with our Beatles songs, with the road supplying occasional bumpy drumrolls. Twenty years later people who rode that bus with us, people whose faces and names I'd long since forgotten, would accost me in incongruous places, saying, "Hey, you're one of the Selgin boys, aren't you? I remember how you guys used to sing in the back of the bus!"

Such reminders always come as something of a shock, since no matter how often I'm reminded something in me refuses to believe. To me such memories are pure wish fulfillment. What I recall of my childhood with my twin isn't perfect harmony; it's complete dissonance. And fights: relentless fights fueled by the resentment bred by being constantly lumped together—*the Selgin boys*—as inevitably as peanut butter and jelly, as yin and yang, as Laurel and Hardy. For a while it felt good, apparently, until we discovered our separate egos and rebelled, going out of our way to play against the stereotype promulgated by a certain chewing gum commercial, refusing to dress alike in tennis togs like the Doublemint twins, or smile their sunny smiles (as if being twinned were the solution to all of life's woes). Our relationship was more like open combat.

To this day I have a recurrent nightmare about my fights with George. In the nightmare I'm on the ground surrounded by people pointing and laughing at me as I sit there, covered in grass, dirt, blood, and tears. Presumably George and I have just engaged in one our Spartacus-like displays (as popular, in their way, as our school bus harmonies), though in the dream my brother is nowhere to be seen. The inescapable Freudian implication being that I've just beaten the crap out of myself.

George and I grasped at anything we could to set ourselves apart from each other. Since he was astigmatic and had to wear glasses, George took on the role of bookworm, while I in turn seized upon my left-handedness as my most distinguishing trait, in spite of my grandmother doing her best to repair what she saw at worst as a freak of nature, at best a nasty habit, like picking your nose.

Nonnie had her own little apartment tucked away in the back of our Connecticut home, a single small room with a hot plate and a refrigerator. It was its own little world, with its own smells, its own sounds, its own stains, its own dust. To get me to write with my right hand, Nonnie bribed me with bowls of her homemade rice pudding, topped with a fetching little swirl of raspberry syrup and half a maraschino cherry. (In time I'd discover that the rice pudding had its genesis in a can marked "Comstock," but that day had yet to dawn.) Nonnie would sit me down at her doilied card table with a pencil and paper and feed me Italian phrases to transcribe, saying over and over to me, "*A destra, Pierro, a destra!*" giving my left hand a slap when I'd reach for the pencil or my rice-pudding spoon with it. She called me *Il mancino*—the left-handed one.

I don't blame my grandmother. She was only following a time-honored tradition, after all, one as old as the prejudice against left-handedness itself, one stretching as far back as the ancient Greeks, who posted sentries at their temples to make sure those who entered did so right foot first, so as not to offend the gods. Centuries later the Catholics took things further, burning left-handers as witches at the stake. In Victorian times left-handed children would have their left hands strapped behind their backs by means of a ghoulish leather

straightjacket-like contraption. It was not unusual for schoolmarms
and headmasters to cane pupils for using their "wrong" hand. To cure
their children of left-handedness, the Zulus of southern Africa would
plunge the aberrant member into a hole dug into the earth and filled
with boiling water, scalding it so severely the child would be forced to
switch hands.

Thankfully, my grandmother wasn't a Zulu. Still, when my mother
found out what Nonnie was up to, she threw a fit. I stood by Nonnie's
door listening to Mom's Italian curses resounding off her dusty walls.

My mother needn't have gotten so upset. Except in so far as it
would win me an occasional bowl of ersatz homemade rice pudding,
I had no intention of betraying my left hand. To have done so would
have been to surrender the best part of myself, the part that kept me
from being George, who, despite having been born first, was (I'd concluded) but a cheap knockoff of me, the original. Like those polymer
security threads embedded in our paper money, my left-handedness
was proof of my authenticity. No one, not even a Zulu, could or
would take it away from me.

The emergency room doctor who stitched up my wounds said I might
want to visit a neurologist to determine whether there was any nerve
damage.

A week after the stitches came out, I did so. I couldn't wiggle my
thumb; otherwise everything seemed normal. The hand specialist I
saw—I'll call him Dr. Chiu—had his office in the lower Thirties, off
First Avenue. I arrived there on a blustery Wednesday afternoon two
weeks after Christmas. The waiting room wall featured a big poster
showing a human hand, splayed open to show its hidden circuitry:
a bewildering network of red and blue veins and arteries, yellow and
purple nerves, green tendons, clay-colored muscles, and layers of
golden fat. It looked like a New York highway map around where the
Grand Central Parkway meets the Long Island Expressway. It was, I
noted with some dismay, a right hand.

Sitting in the waiting room with me were all kinds of people with
things wrong with their hands. The guy next to me was about fifty.
He wore a green corduroy jacket and had his right hand wrapped in
a clear plastic bag, like a sandwich. Across from me, the right hand
of a teenager wearing a New York Jets jersey was splinted and bound

and lay draped over his thigh like a dead albino reptile. Standing in the corner by the receptionist's desk was a tall, thin woman with a blonde bob that looked like a cheap novelty-store wig. Her arm was in a sling, her right arm. I was the only person in the waiting room with something wrong with his *left* hand. I flashed on a world wherein people were divided not by color, religion, or sex, but by left and right, with signs on doors, shop windows, and drinking fountains saying, "Rights Only." Someone tapped my shoulder.

"Mr. Selgin? Dr. Chiu will see you now."

The nurse escorted me to a small room and told me to sit down and push up both sleeves of the white turtleneck I wore. Using a series of electrodes terminating in clear plastic suction cups, she connected both of my hands to a machine the size and shape of a toaster oven, with an ovoid central screen surrounded by dials and meters.

Minutes later Dr. Chiu entered, a small man with a goatee. He looked like Dr. Rey in van Gogh's famous portrait. He handed me a rubber-coated tube with a long curled cord connected to the voltaic toaster. On his command I squeezed the tube as hard as I could with my left hand. Dr. Chiu murmured something faintly approbatory and made a note on his clipboard. He had me do the same thing with my right hand, then murmured something else and jotted another note. Then the left again, then the right. Throughout the test Dr. Chiu kept nodding and saying, "Ah ha," "Umm" or "Hmm."

Afterwards the doctor did another test using a different machine. This time, instead of suction cups, the device and I were united by a series of long, fine needles, which Dr. Chiu, with gentle gyrating motions, inserted into various muscles of my left hand. It wasn't painful; all I felt was a slight electrical tingle. Still, the sight of my left hand run through with a half-dozen needles, like a voodoo doll, distressed me. It took all my self-control not to tear the needles out and run screaming out of that room.

Finished, Dr. Chiu lowered his clipboard, sat down with his knee touching mine, and spoke of the motor component of the ulnar nerve, fourth-degree damage, the epineurial covering, disruption of something or other and the blood-nerve barrier, and how conductivity was no longer possible.

I didn't have to ask Dr. Chiu what all of that meant. Obviously my hand was very fucked-up.

Dr. Chiu recommended surgery. He happened to be a microsurgeon. "Of course," he said, "I cannot guarantee anything."

"Of course," I replied.

In high school I was one of the few (four, to be exact) honorary members of the Pthwecp Club. Though the origin of the club's peculiar name escapes me, I still remember the requirements for admission:

a) having the first name Peter
b) a surname starting with S
c) brown eyes
d) curly hair
e) artistic inclinations
f) being left-handed

What became of Peter Smith, Peter Sloat, or Peter Scalzo, my fellow Pthweeps, I have no idea. I was never all that close to them. Still, I was glad to belong to a club, any club, that excluded my twin.

Poor George. By then I really had it in for him. It was no longer enough to simply distinguish myself from him; I wanted him out of the picture completely. My plan was as simple as it was sinister. I'd outshine him so thoroughly that he would first shrivel up into a nonentity before disappearing altogether. To that end I parlayed my drawing skill into a means of winning friends and influencing enemies, doing swift, devastating caricatures of teachers and fellow students, drawings that I'd tape to walls and lockers and otherwise disseminate. That left hand of mine, it could draw like nobody's business. I trained it like a prize hunting dog—like a black Labrador, if you will—to fetch me anything in the form of a rendering. My twin could draw, too. But where George hid his light under a bushel, I paraded mine shamelessly, making it known to all concerned that I, not George, was the true artist, that he was but a pale imitator. To further up my wattage, I auditioned for and got leads in school plays. When George and I both tried out for *West Side Story*, I got cast as Tony, the lead, while George got stuck playing one of a dozen Sharks.

Artistic triumphs weren't enough. I had to best my twin in all areas (except academics where, being the bookworm, he outclassed me, but then no one cared). If George got a girlfriend, I made sure to get a better—anyway a prettier and more popular—one. When he bought a spiffy car—a '65 Barracuda, bronze with a slant-six engine and a stargazing rear make-out window, I bought an even spiffier MGB convertible, to which I added wire wheels and a flashy red paint job.

Was it a mere coincidence that I, the left-hander, turned out to be the evil, sinister one? Cain to my brother's Abel?

After graduating I spent a year driving trucks and moving furniture for Ethan Allen, then did my perfunctory tour of Europe. On my return I enrolled at the Pratt Institute, an art school in Brooklyn, where the sooty atmosphere of the studio classrooms depressed me. I hated charcoal dust and the smell of turpentine. My fellow art students thought me supercilious, distant, and disturbed. I can't imagine why, unless it was that time when I dangled myself by one arm from a balcony railing at a dorm party. The dorm was in a high-rise apartment building, the balcony on the twelfth floor. I never saw a party clear out so quickly. Afterward I told people I was drunk. I wasn't; I just longed for attention. The imperative to upstage my twin had mutated into a desire to upstage everyone. Need I point out that the hand by which I clung to my life was my left one?

In February, days before my twenty-fourth birthday, Dr. Chiu operated. I was under the knife for six hours. I awoke in my bed at Cabrini Medical Center to find my prior roommate, an elderly Hispanic with a green eyepatch, gone, replaced by a man who looked like the Pillsbury Doughboy, whose name was Günther, and who had survived the bombing of Dresden. Günther's first words to me were, "Don't move it."

"It" was my left hand which, after I blinked a couple times and it came into focus, looked in its heavy white wrappings like a beached beluga whale. Günther asked me if I was left-handed. I nodded. He shook his head and smiled. Günther had a strange bloated face, as if all of its muscles had melted into fat deposits. But then I was still groggy and nauseated. Günther must have seen that I was queasy. He picked up a hospital menu and recited it to me with his thick German accent.

"Ledz zee now, Beeder," he said. "Vhut zounds gut fuh dinnah? Jicken zalad, zliced beeds, gole zlaw, aw de peas 'n' garots?"

It worked. I lurched over the side of the bed and threw up.

Unlike some people, I wasn't hung up on being left-handed. I didn't go around claiming da Vinci as my rightful ancestor, and Einstein too, the implication being that we left-handers are all born geniuses and Renaissance men.[2] Nor did I take umbrage or solace in having this very little something in common with Benjamin Franklin, Alexander the Great, Harpo Marx, Ringo Starr, Julius Ceasar, Ty Cobb, Napoleon, Betty Grable, W. C. Fields, the Boston Strangler, Jimi Hendrix, and Presidents Ford and Reagan (Bush and Clinton were yet to come).

I was never the sort of left-hander who cries "Foul!" when confronted by a pair of right-handed scissors or trousers with no back pocket on the left side. Nor did I lose sleep over knowing that, because I'm left-handed, the writing on a pencil shaft faces away from me when I write; or that 99 percent of all boomerangs manufactured in the world are useless (if not lethal) to me; or that, should I need to carry a bicycle, I'd have to do so on my right shoulder, because if I carried it on my left—as would be my inclination—I'd get grease stains all over my clothes; or that, discharged by me, a semiautomatic weapon will tend to blow its hot casings past my left cheek, possibly resulting in second- or third-degree burns. None of these things bothered me very much. Even spiral notebooks caused me little if any grief, despite the fact that the spirals interfered with my handwriting each time I'd start on a fresh front-sided page.

Not that I wasn't fond of my left hand. I was; I still am. You might say I'm attached to it. It is, after all, the hand that launched a hundred rock-embedded dirtballs at my twin's skull. It's the hand that split open Bobby Muller's lip after enduring months of face-slappings from him at the bus stop for admitting that I didn't believe in God. It is the very hand with which I brought myself to my first bewildering orgasm, and with which, a few years later, I'd reach deep into my high school sweetheart's Wrangler's and bring her to *her* first bewildering orgasm. With that hand I'd sketch hundreds of illicit, unflattering likenesses—a skill closer to archery than to draftsmanship, and one requiring a great deal of dexterity—an odd word, considering. This hand could draw a sinking *Titanic* like nobody's business. It did a fair *Lusitania*, too.

Soon after Günther got me to throw up, Dr. Chiu dropped by. He explained that, as he had suspected, the nerve had not been "transected," but that a layer of "scar and neuromic tissue" had built up around the affected area, putting pressure on the myelin sheath and thus "preventing conduction." He said he had done his best to scrape the scar tissue away, but warned me that it might grow back.

"We'll just have to wait and see," he said.

My right-handed twin having taken the straight and narrow path to academe, I did the opposite, switching schools and interests as often as most people change the oil in their cars. After quitting art school I bummed around. I would have joined the air force but for my mortal fear of discipline. Instead I hitchhiked. On my way nowhere I met George at his undergraduate school, where we got into a fight over a pen he claimed I'd stolen. George collected fountain pens, antique ones. He had at least fifty of them. The one I took didn't look that expensive to me; the nib wasn't even pure gold. Of course I denied it. He called me a moocher and a libertine—words I had to look up later. I called him a greedy capitalist pig. He said, "Hit the road, asshole." I did, crossing the dusky campus with tears in my eyes and without having said goodbye—but not before quietly slipping George's fountain pen back into his desk drawer.

There followed two semesters at Bard College, at Annandale-on-Hudson, plodding through *Ulysses* and spending the rest of my time doing push-ups and sunning myself on the campus quad, trying to forget that my leisure cost me and my folks $8,000 a year. Genius didn't come cheap. When a then twenty-five-year-old President Leon Botstein refused me a scholarship, I quit Bard in disgust and hitchhiked south to New York City, where I parlayed my skills as an actor, and got nowhere. A failed foray in Hollywood brought me back—by way of a series of increasingly sordid low-budget movie jobs—to the nutmeg state, where at the state college I met my future songwriting partner, who taught me my first three guitar chords, and with whom I would go in on a fateful Westchester housesit.

An hour after my brief visit with Dr. Chiu, with my left hand still paralyzed and swaddled in surgical gauze, and still feeling groggy from anesthesia, I was discharged from the hospital into a polar-bright winter afternoon. The remains of snow from a blizzard the week before lay in stained patches along sidewalks and gutters, while the low-angle sun blazed off car hoods and windshields. With nowhere to go,

I wandered the city streets, feeling the eyes of its countless windows looking down on and judging me, condemning me, me and my left hand—punished, at last, for our conjoined sins. The job that my grandmother and her rice pudding began in her dusty room twenty years before, God and a black Labrador retriever named Gus finally finished. My left-handed days were over. Time to straighten up and fly right, so to speak.

These weren't happy days. Since Mark and I had nowhere else to go, Mr. Cheswick, the manager of the copy shop where we worked, let us sleep on the industrial gray carpeting next to the hulking machines. With my left hand out of service I was reduced to making copies a page at a time, hence useless as an employee. After a week, Mr. Cheswick said he was sorry, but he'd have to let me go.

Seeing my bandaged left hand, the clerk at unemployment asked me if I was left-handed. I told her I was. She said if I couldn't work I couldn't get unemployment benefits. I asked, What about disability? She said it would be three months before I'd get a check. By then I'll be able to work, I said. She said in that case you're not qualified for disability, either.

The rehab nurse told me to rub Vaseline Intensive Care lotion into my scar. "You should massage slowly, in circles, like so," she said, looking into my eyes as her fingertips worked the semen-like unguent into my palm and wrist. "You can ask your girlfriend to do this part for you."

"What if I don't have a girlfriend?"

She handed me a ball of yellow-green putty and told me to squeeze it every day. "Like this," she said, showing me.

One month after my surgery I met again with Dr. Chiu, who hooked me up to his machine. The results were gloomy. The nerve showed no signs of renewed life, and already there were signs of muscle atrophy. The operation had failed. With luck and practice, Dr. Chiu said, I might regain 50 percent of the use of my hand.

"Will I be able to draw again?" I asked.

"That would depend," said Dr. Chiu, "on your artistic standards."

I began to give serious thought to my right-handed future, wondering if it was too late for me to go to law school or become an accountant.

Maybe I'd go back to moving furniture for Ethan Allen. Or maybe (I considered in one of my gloomier romantic moods) I'd get a job down at the Fulton Fish Market, unloading crates of ice-packed fish from the backs of 3 A.M. trucks. I pictured myself among fishmongers in plaid coats, warming gloved fingers over an oil drum fire, Leonard Bernstein's theme to *On the Waterfront* swelling in my sappy head.

In March, Mark left New York. A country boy by nature, he couldn't stand life in the city. The air infected his sinuses and gave him miserable headaches. And besides, our dream of becoming the next Simon and Garfunkel was ashes, and we both knew it. Even if I could somehow play the guitar again, it wouldn't matter. By then I'd lost heart.

I tried drawing with my right hand, but it was like trying to sing with my fingers holding my tongue, or run with my shoelaces tied together. I couldn't be right-handed any more than the earth could spin the other way on its axis.

The week after Mark left, walking down the ill-lit and loosely treaded stairs of the Gramercy Park Hotel where I'd taken a room the size of a closet, I tripped and broke my leg. I spent the next three weeks hobbling around the city, the right leg in a cast and my left hand and arm still wrapped to my elbow.

One night, still on crutches, I hobbled to the East River, to where in my wanderings the day of my release from Cabrini I had located a breach in a chain-link fence. It was still March, and there had been another big snowstorm. Huge floes floated like the ghosts of ships over the black water. I made my way out to the end of a pier, my crutch tips breaking through the rotted wood every dozen or so yards, to where I stood looking out across the water, at the lights of Brooklyn shattered in inky waves. It wasn't the first time I'd thought of killing myself, but other times I'd done so only in passing, and never with the opportunity so conveniently at hand. As I leaned forward on my crutches, I knew that with an arm and a leg out of whack and winter boots on and the water freezing, even a strong swimmer like me would be done for in minutes. It was more than tempting; it seemed preordained, a fitting end to a wrong-headed, left-handed life.

Then my mind flashed a photo of me and George, the Selgin boys, topsy-turvy on the front lawn with curly heads touching and big cheesy smiles, one of those corny photo ops parents of twins always insist upon, taken in the years before the edict to wipe each other out was issued. I looked up at the clouds sweeping the night sky, pulled back from the brink, had a good bawl, and hobbled back to my hotel room.

I sued Miss Leachman. I had to. I owed over $10,000 to Cabrini and Dr. Chiu. The case would drag on for years, with Miss Leachman's lawyers deposing my high school music and art teachers to see if I'd had any real talent. In the end the insurance company settled, but only after the jurors had been sworn in. My lawyer, a woman not much older than I was, urged me to hold out for more money. But I wasn't feeling greedy, and told her so. I never saw a more disgusted look cross a lawyer's face.

In the two years following my surgery, the surviving muscles in my left hand rallied, taking the place of those that had died. With practice I was able to write left-handed again, but in a craggy, childlike scrawl that gave way quickly to cramps and that I alone could decipher. In time I drew, too, tentatively at first, crude sketches devoid of facility, let alone glibness. But then I realized: facility wasn't everything. In fact it is very little. Under what had been slick surfaces I uncovered new, hidden depths.

More than twenty years have passed since Gruesome Gus's incisors tore into my left wrist. Since then a lot has changed. I no longer see my left-handedness as a means to prove anything to anyone, myself included. Nor do I see it as a way to eclipse my brother, a highly regarded professor of economics, whom I love dearly and get along with very well.

I no longer feel blessed or cursed by being left-handed; it's just the hand I happen to use. Still, it's been a faithful servant, this left limb of mine, and I'm glad to have stuck with it all these years, through thick and thin. However much we've both changed, my left hand and I are happily reunited.

And though I now earn my living as a painter and illustrator, my work has nothing in common with what I did before. For better or worse, my drawings have turned naive, even primitive. My lack of dexterity has freed me from glibness, which in turn has delivered me from the temptation to force attention to myself by showing off. For the artist, to master humility is every bit as important as mastering perspective, proportion, or a graceful line. The hand holds the instrument, but if we're lucky the heart guides it, not the brain or the ego.

On the ceiling of the Sistine Chapel in Rome, in the central panel of the most famous painting by Michelangelo (that other Renaissance lefty), God, floating on a cloud of purple silk, bestows life on the first man, Adam, through the fingertip of his right hand. Adam, however, who has been created in God's image, accepts the gift with his *left* hand. Michelangelo knew what he was doing. According to the Roman poet Isidorus, a secret blood vessel runs directly from the index finger of the left hand to the human heart—the heart, not the brain.

God wished to bypass the intellect and launch his spark straight into the heart of man, who reaches out to lend Him a hand. The left one. It was good enough for Adam, and it's good enough for me.

NOTES

1. Cruel children that we were, we invented this bit of doggerel to go with her name. "Miss Hatt is Fat / she's a Dirty Rat." I'd like to apologize for this tiny bit of evil visited upon a thoroughly nice bus driver, and let it be known to all who read this that, though she *was* fat, Miss Hatt was *not* a rat, nor was she dirty. She was a fine bus driver and I miss her.

2. In fact both men were probably ambidextrous.

Painting Icebergs: A Titanic Obsession

Uncles and Aunts, little children lost their pants.
It was sad when the great ship went down.
—Children's Nursery Rhyme

n the mid-1990s, Fred, my therapist, suggested that I do a self-portrait of myself as a naked child. The assignment was designed to liberate an innocent, joyful, spontaneous spirit from that of the anxious, striving, and self-conscious man I had by age thirty-eight, unfortunately, become. Like eating vegetables, meditating, and all things meant to do me good, I resisted the assignment at first. I didn't want to paint myself at all, never mind as a child. I pictured those cloying, doe-eyed paintings of children that pediatricians used to decorate their waiting room walls. Session after session Fred kept asking me, "So, Peter, have you done the painting yet?" And session after session I would say no, but that I would. Finally, Fred stopped asking.

During that same period, while in Philadelphia for a pharmaceutical products convention at which I'd been hired to draw caricatures, I wandered into an antique shop in the historic district, a dusty, cramped little shop where, leaning against a ratty piece of furniture, something caught my eye, or rather two things caught it: a pair of paintings.

The paintings were executed in an unusual technique. They were shiny, very shiny, with absolutely no texture, their surfaces as smooth as glass. In fact their surfaces *were* glass. They were reverse paintings—oils executed on sheets of glass. The technique, which the French call *verré églomisé*, has been around since the Middle Ages, at least, when the Byzantines used it for their icons and to depict other sacral subjects. With the Renaissance it spread to all of Europe, where it was later adopted by nineteenth-century horologers for decorating the faces of their clocks. It wasn't long before folk artists and artisans embraced the method, which gave rise to a cottage industry, with one factory in Bavaria producing over four thousand glass paintings in a single year.[1] They're sometimes called reverse paintings, since the side of the glass that gets painted on isn't the side that's displayed.[2]

The style of the paintings was no less remarkable. Though the subjects they depicted were as gloomy and grim as could be, the manner in which they were depicted was anything but grim. Indeed it was refreshingly innocent and naive, like a child's dream. For all I knew they might have been painted by children, only they were a little too tidy, too fastidious, their colors, however fanciful, too measured, too restrained.

But the most unusual thing by far about the two paintings was the subject matter. In one a ship in silhouette bore down on a mammoth silver iceberg. In the other the same ship was shown sinking, plumes of bluish-gray smoke rising from its four funnels against the now silhouetted black iceberg.

The ship, it goes without saying, was the *Titanic*. The paintings were done the same year she sank, in 1912, from do-it-yourself kits slapped together by entrepreneurs eager to exploit the sensational tragedy, which, for a brief time, created its own little industry.

For a long time I stood there, gazing at the two paintings, mesmerized. What I felt was beyond covetousness, beyond the feeling that I *had to* own them. It was more like a premonition, an inevitability, a sense that the paintings were mine and mine alone, that they always had been, and always would be.

As a child I'd always been fascinated by ships, and especially by ocean liners, a fascination ignited by my first visit to New York City with my papa when I was five years old, when I saw a group of them, the *Queen Mary*, the *France*, the *United States*, lined up in their berths, looking, with their vanilla-white superstructures, their yellow masts and cherry-red funnels, like colossal floating banana splits. That things so enormous could move, let alone float, astounded me. No more than a year or two later, I first saw, on the boxy wooden Magnavox in our living room, the film version of *A Night to Remember*, Walter Lord's minute-by-minute account of the sinking of the *Titanic*. The image of the doomed liner's counterstern rising out of the water, looming with its lights still ablaze against a starry sky, made an indelible impression on me; very possibly it was my first experience of awe. The first long paper I ever wrote for a school project was about the *Titanic*, a book report on *A Night to Remember*, complete with a cutaway illustration of the ship—its details thoroughly improvised.[3] On the brown shopping bag covers of my grade school textbooks, and on the wide-lined pages of my composition notebooks, I sketched the sinking *Titanic* over and over again, as if somehow by sketching it I could bring the events of that cold April night closer, and own them somehow, or at least make them more my own. And though in my sketches I always made sure to include minuscule bodies plunging into the sea, I never really gave any thought to the people on the ship; I never stopped to consider the horror; I never concerned myself with the human side of the tragedy. I thought only about the ship, about its four tall majestic funnels, its gleaming propellers, its countless portholes, and that curved, looming, massive hull.

The paintings in that Philadelphia antique shop were about four feet long by a foot and a half wide, with cheap gold-painted plaster frames. My then wife and I had just bought our first apartment on the Upper West Side. It featured a sunken living room with a dining alcove in the area above it. We painted one wall of the alcove bright red, and docked our most extravagant and expensive furniture item there: a 1920s maple English bar unit, with a hinged top that opened to a Busby-Berkley display of blinding light and mirrors etched with droll cocktail shakers and floating martini glasses. One of those two paintings, I thought, would look magnificent over it.

As I mentioned, the paintings weren't historically accurate. All the details were wrong. The funnels were much too large, the iceberg was a stupendous exaggeration, the colors, however restrained, were sentimental: silvers and blues and blacks, with just a touch of red in the funnels. It was a child's dream of the *Titanic* sinking, a work of supreme naiveté. It reminded me of the sketches I'd done in grade school.

The antiques dealer wanted $900 for both paintings. I asked if he would consider splitting the pair and selling me just the one of the sinking ship, but he wouldn't, so I let it go. Even at half the price it would have been too rich for my blood

But the painting wouldn't let me go. It haunted me, so much that,

one night after a day spent working on an oversized corporate caricature commemorating the principle actors in a bond merger,[4] I sat
down in my studio with some acrylic paints and brushes and tried to
recreate from memory the forsaken *Titanic* painting. The result fell far
short of my aim. So I tried again, and again. Rather than attempt any
kind of realism, I aimed for what I'd seen in those paintings: a child's
interpretation of the *Titanic* disaster, with everything charmingly, dis-
armingly skewed. I stayed up all night working. By sunrise, like Monet
with his lily pads, Degas with his ballerinas, and Morandi with his
dusty brown bottles, I'd found not only my perfect subject, but the
perfect style to go with it. That night the naive artist in me was born.

Over the next twenty-eight months, there followed a hundred and
four paintings of the sinking *Titanic*. They lined every wall and shelf
and filled every closet of our Upper West Side apartment (with its
highly appropriate sunken living room). I worked in all different sizes,
in all different colors, proceeding according to whim and fancy, my
only constant directive to myself being to *do it wrong*. To hell with perspective, to hell with light, to hell with proper proportions, to hell
with rules, to hell with everything they ever taught me in art school.
Create purely from joy and inspiration, spontaneously, and damn (so
to speak) the icebergs. And though my subject remained consistent,
there seemed to be no end to the possible variations. While there may
be a limited number of ways to do something right, when it comes to
doing something wrong, apparently there is no such limit. Anything
was possible. Indeed, everything was not only possible, but inevitable.
While working I would say to myself, "Yeah, sure, why *not* do it that
way? Why not choose this or that color? Why not make the funnels
green? Or paint a dozen instead of four? After all, assuming you keep
painting the *Titanic* for the rest of your life, you're bound to paint one
with a dozen green funnels." It was like that old chestnut about the
infinite number of monkeys banging away infinitely on an infinite
supply of typewriters, thereby eventually producing *King Lear* or some
other masterpiece.

But my goal wasn't to produce a singular masterpiece; mine was a
quest for variety and abundance. How many ways could I paint this
picture? For years I had drawn and painted, but never in my life had I
done so with such joy and ease. It was as if a burden had been lifted—

a heavy burden about the size of the *Titanic*'s hull, the burden of great ambition met with grim determination, of youthful dreams evolved into adult anxieties, of high hopes turned into stomach ulcers. The more I painted, the happier I felt. Except when I was a kid I'd never felt happier. All thanks to a sinking ship. I'd found my obsession.

In obsessing over the *Titanic*, I can hardly claim originality. The sinking has obsessed generations. It is the Belle Epoque's answer to Noah's Ark. As legends go, it looms as large. It has all the necessary elements: a drama of disaster unfolding upon a world stage. As with Noah and his ark, it is a tragedy wherein a select few prevail, while the rest are doomed. And while the story of the *Titanic* may not take in the entire globe, it takes in quite a big chunk of society: rich, poor, heroic, cowardly. The ship's passenger list represented almost as many specimens of humanity as the beasts aboard Noah's vessel stood for all species. Indeed, had the *Titanic* story never happened, to be sure, sooner or later, someone would have invented it.

In fact someone did. In 1898, fourteen years before the *Titanic* went down, a struggling author of seafaring tales named Morgan Robertson penned a novel about a magnificent liner's fateful encounter with an iceberg in the North Atlantic on a freezing cold April night. As Walter Lord describes it in his chilling forward to what remains by far and away the best book about the *Titanic* disaster[5]:

> The real ship was 882.5 feet long; [Robertson's] fictional one was 800 feet. Both vessels were triple screw and could make 24–25 knots. Both could carry 3,000 people, and both had enough lifeboats for only a fraction of this number. But then this didn't seem to matter, because both were labeled "unsinkable."
>
> On April 10, 1912, the real ship left Southampton on her maiden voyage to New York. Her cargo included a priceless copy of the Rubaiyat of Omar Khayyam and a list of passengers collectively worth $250 million dollars. On her way she too struck an iceberg and went down on a cold April night.
>
> Robertson called his ship the *Titan*; the White Star Line called its ship the *Titanic*. This is the story of her last night.

The title of Robertson's novel was *Futility*, and, as Lord points out, it was meant to underscore the folly of all human attempts to rise above their limits and rival their gods, the hubris and vanity inherent in all human ambition and enterprise.

I remember reading in the fall of 1985 about Bob Ballard's discovery of the *Titanic* wreck two and a half miles under the Atlantic. It made the *Times* front page. The news horrified me. A disaster in its own right, it seemed to me. Where the article continued in the science section there was a photograph of the grinning oceanographer wearing his signature baseball cap. I took an instant dislike to Mr. Ballard, who seemed to me the sort of scientist whose empirical enthusiasms date back to frying toads on the barbecue grill. And now this grandstanding oceanographer with a pubescent boy's wanton gleam in his eyes had gotten his empirical hands on the *Titanic* and would torture every last remaining secret out of her, bolt by bolt. Those fabulous mysteries would no more survive the glare of Ballard's submarine searchlights than its waterlogged hulk could survive a sudden influx of oxygen. Along with the rest of the world, I'd happily pictured the ship down there, still more or less intact at the bottom of the sea, her slender, graceful, buff funnels—three of four, anyway—reaching toward the sun-wrinkled surface like the pipes of Nemo's organ. *In a solitude of the sea / Deep from human vanity, /And the Pride of Life that planned her, stilly couches she.* Coal bunkers groaning, engine cylinders still gleaming in their casings, brass propellers miraculously void of barnacles turning golden figure eights down there in the steel-blue depths: a ship no less intact than her myth, growing more unsinkable year by year. Then along comes Ballard with his baseball cap in his toy submarine to reduce it all to heaps of rust-oozing junk mired in ocean muck.

"Why it's amazing how good she still looks," he and others proclaimed, or some such supreme idiocy. She didn't. She looked awful, as bad as any rotting corpse exhumed after seventy-five years. Save the macabre thrill of watching some extremely high-tech oceangoing grave robbers at work, there was nothing to celebrate here. And notwithstanding all the high-minded talk of preserving the wreck and respecting her dead, it was but a matter of time before entrepreneurs like George Tulloch with their own submarines had at her, selling golf-ball-size bits of bunker coal to suckers for twenty-five dollars a pop. Get yours while supplies last! Only 250,000 chunks left!

For better or worse, Ballard's discovery rekindled the public's fascination with the *Titanic*. Soon there was a Broadway musical (in which, during previews, the model ship on stage refused to sink), followed by Cameron's $200 million epic for which he practically resank the ship, painstakingly synthesizing her vertiginous final plunge into the sea, bodies and deck chairs sliding, funnel cables snapping, tortured deck timbers and hull plates snapping, the great ship splitting in half—all in service of a cheesy, comic-book melodrama. I enjoyed and hated the film, mentally retrofitting *A Night to Remember*, the 1958 classic based on Walter Lord's book—a sober docudrama—with Cameron's far superior special effects.

Suddenly the whole world shared my private obsession with the *Titanic*. Thanks to the tidal swell of interest in the ship, generated by Ballard's discovery and Cameron's movie, my paintings had their moment in the limelight, with spots on TV and radio shows, and an editorial in the *Wall Street Journal*. My paintings had gained their fifteen minutes of fame. Unwittingly, I both contributed to and took part in the *Titanic* feeding frenzy. I was one of the myth's perpetuators, and one of its teeming exploiters.

Having finished my first seventy-five *Titanic* paintings, I decided to hold a salon at our apartment. My wife made period hors d'oeuvres to go with the champagne. I hung a trumped-up *Titanic* life preserver (the real ones didn't say the ship's name) on the apartment door, and hired a solo cellist to play ragtime and *Nearer My God to Thee*. The event took place on a Saturday afternoon. Over two hundred people stopped by throughout the day, some coming from as far as Vermont, Washington D.C., and Georgia.

Of all the people we had invited, only one disappointed us by not showing up, a man who lived just across town on East 68th Street. Due to an infirmity, he had responded with regrets to my faxed invitation. However (his typed letter went on to say), if I offered him a rain check he would do his very best to come by some other time.

Two Sundays later, in a wheelchair pushed by his attendant, Walter Lord arrived, trembling with Parkinson's disease, but alert and eager for my offerings. Tea and crumpets were served. One by one, as he sat at the dining room table, I took the paintings down from the walls and displayed them for him. With each painting he nodded, though it was hard to say for sure whether his nodding signified approval or was a symptom of his disease. When asked by me to explain his own obsession with the *Titanic*, Mr. Lord gave this simple answer. "Well," he said with a snort as though it were perfectly obvious, "if there's anything better than a big ship, it's a big ship that sinks!"[6]

In our obsession, Mr. Lord (who died in 2002) and I were far from alone. Few are not drawn to the story of the *Titanic* and of the concatenation of coincidences and misfortunes that, in retrospect, seemed to have been orchestrated with a watchmaker's precision by fate with no other intent but to doom her. If only this, if only that. But that night the *if onlys* were all as fast asleep as the Marconi man aboard the SS *Californian*, drifting with her engines off a mere dozen miles from the doomed liner's last stand. The *if onlys* and *what ifs* were aroused only in and by retrospect. Such is fortune. For the salient feature of all legends and myths is that they *need* to have happened. Something in our collective unconscious yearns for, insists upon, them. And what myths reality does not provide, we concoct (The Abominable Snowman. Elvis lives!). Even when, as with the story of the *Titanic*, reality is generous to a fault, providing us with as much irony, awe, and horror as we could ever wish for, still, we feel the need to enlarge, to embellish, to augment, to improve, to perfect. To turn tragedy into a masterpiece.

People need disasters; we need tragedy; we need horror. But we need to enshrine—to protect and preserve and hold—it in legend or myth, like the bones of a tyrannosaurus in a museum, where it can instruct and fascinate while posing no danger. We all yearn to get up close to horror, where we can see and touch and begin to experience it as something other than a vague abstraction, if only to begin to grasp it, to *know* exactly what we fear. Life is one long freeway pileup and we're all of us rubberneckers, with doom our own ultimate destination and no chance of escape. We're *all* passengers on the *Titanic*.

But for the people of 1912 who lived through that disaster, the sinking of the *Titanic* was no metaphor. It was a living nightmare, a shockingly gruesome reminder of the potential for suffering within a matter of hours and on a massive scale. Yet, given sufficient time and distance, even the most gruesome tragedies take on the patina of myth by way of nostalgia. They become quaint, friendly. Compared with our own contemporary disasters and tragedies they seem tame, innocent. So we take a kind of cold, perverse comfort in them. They belong, after all, to the myth of the good old days. Compared with 9/11, the sinking of the *Titanic* is a *chaste* tragedy. Still—despite all attempts by oceanographers, scientists, and historians (including Walter Lord) to put to rest any doubts as to what, exactly, happened on that cold April night, thereby sinking all *Titanic* myths once and for all— the ship, along with her cargo of legend and lore, keeps bobbing up to the surface again and again, refusing to stay sunken. The supply of facts may be limited; however many millions of bolts were driven into the *Titanic*'s hull, there were only so many. But the imagination knows no such limits, nor does the human hunger for legends and myths.

Children are especially susceptible. One day as I was walking through Grand Central Station with one of my *Titanic* paintings under my arm, transporting it to a gallery downtown, a toddler, walking hand in hand with her father, caught what must have been a very brief glimpse of what lay on the canvas.

"Daddy, daddy!" she cried out, pointing, "It's the *Titanic!*"

In that girl's unmitigated joy I recognized my own childhood fascination with the ship, my own wonder at the sheer magnitude of that colossal vessel, its scale matched only by that of the disaster that sent it and fifteen hundred souls to the bottom of the ocean. But the child saw nothing tragic in my painting. She saw only awe, wonder, spectacle. Where others might have seen disaster, she saw a miracle. Her jaw hung, her cheeks glowed, her eyes blossomed, lit up with a child's categorical delight. Yes, life can be grim. But in spite of its grimness, or maybe part and parcel to it, it's also spectacular. That little girl in Grand Central Station, she knew this. She couldn't have been more than four years old, yet she knew, as all children know, as all children seem to know, that horror and beauty are not mutually exclusive. It isn't horror that deprives us of innocence. Nor is experience itself opposed to the sense of awe and wonder. If we've lost our childhood innocence, if we've surrendered it to something grim and obligatory, it's because we assume that this is what we're *supposed* to do, just as we assume that, in public, we're supposed to wear clothes, and, when life turns grim or tragic, our emotions, like our clothes, should be black. But children don't mourn. Not just because they don't have to, but because they know better. They mostly see the wonder in things. That, above all, makes them children.

As I neared the end of my painting series, instead of painting the *Ti-tanic* sinking, I began painting it in other poses: at dockside on a bright sunny day, breezing past the iceberg, and even one of her steaming safe and sound into a sleepy New York Harbor at night. The last painting I did was of the *Titanic* and Noah's Ark meeting at sea, with the former vessel transferring her passengers to the latter. Then I was through.

One day, a few months before I stopped painting the *Titanic*, I brought one of the earlier paintings, a small one I'd done using a scratchboard technique and bright earth colors,' to Fred, my therapist.

"Congratulations," he said, smiling as he peered at it over his bifocals.

I'd done the assignment.

NOTES

1. 1814

2. The paint is likewise applied in reverse. Unlike a typical painting, where the first strokes are normally covered up by subsequent colors and strokes, with a reverse painting the first strokes are also the first to meet the eye, with the background (or the under-painting) painted last. For the artist to see his creation while creating it, he had to mount a mirror on the wall behind it.

3. Down to the wallpaper on cabin walls.

4. Such works of art, for those who may be interested, are called tombstones.

5. One that treats the simultaneous events of that night almost cubistically, like a still life by Georges Braque or Juan Gris.

6. Weeks later, on a visit to Lord's East Side apartment—itself a film set of the *Titanic*'s first-class dining salon, with its coffered ceilings and panelled walls—while looking over his collection of ephemera, high on a closet shelf I noticed a thick wad of paper. "Take that down," he said. I did. It was the handwritten manuscript of *A Night to Remember*, on yellow legal paper bound with two red rubber bands. "How many drafts did you end up doing?" I asked. Lord looked at me, perplexed. "Drafts?" He'd given the holograph to a secretary to type up, and that was that.

7. "Clay Titanic," I called it.

Dirty Books

ooks are filthy. I learned this when I volunteered to help reshelve them for a renovation project at the Mercantile Library in Manhattan. The library, which was founded by merchants (hence the name) and predates the public library system, has one of the biggest fiction holdings in the country. For decades the books were kept in cave-like stacks, arranged eccentrically by title, and mostly inaccessible to the library's patrons. To get a book you had to fill out a call slip and hand it to the librarian, an elderly woman who, with the desultory air of someone requisitioned to descend into the ninth circle of Dante's *Inferno*, would relinquish her front desk and ride the elevator down into the dungeon-like stacks, or send an intern to do it, if one was available. The renovation would change all that, with stacks well lit, arranged with Melville Dewey's blessing, and accessible to all.

Since discovering it ten years ago, I've loved the Mercantile Library (known to its members as the Merc). When I'm in Manhattan I consider it a second home, a rare oasis in the heart of the city, a book-lined refuge in that desert of noise and commerce known as Midtown, steps from Grand Central Station. At first you can't believe it's there, wedged among skyscrapers and other "monuments to men's mysteries" (as Saul Bellow describes them in the opening of *The Victim*, his first novel). But even once you accept that the Merc isn't a mirage, there's that nagging suspicion that, like the hero of *Slaughterhouse-Five*, Billy Pilgrim, it has become unstuck in time. Though the librarian has a computer on her desk, there are no other computers or machines of any kind to be found there, no copiers or microfilm viewers, no books on tape or videos or DVDs, just printed books and lots of silence.

At the front door I was greeted by Brenda, the head librarian, a willowy blonde who rode with me up the library's creaky, slow elevator to the fourth floor. There I was introduced to the intern, Stacy, a perky brunette who handed me a pair of white surgical gloves along with my marching orders. My task: remove all books by authors with surnames starting with M through Z from the shelves, sort them, put them on a cart, trundle them up to the fifth floor, and reshelve them.

It seemed easy enough at first. I chose a place among the stacks still groaning with novels arranged by the old system, with titles all beginning with E, and set to work, extracting the books according to their authors' last names. Since I was free to start anywhere I wanted, I restricted myself to M authors (Morris, Miller, McBain, Morgan, Maugham . . .) But then I noticed there were a lot of S authors (Smith, Scanlon, Shaeffer, Solowitz) and started pulling those down, too. And get a load of all those P's (Peck, Porter, Platt, Patrick . . .) and R's (Reilly, Roth, Reilly, Rhodes—there must be thousands of writers named Rhodes!) and W's (Wallace, Winchell, West) . . .

My head started spinning. I kept moving books around, taking them from one shelf or pile and putting them on another without reason or rhyme. I was trying to come up with a system, but no sooner would I devise one than I would break its rules. It was sweltering hot in the stacks. Somewhere an air conditioner thrummed, but it made little difference. Sweat dripped from my nose. I had to be careful not to drip on the books. Meanwhile, the books swirled around me, along with the first letters of their authors' last names, like letters in a bubbling pot of alphabet soup.

Then there was the dust. At first I couldn't see it, the stacks were so poorly lit, but when I went to get a drink of water, I looked down at my surgical gloves. They were black as if I'd been shoveling coal. Some of those books hadn't been touched in decades. The oldest ones disintegrated as I took them down, having been held in place only by those books surrounding them. They turned to brown dust in my hands, their covers snapping to bits and fluttering to the floor to join the rest of the brown pages and covers turning to mulch down there, autumn leaves on a forest floor.

The smell, too, was powerful, the musty, nutty, mushroomy smell of old books, a smell that took me back to the summer of 1971, when I was thirteen years old, the summer I lost my literary virginity.

I'd been alphabetizing Mr. Boyd's books. Mr. Boyd lived in a cedar-shingled house at the top of a wooded hill (this was in Connecticut, where there were lots of woods). Mr. Boyd couldn't see his closest neighbor and liked it that way. He was a misanthrope and a miser. He looked like Lee Marvin in *Hell in the Pacific*, but bald, with big ears that had clumps of hair sprouting from them, and a hanging, thick, toad-stool-like, eternally moist lower lip.

Since the death of Sally, his wife and my mother's close friend, Mr. Boyd had elected himself a member of our family, showing up uninvited for lunch and dinner and sometimes even in the morning for breakfast. He would stomp around our kitchen in his yellow brogans crusty with mud from one of the construction sites that he owned, depositing little bits of dirt that our dog would try to eat. He would help himself to my mother's coffee, then complain that it was lukewarm and too weak, and insult my father, calling him an "absent-minded professor" and "the world's greatest egocentric." Still, I had a soft spot for Mr. Boyd. I liked how he always whispered so you had to lean close to hear him, and how his big hands trembled when holding a carving knife or turning a screwdriver. He told funny stories about being in the navy (my "egocentric" father never went to war) and about his morbid fears of heights and water. He had a great laugh that started with a snort and ended in his eyes.

That summer, after I'd painted the trim on his cedar house and cleared his yard of fallen branches left by winter storms, Mr. Boyd asked me to rearrange the library that he kept in his basement, in the same room where, on sweltering hot summer nights, he slept on an army cot to save on air-conditioning. There were hundreds of books in there; Mr. Boyd was well read. Most were cheap Signet drugstore paperbacks from the 1940s and 50s, their pages brown and brittle with age. As my compensation for alphabetizing them, Mr. Boyd said I could borrow any that interested me—an offer I greeted with scant enthusiasm, since back then, unless they had pictures in them, my interest in books was just about nil.

I was barely literate; subliterate, you could say. My parents were Italian. My mother's English was poor. My father disapproved of her speaking to my brother or me in Italian, so she never read to us from Italian books (only our grandmother could get away with that). As for my father, a polymath genius and inventor, though he wrote many books—on physics, on etymology, on psychology, on philosophy—he didn't bother to read to us or encourage our reading; he *was* egocentric. As for the books in our house, except for my mother's *gialli* (Italian pulp magazines), they were mostly our father's books, and mostly in French or German, his favorite languages.

Am I blaming my subliteracy on my parents? I don't mean to. My brother grew up in the same house, and he was well read. The only books I read were *MAD* paperbacks, and mostly to study the cartoons. The point is that until that summer, books—at least those in English—hadn't been a big part of my life. I never cared much about them.

Rearranging those books in Mr. Boyd's basement library changed everything. As the books fell apart in my hands, I wondered what was inside them. That they were in such awful shape only made them that much more intriguing to me. They were like the bones, pottery shards, and other relics at an archeological dig. The voices of all those decomposing books and the authors who wrote them seemed to call to me, begging for one last pair of eyes to read them before they turned into dust. If I didn't read them, who would? Not Mr. Boyd, who hadn't touched them in years, and who kept them only for the same reason he kept old cars, newspapers, empty jars, and scraps of Saran Wrap and aluminum foil: because he couldn't stand to throw anything away. Because he was a miser.

And so, while alphabetizing Mr. Boyd's books, I'd dip into the ones whose covers or titles attracted me. I dipped into *The Heart Is a Lonely Hunter* and *Invisible Man* and *The Naked and the Dead*. I read the first sentence. If it was any good, I'd read another, and another. If I got through a whole page without getting bored, I'd put the book down—carefully, like the body of an injured bird—on the fusty tartan blanket that covered Mr. Boyd's cot, alongside other books that held my interest, a sort of triage station of books in an emergency ward. At the end of each day, I'd choose a patient to take home with me and revive.

Though most of Mr. Boyd's books were novels, there were many nonfiction titles too, like *For 2¢ Plain* by Harry Golden, and *Endurance* by Alfred Lansing,[1] and *May This House be Safe from Tigers* by Alexander King. But mainly my interest was drawn to the novels. The first novel I took home with me was *The Man with the Golden Arm* by Nelson Algren. It's about a heroin junkie named Frankie "Machine"

Majcinek, and takes place in Chicago's then slummy South Side. That night I sat up in bed reading the whole thing. It was the first grown-up novel I'd ever read from cover to cover by my own volition. Some sentences I read a few times, not because I didn't understand them, but because I wanted to savor them, to turn them over and let them melt slowly, like butterscotch Lifesavers, on my tongue. I loved how the paragraphs looked, too, packed tightly on those brown, brittle pages that broke free of the book's spine one by one as I turned them. And I loved that smell they gave off, that damp, musty, fusty smell— a smell that I equated with the slums of Chicago, circa 1947, with sagging tenements and blinking neon beer signs and whores with heart-shaped faces. By the time I put *The Man with the Golden Arm* back on Mr. Boyd's shelf (between James Agee's *A Death in the Family* and Saul Bellow's *The Victim*) there wasn't much left of it.

It took me half that summer to rearrange Mr. Boyd's books. For every minute that I spent alphabetizing, I spent ten minutes reading. Mr. Boyd didn't seem to mind. Every so often he'd look in on me. Catching me sitting on the edge of his cot, turning the pages of a book, he'd throw me a smirk, his gristly lower lip creeping up one side of his face like a banana slug drunk on beer.

I read *A Face in the Crowd* by Schulberg, *The Grass Harp* by Capote, *Lilith* by J. R. Salamanca, *Intimacy* by Sartre. *The Big Sky*, *The Maltese Falcon*, *The Postman Always Rings Twice* . . . To read novels was to run far from home, to hop freight trains and shoot heroin and murder someone's husband for their life insurance and fall in love with dark angels. It was assaulting a Japanese-held island during World War II, and stumbling around in a drunken stupor on dim-lit, rain-soaked, garbage-littered streets—all while snuggled safely under the sheets of your bed with the lamp burning and the ceiling fan mumbling in its louvered nest at the top of the stairs, with the curtains blowing and the crickets chirping outside.

One day while sorting Mr. Boyd's books I came upon one with a purple cover showing an old-fashioned engraving of a man in a top hat with a bushy, neat mustache and holding a smoldering fat cigarette or thin cigar—I couldn't tell which. The book was titled *My Secret Life*, and though its author was "Anonymous" I took him to be the nattily dressed man on the cover.

According to the back cover blurb, the book, which was a good two inches thick, contained "the anonymous confessions of a wealthy Victorian who lived for sex alone." What's more it was "complete and unexpurgated," a phrase that gained quick entry into the rapidly growing pantheon of titillating words and phrases that had accrued in my vocabulary lately. For reasons having little to do with literature, this book, which I took home that night (furtively, this time, under my windbreaker), became a favorite of mine. As soon as I got it home I set about hiding it—first in a dresser drawer under a pile of moth-balled sweaters, and then, knowing my mom would eventually find it there—behind a trunk in the attic.

For two or three weeks, whenever the opportunity presented itself, I'd take *My Secret Life* out and carry it deep into the woods behind our house, up to Eagle's Cave—a deep crevice formed by the gla-cial tumble of rocks during the Ice Age. The cave's entrance was just barely large enough for a thirteen-year-old body to squeeze into, yet too small to detect unless you knew exactly where to look. From the beer and soda bottles and campfire ashes on the floor, and the graffiti on the walls and ceiling, it was obvious that other boys knew about it. Yet, the odds of anyone coming around while I was in there were very small.

I brought a flashlight, matches, and birthday candles with me, and lit them one by one to see the pages as I tunneled my way through *My Secret Life*, digging for the smutty parts like a Perigord pig digging for truffels. It turned out that there were quite a few, the book being a kind of Sears & Roebuck catalogue of every conceivable—and, to this thirteen-year-old, *inconceivable*—act of sex, but without pictures.

For two weeks, by candlelight in that clammy crevice, I read all 2,000-plus pages of *My Secret Life*, dog-earing for future reference those passages that I found particularly edifying. One passage earned so much attention from me that it finally broke free of the spine, sur-rendering itself into my hot, greedy hands.[2]

Fearing that he might note its absence, I eventually replaced *My Secret Life* on Mr. Boyd's shelf, keeping only that one special page, a carnal talisman. I folded and tucked it between the pages of one of my *MAD* magazines, between its movie satires and Don Martin cartoons. Seized by a sudden hunger for Victorian prose, I'd sneak off and read the passage again—and again, and again—until finally the sweat from my fingers ate clear through the page. It hardly mattered, since by then I had memorized every word.

And even if I hadn't, it wouldn't have mattered, since by then the smell of an old book, of any old book, would have been sufficient to inflame my imagination. That musty, mushroomy smell, the smell of words rotting on paper, had become linked in my mind with my sexual fantasies, which in turn became linked with the splendors of the written word and of the books that contained those words.

Summer came to an end, and with it my working for Mr. Boyd. September brought school and other new pursuits, including an enhanced interest in the opposite sex. As suddenly as I'd started reading books, except for school assignments I stopped reading them and went back to being a subliterate boy, only now I was a *horny* subliterate boy. Compelled by one of my schoolteachers to read a book, I would do so, but with no special interest, and even sometimes with the nausea attendant to oppression.

What had happened? Had I regressed, or was there some other explanation? Perhaps I'd been spoiled. After all, what happened to me that summer would never happen again. That first rush of voluntary reading had been like losing my literary cherry, something you can do only once and on your own, with no one supervising or protecting you. It had been my own private, personal doing, not that of a schoolteacher. It had been my secret. And everyone knows secret love affairs are always the best. As I kept sorting books at the Mercantile Library, smelling their smutty, nutty mustiness, it occurred to me that it had not been the smuttiness alone of *My Secret Life* that had turned me on to literature. Nor was it anything forbidden about the books that I read that summer. It wasn't even their perfume that excited me so. It was the simple fact of spending time alone with all those complete strangers through their words, in worlds that they had created for me alone, or so it had seemed.

The sublime interlocking of reader and writer—as intimate in its way as any sexual coupling: *that's* what had aroused me. Those cheap, crumbling old paperbacks, I'd loved them in every sense of that word, the kind of devotional love that a pubescent child feels toward the older, more experienced man or woman who initiates him into the wider ways of the world.

Those crumbling old books, they had been my secret lovers. That I discovered them while discovering my sexuality made for a heady summer, one that comes back to me whenever I breathe in the fusty, smutty air of old books.

NOTES

1. Who happened to be the editor of the Bethel Home News. He lived in a shack next to a brook, drove an orange BMW, and never—as far as I know—wrote another book.

2. I recall only that it concerned two "gay" German women and a drunken sailor, and that the scene ended with one of the ladies crying, "*Nicht gut! Nicht gut!*"

My Locomotive God

O n Sunday mornings when I was a kid, when most fathers took their kids to church, mine took me to explore the beds of abandoned railroads. We'd start out very early in the morning, with the town's half-dozen church bells still tolling, filling the New England sky with sounds of holiness and grace. My papa wore his crumpled Mr. Magoo cap and thrift-store sneakers. He brought his compass and a rolled geological survey map, with tiny black squares standing for houses, and a red pen with which, across the map's filigreed surface, he would trace the routes of the old Shepaugh and Housatonic Valley railway lines.

I, too, equipped myself. I wore my red PF Flyers and a matching red windbreaker, and carried the perpetual hope that, this time, at last, we'd encounter the remains of a rusty locomotive, complete with boxy headlight, brass cylinders, triangular smokestack, and cowcatcher, just like the one on *Petticoat Junction*.

Our explorations took us to quaint towns with names like Washington Depot, Old Hawleyville, and Sandy Hook. We'd hike through scruffy old apple orchards and industrial parks and the backyards of people who lived in those tiny black squares. Their dogs would bark viciously at us, and sometimes the people themselves would come out to yell at us. My papa, a lifelong socialist, had no respect for the concept of private property.

Suddenly the trail would grow cold, and we'd pick it up again a half-mile away, on the far side of a river, or in the woods skirting some farmer's field. We came across many interesting sights: the ruins of trestles, Civil War foundries, and smelting ovens, even a few forgotten tunnels.

I enjoyed our abandoned railroad explorations. Still, after hours of hiking, my legs would turn to rubber, and I'd want to go home. To spur me on, my father would summon a rusty locomotive, the one that was always right there, waiting for us around the very next bend, but which somehow, despite my father's repeated promises, never seemed to materialize.

As the sun went down we'd head back to my father's Studebaker, me crying the whole way, saying, "But you *promised!*" To which my father would proclaim with a smile, "My promises are worth nothing!"

That rusty locomotive was like God: ever present but never visible or attainable, a matter of faith.

My father was an atheist, as far as I know the only atheist in Bethel, Connecticut, the town where I grew up. He was also, aside from my mother, the only Italian immigrant—though he spoke better English than Walter Cronkite—the only full-time inventor, and the only certified genius. He aced the Mensa test with a top score in half the allotted time. One time he took my brother and me to a Mensa gathering, one of their picnics. It was like going to the genius zoo. At some point an argument broke out between a physicist and a philosopher. The subject of debate: whether or not a can of baked beans put unopened on the barbecue grill would explode. As my brother and I looked on from an instinctively safe remove the two brains went at it, talking of molecules and vacuums and critical excitation, gesturing boldly to illustrate their opposing theories. Suddenly there was an enormous explosion. Afterward we watched as the two geniuses, along with a handful of bystanders, picked scalding beans out of their clothes, hair, and eyes.

"Idiots," said my father.

My father was a proud, passionate, unapologetic atheist. To call him an agnostic would insult him. To witness the depths of his distaste for religion you had only to switch on the TV to one of those afternoon evangelists, then stand back and await his thunderous oaths, his *viles* and his *loathsomes*. The words "Jesus" or "Christ" stretched to more than one syllable by men in pale suits with thick wavy hair and capped teeth would deliver him to apoplexy's door. Televangelists were to my father what a scarlet cape is to a bull. His face would turn red, his cheeks would puff out like the jibs of a clipper ship, his lower lip would start to quiver and sparkle. As quickly as possible we would change the channel.

In our house, crammed with books on every subject, there was never a Bible to be found. There were books on science and art and psychology; there were novels and plays, dictionaries, encyclopedias, books about cars and planes and ships (and locomotives), books in English, in German, French, Spanish, Italian—all languages my father spoke fluently. But no Bible. My father, who spent so much of his time reading and writing books, had no use for that particular one. When I once pointed out its absence, he made a face like he smelled something sour and waved the notion away. "Ach," he said. I might as well have suggested that he take out a subscription to *Swank*. On second thought, he'd have gone along with that.

Papa hated almost everything to do with religion. I say almost since he had a soft spot for stained glass windows. Every now and then he and I would drop into a church together, on weekdays usually, when few people were inside, strictly to admire the stained-glass windows. We'd stand side by side in the cathedral's sepulchral hush, looking up at the tutti-frutti displays, oblivious of their symbolic content, of the stations of the cross and the angel of the annunciation. If my father saw those things he never mentioned them to me. To me he spoke only of bandwidths of spectral color, of the prism's ability to parse light, of the eyes' cones and receptors. The Color Coder, the most enduring and versatile of my father's inventions, was used by industries to measure and compare colors for quality control purposes, to make sure that one batch of peanut butter was the same exact color as the next, and so on. In the Building, the laboratory where Papa did his inventing, I'd dig through his boxes of test samples, plastic chips of every hue, each like a sweet spoonful of eye-pudding. They were the colors of the world, of my life, of joy and happiness. The stained glass windows were like transparent versions of those samples, trapping the light from outdoors, investing it with magical colors. As we stood holding hands inside the churches, my father didn't have to preach the gospel to me; it preached itself straight into my heart through those windows.

Once, as we were leaving a church after one of our visits, my father shook his head, sighed, and muttered, "Such a shame, all that beauty wasted on such crap."

The Building—my father's laboratory—sat at the bottom of the hill where we lived: a shack of peeling yellow stucco and steadily rotting wood. My mother referred to it as "the Building" as though it were the only standing structure in the world, let alone in Bethel, Connecticut. I couldn't wait to visit my father there, in his crumbling sanctuary, the cathedral where I'd come to worship him.

After school, when the bus dropped me off, I'd hurl myself up our long, unpaved driveway, under the swaying branches of the six large willow trees lining it, to the Building's front door, on which I'd knock tentatively. I don't know why I felt so shy about visiting my father, since he always welcomed me with a smile, saying in the mid-Atlantic accent he acquired some time between abandoning Italy for England as a teenager and coming to America as a young man. "Ah, Peter, my boy! How good of you to visit!" Maybe it was my sense of reverence that made me feel shy, that told me that I was entering hallowed ground, a place of secrets shrouded in the eerie green light of my father's oscilloscope, buried under the sounds of static from his radio that played nothing else, aswirl with eddies of dust. The Building was my church, perfumed with the frankincense of solder flux and smoke, and the myrrh of scorched metal, aromas that joined and clashed with the smells of my father's generous farts, and the smell of orange rinds exuded by his wastebaskets.

Cautiously, since the wooden floors were rotted ("Careful, my boy; this is a holy shrine!"), I'd proceed toward him at whatever task occupied him, my PF Flyers sending up puffs of ruddy dust where they'd form new holes in the rotting floor. I'd find him at his typewriter (already an antique in 1966, and on which he wrote a dozen never-published books) or at the drafting table or behind the band saw or the drill press. Or he'd be stooped over the oscilloscope, soldering gun in hand, his features awash in that green light, so he looked reptilian. Or, if I was lucky, I'd find him behind the lathe. I'd watch the metal-stained fingers of his left hand curve over the smooth spinning chuck, while his other hand manipulated an array of chromium dials and le-

vers, guiding the bit that sliced into spinning metal like the prow of a
ship through heavy seas. I'd watch as the bit spewed bright, steaming
turnings[1] of aluminum, copper, and brass. Afterward I'd sweep the
turnings into a dustpan, and pocket the longest and brightest for a
collection that I kept in an ornamental wooden box behind my bed.

Dressed in his ratty cardigan and stained khaki shorts, wearing his
Magoo cap indoors, Papa showed me his latest inventions: a machine
he built for Levi Strauss for measuring irregularities in bolts of denim,
another for sorting shoe soles by thickness, a third for matching the
colors of real and false teeth, a fourth for determining the fat content
in batches of ground beef, a fifth for checking the ripeness of fruits
without cutting into their skins or bruising them.

The Building had no septic system. At dusk, on the way up the
steep driveway to the house, we'd stop to empty our bladders, standing side by side as when admiring the stained glass of churches, my
father's stream arching, twisting, steaming, glittering far above and
beyond mine, resembling the brass turnings from his lathe. If I missed
having God in my life, I didn't feel it back then. At age six or seven
my papa was all the God I needed.

As I grew older certain questions began to nag me to which my father's atheism offered no answers. Why had I been born? Why the
earth? Why the sun? Why life? And, more vexingly, why death (our
dog, Pal, had just died)? What, assuming it had one, was life's purpose? Not only did my father lack answers to these questions, he
scoffed at my asking them. Or he'd take a deep breath and say, "The
purpose of life, Peter boy, (deep breath) is to breathe. The rest is icing
on the cake." Such answers failed to satisfy me.

Other cracks were beaten into my skepticism by people like Bobby
Muller. Bobby Muller: the perfect name for a Catholic school bully.
He shared the bus stop with my brother and me. He was twelve years
old, two years older than us, and a better fighter, which isn't saying
much. Somehow Bobby Muller had gotten wind that we were atheists.
That he had to share a bus stop with twin heathens outraged him. He
conducted his own personal Spanish inquisition there at the corner
bus stop, squaring up to us with his pug-nosed, acne-ridden face and
asking with a sneer, "Do you believe in God?" Having been taught
to tell the truth, George and I would answer, "No." And Bobby

Muller would punch us. Sometimes he'd punch me, and sometimes he punched George. Odds are he couldn't tell the difference, since we were twins. For some reason he never punched us both on the same day.[2]

While one of us was being punched by Bobby Muller, the other stood by and watched. What choice did he have? Not only did we not know how to defend ourselves; we were guilty as charged, guilty of not believing in God. Even at age ten, already I harbored the sense that my disbelief was, if not abhorrent, aberrant, at odds with the world and just about everyone living in it. We were the only atheists I knew, the only ones who didn't go to church or take communion or go to confession, who weren't even sure what those words meant. We'd never tasted the host or drunk the blood of Christ or clasped hands in prayer or said a Hail Mary or Our Father or even a Now I Lay Me Down to Sleep. At our mother's insistence, we'd been baptized and named after saints. But after that: nothing. Under the strict influence of our father's secularism, my mother let her Catholicism lapse. Following our baptism, excepting the occasional funeral or wedding, and to admire the colors of the stained glass windows, no Selgin ever set foot inside a church again.

And so I couldn't even turn to my mother for an exemption from hell, where I began to assume I was headed. It seemed to me, even as I suffered his blows, that Bobby Muller should not be blamed for my father's transgressions, or mine, that after all Bobby was only serving a higher authority, doing God's work, trying in his crudely violent way to shepherd a few of His lost sheep.

But Bobby Muller's crude methods backfired. The more severely he punished me, the more fervently I clung to my skepticism. If I believed in *any* god, it was one who looked exactly like Bobby Muller, down to the pimples on his face and the green plaid neckties he wore with his white oxford Catholic school shirts. God had acne and red hair and I detested him.

There were others besides Bobby Muller doing God's work, or trying to. Like the Rowlands, the parents of my best friend Chris, who, though no great believer himself, set the standard for me of how decent Christian WASPs should behave (as opposed to Italian heathens). When I'd eat dinner at the Rowlands, at their dining room table set with ringed napkins, lace doilies, and hand-dipped candles, I would invariably dig into my food and start chewing as they bowed their heads in prayer. As discreetly as possible I'd swallow my mouthful, lower my fork, bow my head, and murmur a meaningless string of words, certain that otherwise Mr. and Mrs. Rowland would mistake me for the antichrist himself. Except for an occasional "Pass the butter, dear," the rest of the meal would proceed in complete pious silence, giving me yet another reason to suspect that all of us Selgins were devils, since at our pagan kitchen table, conversation with meals was not only routine and extremely loud, it was aggressive and even violent, with everyone shouting at once, and not just shouting, but calling each other names, joking, laughing, cursing, arguing, accusing, ridiculing. The words "Pass the butter, please" were among the few that never crossed our dinner table (we weren't that polite, and we didn't eat butter).

The contrast between our two households, the Rowlands and the Selgins, couldn't have been more severe. For me it exemplified the difference between people who believed in and feared God and those who didn't, which is to say *decent* and *indecent* people, with the negative judgment falling squarely on the nonbelievers, since there could be little doubt as to which group had better manners.

One evening my parents invited the Rowlands for dinner. It was the first time they'd come over, and would be the last. At some point during dessert, as my mother dished out her famous *zabalione* from a great yellow bowl, my father told one of his famously bad, off-color jokes—nothing too bawdy; he'd managed to restrain himself that far. Still, it was a bad joke, a very bad joke, designed to make us groan, and neither my brother nor I could contain our disapproval. In unison we both burst out with a loud "Pig!"

This was in 1970. Mr. Rowland was a starched, staunch, pipe-smoking Eisenhower Republican; Mrs. Rowland was a dyed-in-the-wool, Taylor cream sherry-nipping New England Puritan. Aside from the Bible and a complete edition of Fennimore Cooper's *The Leatherstocking Tales* illustrated by N. C. Wyeth, the only items of literature in the Rowland house were L.L.Bean catalogues and back issues of *Yankee* and *National Geographic*. Needless to say, the Rowlands were scandalized. Afterward, in the kitchen, like a team of missionaries they took my mother aside and said, "Oh, Mrs. Selgin, *how* can you let your children speak that way—to their *own father?*" My mother had to explain to them that in our family "pig" was a term of endearment, that each of us had his or her animal moniker: "toucan" (my mother's, for her long Roman nose), "fish" (George, since he loved to swim), and "tarsier" (me, because I have big eyes). This explanation cut no mustard with the Rowlands, who, needless to say, never came over again and who thenceforth restricted their son's visits as well—convinced, no doubt, that otherwise we'd deliver him straight to the devil.

Which was where I myself was headed, so I'd come to believe. After all, I knew right from wrong. I didn't kick dogs or pull canes out from under old ladies. But still I couldn't trust my morality. It felt wobbly, brittle, a house built on stilts. One day it would collapse and I'd be a child molester, or a serial killer, or just a plain old run-of-the-mill bad person. How could it be otherwise? We were *atheists*. My friends and their families all went to church. At a bare minimum they attended Easter services and paid lip service to Ash Wednesday and Good Friday—which, to us, was no better than any other Friday. When Christmas came around, we put up a tree and decorated it with tinsel and colored lights, yet for me there was the nagging suspicion that our Christmas tree never looked quite *right*, that something about it would give it—and us—away. Who were we trying to kid, anyway? We didn't believe in Christ any more than we believed in Santa Claus. We were godless heathens and everyone knew it. Atheist creeps. We didn't *deserve* a Christmas tree. We didn't deserve Santa or his gifts. We had no right to them. A pile of twigs, that should have been our tree. A bunch of bleached bones, a pile of pagan stones.

Despite my doubts, discomforts, and fears, I never once considered turning to God. It seemed to me that, as disingenuous as our Christmas tree was, my turning to religion would have been even phonier. The simple truth was I didn't believe. I *couldn't* believe. It wasn't a matter of choice. You either believed or you didn't. I didn't. As for making myself believe, if you had to force yourself you'd already failed.

What was "belief," anyway? What did it mean to "believe" in something, as opposed to simply knowing it for a fact? The question irked me. I began to suspect that my skepticism extended far beyond God or religion, that I didn't believe in *anything*, and never would, that I was fundamentally incapable of belief.

In his famous essay, *The Necessity of Atheism*, which I first read in high school, eighteen-year-old Shelley makes the point concisely. I thought then and still do now that belief and disbelief are not acts of volition, but passive fruits of faith or skepticism, therefore not subject to regulation by the mind. We don't choose our beliefs; they choose us. To attach any degree of criminality or morality to either is a mistake. Bobby Muller hadn't read his Shelley, apparently.

To find out just how incapable I was of believing in anything, I performed a little experiment on myself. I asked myself whether I believed in certain things for which the factual evidence was either unavailable or not close at hand. For instance: *Do you believe the earth is round?* (Of course the evidence existed, but it wasn't at hand.) The answer, to my relief, was "yes." Then I asked myself: *Do you believe in miracles?* To this I had to give more thought, since I'd never experienced a miracle, as far as I knew, and wasn't sure I'd recognize one if I did. But then I concluded that the *reason* I wouldn't recognize a miracle was because I'd never live to see one; therefore, what was the point in believing in them? The answer, then, had to be "no." Third question: *Do you believe in your own future?* Now I was starting to get anxious, since I knew this third answer would be the capper. If I said no to this, there could be little room to doubt that I was incapable of believing in anything. And so I thought very hard about it. While thinking, the image of a clear blue, cloudless sky entered and filled my mind: an endless, pristine expanse without horizon or foreground, void of sun or moon or even a single navigational star. If I believed in a future, any future, then this was it, this nothing: a transparent blue wall. I shook my head, no.

There was my answer.

I was fifteen years old at the time. So began what I call my agnostic phase: since if, as I'd concluded, I was incapable of believing in anything, that had to mean that I was incapable of believing in *not believing* in God. That being so, it made more sense for me to consider myself agnostic, a word I looked up in the dictionary and which, according to *Webster's Collegiate*, means "one who holds the view that any ultimate reality (as God) is unknown and probably unknowable." Which struck me as perfect, and a much better designation than *atheist*, which the same dictionary defines as "one who denies the existence of God"—a less passive stance and one ill fitting someone like me, who, back then especially, felt too uncertain and powerless to act on any set of beliefs, let alone go around denying other people's. No, I told myself. I am NOT an atheist. But the truth is I didn't—couldn't—believe that either.

Even death, the most certain of certainties, didn't get in under the radar of my unholy skepticism. One day at the height of my Doubting Thomas period I was taking a shortcut, cutting through a cemetery in town, when I discovered, with a mixture of horror and amusement, that some of the gravestones weren't of granite or marble, but cast in aluminum and given a warm patina to resemble stone. They were *hollow*. I went from tombstone to tombstone, testing with bare knuckles, listening for the telltale echo. At least two-thirds of the headstones I tested were fake, as bogus as a Selgin Christmas tree. Even death, the one thing that seemed sure and solid, that could be counted on, had a hollow ring to it. *My promises are worth nothing.*

What saved me from drowning in skepticism? My belief in the mystical power of Art. A contradiction in terms, since (again, according to Webster) to be mystical a thing must have a spiritual meaning or reality that's not apparent to the senses or obvious to the intellect. The works of art that I admired most violated both of these rules. Yet I couldn't imagine anything more spiritual than a painting by van Gogh, or Stravinsky's *Firebird*, or a good Beatles song. At sixteen I had no idea what I wanted to do or be, but I knew I'd be an artist, I knew I'd make things that would touch people's emotions, that would fill them with something like wonder. The unconscious hope behind this conviction was that in doing so I might fill my own skeptical soul with meaning, and save myself from falling into that deep blue nothingness, the nihilist's hell that I once saw as my only possible future.

Thirty years later, I still worship at the secular altar of art. I write and I paint, and most if not all my friends are artists. As I write these words, a painting-in-progress of New York Harbor sits on my easel, a fanciful harbor with a duo of red-funneled liners jockeying for position among tugboats and skyscrapers. The style I paint in is either faux naive or neoexpressionist, with bright colors peeking out through more somber tones, the paint scumbled and encrusted, the shapes outlined in thick black strokes like the bars of lead in the stained glass windows my father admired.

How nice it would be to believe in a personal God, some ultimate benevolent force looking over things, making sure everything has its purpose, however terrible. How nice to question things a little bit less, to feel that warm glow that I imagine most believers must feel, and not only to feel it, but to emanate it, to shed its beautiful bright colors, whereas we atheists radiate no such colorful brightness. Gloom tends to be more like it. If atheists had churches, the windows would be stained black.

But then sooner or later each of us finds our own god. Whether it's the god of the Bible or of the Koran, the god of love or lust, the god of science or art or nature, the god of fame, fortune, friends, family, fear—or a combination of these. William James said that "even disbelief is a form of belief." I believe him. To live well is to believe. Every day, when I write or paint or go for a walk, I practice my faith: I'm humbled; I worship. I think my father felt this way about his work, making his inventions down in his laboratory. Passing by on my way up the driveway, through his window I'd see Papa there, at his typewriter or his drafting table or soldering a circuit, lost in thought, a dreamy smile on his face, locked in a bliss of concentration like a monk deep into his prayers.

My father has since passed away. Sadly, many of his inventions failed to pay off,[3] at least not to his satisfaction. To watch him grow old was no pleasant thing. That gentle smile I knew as a child wore thin in his seventies, and by the time he turned eighty no longer hid the sadness of a certified genius who, when all was said and done, considered himself a failure. He still smiled, but his smile no longer hid those feelings. As piece by piece a series of strokes took him from us, my mother did her best to keep him at home until she was forced to put him in a nursing home. If she chose one named for Pope John Paul II, we couldn't blame her. It was the best place she could find for him. We asked the management to kindly take the Pope's portrait down from his room. There's such a thing as too much irony.

At the memorial service there was no preacher. It was a humble ceremony. Before a small table arranged with mementos of his life each of us rose and said a few words. I said that, although he was an atheist, my father was one of the most Christian men I'd known—who couldn't hold a grudge, who loved the lowly serpent, who never raised a hand in anger, who, unlike many self-described Christians, actually did turn the other cheek. Kierkegaard said, "A Christian is nevertheless something even more rare than a genius." In his own way my father was both.

The ceremony over, I gathered the artifacts from the table: my father's typewriter, a Color Coder, one of his last manuscripts, his German dictionary, a brass turning from his lathe, the geological survey map on which, thirty years before, he'd traced in red pen the routes of the old Shephaugh and Housatonic Valley railway lines.

My father, the engineer of that chimerical rusty abandoned locomotive, the one I never got to see, but that rolls through my dreams.

NOTES

1. "Curlicues," I called them.

2. Maybe he reasoned that since we were twins, punching one of us was as good as punching the other.

3. Among them was the first machine that could give change for a dollar bill. But the patent attorney with whom my father partnered was a criminal who underhanded the technology to several firms that replicated it. As other dollar-bill-changing machines started popping up around the country like mushrooms after a spring rain, my father and his crooked partner instigated a patent infringement investigation, which proved too costly, and in the end my father gave up. Thus, the man who invented the first dollar-bill-coin-changing machine never made a nickel from it.

The Man from Stanboul

arning: *some of you may want to skip this essay, which treats the male human body and some of its more intimate parts and functions. Some may feel that what follows falls squarely under the heading of too much information, that it's none of their business, and disgusting to boot, and that I should keep such matters to myself. I beg to differ. I say my body with all its flaws and idiosyncrasies is no less worthy of sharing with you than my soul, and furthermore that the two are connected, so you can't have one without the other. If you insist on believing otherwise, by all means pass over this essay, which begins with the following limerick*:

> There once was a man from Stanboul
> Who soliloquized thus to his tool:
> First you robbed me of wealth
> then you took all my health,
> And now you won't pee, you old fool!

I am the man from Stanboul. Yes, I *cannot pee.* Oh, I can squeeze out a few drops now and then. I can dribble; I can even trickle. Occasionally what passes for a stream drizzles down into the commode. But it is no McDonald's golden arch, let me tell you, not the resplendent yellow rainbow of release I once knew so well, the Victoria Falls of my not-so-distant youth.

Yes, dear reader, I am going to tell you about my body: a marvelous machine, but as capricious as a degenerate Roman emperor and susceptible to malfunction. It grows in places where it shouldn't. Too fecund and inventive for its own good, given time it will sprout enough baubles and bangles of errant tissue to trim a modest Christmas tree.

It is just a little after 2 A.M. In exactly nine hours, at 11 A.M., I will enter the outpatient surgical unit of Montefiore Medical Center here in the Bronx and put a very personal part of myself at the mercy of a beam of concentrated light so powerful it can vaporize flesh.

I'm talking about my prostate, an organ (more precisely a gland) characterized by regimentally indoctrinated physicians as "walnut-sized," though anyone in my shoes will tell you that its size can vary greatly, from walnut to apple to grapefruit, progressing always from small to large. For though men are known to shrink with age, their prostates never do. The gland's purpose: to secrete that milky fluid known as semen, which mixes with sperm from the testicles to form the gooey syrup that initiates life.

The word *prostate* comes from the Greek, meaning "to put before." What my prostate has been put before I don't know, but I can say what it's wrapped *around*, namely my bladder. If there's an argument to end all arguments over intelligent design, this is it: no intelligent God would have been so dumb as to locate this most growth-oriented organ around man's pee hose. Yet that is just what my dunce of a Creator has done. He has pitched this expanding semen factory where I piss, has strangled my urethra with it, has grabbed it like a straw between two fingers and pinched.

The resulting disease is called "benign prostatic hyperplasia," or "BPH." Here the word *benign* means "not a threat to life or long-term health, especially by being non-cancerous," as opposed to "having a kind and gentle disposition." Believe me, there is nothing kind about a swollen prostate. Nor is there anything gentle about being roused ten times a night and forced to drag your groggy bones to the toilet, only to stand there, inert as a statue over a fountain, yet unable to do what fountains do so well. You turn the spigot on the sink, spread your legs like Ty Cobb, close your eyes, and contemplate the fabulous waterworks at Tivoli Gardens, the Great Cascade at Peterhof, the spouting dolphins and spewing gargoyles of the Villa Lante. You stand on a rug to make sure the bottoms of your feet aren't cold, having heard somewhere that cold feet inhibit the bladder. You harbor misty memories of once having peed like King Kong, like Gulliver, like Zeus. Nevermind campfires: your hose could have extinguished the great fires of Chicago and San Francisco. You recall how, as a boy of five or six or seven, you signed your name in snowbanks, the cursive melting and steaming with the heat of your body's golden ink, a fleeting testimonial to the Palmer method. In service station restrooms across America, along highways, behind great oak trees, you let your kidney juice fly. In high school, while waiting in the wings during a performance of *Camelot*, seconds prior to the scene where you, Lancelot, sang "If Ever I Would Leave You" to Guinevere, you poured yourself into a red fire bucket squirming with gum wads and cigarette butts. You think of your dead father, the first man you ever saw take a leak outdoors, of how you and he would stand side by side at the driveway's edge at twilight pulling out father and son dicks: his tawny and uncircumcised; yours minus its protective sheath (thanks, Dr. Spock) and pale and small as the bud of a white English rose. Together you'd aim into the Queen Anne's lace and milkweed. Watching his glittering parabola steaming as golden as the brass turnings that flew from his lathe, you'd say to yourself, *When I can pee that far, then I'll be a man!*

These fond memories do you no good as you stand there blocked as a pipe full of concrete. Should mercy shine upon you, you might acquit yourself of a thimbleful of piss, just enough to wet the rim of the commode and dribble down your leg. You give it another five minutes, your thoughts by now gone abstract: the geometry of bathroom tiles, the fractal algorithms of the water stains on the shower curtain (an action painting worthy of Pollock), the brown tongue of rust under the sink faucet. Urinous puns assail you: *To pee or not to pee. Let it pee. Piss on earth. Pee of good cheer.* Jokes, too. *Patient: I can't pee anymore. Doctor: How old are you? Patient: Seventy-six. Doctor: You've peed enough.* None of this is helpful. You feel, furthermore, that you are being watched, that this is a scene in a supposedly funny movie—one by Neil Simon at the top of his game—of which you are the hapless lead. For your own sake, you crack a little smile in the medicine chest mirror. But your smile isn't convincing and you forfeit your Academy Award.

In despair you take a warm shower, to rinse the urine from your leg and also because the warm water coursing down your shoulders and back helps relax the muscles of your bladder neck, loosening its contractions. Though this often works, it has always been a last resort, in part because you really don't feel like getting wet in the middle of the night, and also because you know how displeased your wife would be if she knew that you peed in the shower, which is *her* bathtub. Yet into the shower you go, and piss you do—not much; but then, it's hard to say, with the water running off you. What spouts from the tip of your dick may be from inside you, or it may be courtesy of the New York City public drinking water supply system: these days the difference may not be of an order of magnitude. Still, just the semblance of fluid draining from your dick is grounds for at least some gratitude.

This comic opera has been performed nightly, sometimes ten times a night—or about once every thirty minutes—with the first overture waking me always at 2 A.M. There is no point trying to sleep between performances. It only makes it that much harder to drag myself to the commode when the time comes. But drag myself I do, as I have this morning (it is now 2:48), since anything beats lying there listening to my bladder crying *Empty me! Empty me!*—like David Hedison in *The Fly.*

My first urologist, whom I'll call Dr. L., wasn't a bad doctor. In fact, I suspect him of being a decent man, though one with little enthusiasm for his work. And who can blame him? What are a urologist's dreams made of? Does the faint tang of urine ever leave their nostrils? What draws them to their work? Was the high point of their youths a day at Splash Mountain or Water Mania?

Dr. L.'s office was on Manhattan's Upper East Side. The waiting room was painted (appropriately) yellow, and crowded with people all of whom wore the troubled expression of the incontinent. If you listened carefully I swear you could hear bladders filling. I was given a form to fill out, asking about my "voiding history"—a phrase that struck me as pertaining more to certain presidential administrations than to my nocturnia. On a scale of one to ten I was to score stress, urge, overflow, waking, dribbling, volume, and frequency. I filled in the answers quickly, with the same sense of resignation and doom as when I took the SAT.

Eventually I got to see the doctor, a bland-looking man with a white smock and whose taste in neckties was questionable. I put out my hand for him to shake, but he was already leading me to his office. I may as well confess here my prejudice against doctors who don't shake your hand. I don't care if they've been shoving their fingers up people's bums all day. The right of refusal should be mine.

We chatted, with him taking notes. I admired his Mont Blanc fountain pen while continuing to disapprove of his neckwear. Having distilled my symptoms into a few sentences onto a sheet of yellow lined paper, the doctor took me into another, far less sumptuous room.

He had me drop my pants and bend over with my back to him, my head thrust forward, my elbows upon a padded gurney. *Now* came the handshake, urologist style.

"Well," said Dr. L., feeling around in there, "your prostate *is* a bit bulky."

Bulky? What did that mean? Did it mean big and awkward, like Dan Blocker? Or broad and muscular, like Charles Bronson?

The doctor asked how old I was, and I told him: forty-eight. (I've since turned forty-nine.) "Hmm," he said. "Young for BPH."

What was he implying? That I'd abused my prostate through too much sex? Or perhaps the opposite: I hadn't given it enough sex, depriving it of its intended function, like a hunting dog kept on a chain in the backyard.

Dr. L. snapped off his rubber gloves. "I'd like you to do a flow test for me," he said, and introduced me to his assistant, Marta, a dark-skinned woman no older than twenty-five, attractive, but with a beset-upon quality and a pugnacious, fed-up look on her face. She led me to another room. "I need you to pee in there," she said, pointing to a rickety folding lawn chair, circa 1967. The plastic webbing had been removed, replaced by a large white plastic funnel such as my wife uses to transfer the extra-virgin olive oil she buys by the three-liter drum into smaller, easier-to-handle bottles. From that funnel my own extra-virgin essence was supposed to drain into a device attached by wires to what looked like a seismograph—but was actually a flow meter—ready to chart my effusions on a tongue-like slip of graph paper.

They might as well have asked me to fill the Grand Canyon to brimming. I teetered over the funnel but couldn't work up a single drop. It didn't help that the doctor's assistant stood just outside the door, so close I could hear her popping her bubble gum, asking me continuously if I was "done yet." I pictured her tapping her professional white nursing sneakers on cold linoleum. *If I can piss just one drop,* I said to myself, *just one miserable little drop to get me started, then, by God, I'll unleash a flood, I'll piss a fucking tsunami!* I tried all my usual tricks: running the water, humming softly to myself, imagining Japanese lily gardens and rain forests heavy with dripping vegetation. Below me the seismograph gurgled and whirred to no avail, like a hungry stomach wanting to be fed.

Fifteen minutes later I finally stepped out of the little room and said to the waiting assistant, "No go." She gave me a look that I imagined she'd given to many a failed lover in bed, that Elizabeth Taylor "I am the earth mother and you are all flops" look. "Guess I must be nervous," I added, which only fueled her contempt.

But there was no time to brood: Dr. L. awaited me in yet another room, one that might well have been labeled "Torture Chamber" for its menacing racks of implements. The test is called a "cystoscopy," leading one to think it has something to do with cysts and scoping them out, when in fact it involves passing a fiber-optic viewing device through the penis and into the bladder. Now, I have nothing against having things shoved up my penis *per se*. But when the thing is the size of the Mt. Palomar telescope I find cause to object. Surely an object so large was never meant to intrude upon such a small (and, may I say, delicate) space? Yet, there is the doctor's frowny assistant slathering it with KY Jelly as one might slather a ballpark frank with mustard.

Dressed in an examining gown, I sat naked on the equivalent of a rubber diving board with a U-shaped opening carved out of its forward end, the better to let my private parts dangle free and unencumbered. Until then I had maintained a modicum of what might have passed for dignity. Now all bets were off. Taking my limp member into her hand with less interest than she would have shown a garden slug, the nurse explained, "This'll make you numb." No sooner had she offered this inadequate prediction than, using a hypodermic, she squirted something into my shaft. I felt a brief shiver of icy coldness, then nothing, only the lingering impression that I had just been violated, along with a sympathetic confusion for my poor penis, which must have thought it odd indeed to have something ejaculate into *it*.

But the real fun had yet to begin. Dr. L. snapped on his gloves again, and his assistant wheeled close a metal cart bearing what looked like a plumber's snake. Dr. L. said, "Bend your knees and try to relax." (Apparently I looked anxious.) "I'm going to explain everything I'm doing." Dr. L. was a man of his word, detailing every inch of the assault as he advanced like General Sherman on Atlanta. "I'm introducing the probe into your penis," he announced. Yet I felt only a vague imposition, a rigid coolness rising from deep in my depths: it must have been that numbing jelly. Dr. L. told me to cough. "Again," he said. "Again." With each cough the plumber's snake advanced another inch. "We're getting to the prostate now," he announced with the cool midwestern drawl of an airline pilot pointing out the Rocky Mountains down below. And how about that royal *we*? Was he referring to him and me, or him and his moon-rocket-sized apparatus?

"You may feel a little something right about now."

Quite so, only the little something was a hurt the size of Alaska. Determined to convince Miss Mercy of my manliness, I contrived to suppress a scream, my cheeks awash in involuntary tears. The doctor's assistant remained unmoved. What did it take to impress some people?

With the plumber's snake withdrawn and the examination concluded, Dr. L. said, "Congratulations, you have a ball-median valve."

Hooray, I thought, and waited for my cigar. Meanwhile, the doctor explained that prostate glands have three lobes: two outer (or lateral), and one median, so named because it sits between the other two. When this middle portion of the gland enlarges, it sometimes sends a knob of tissue up the urethra and into the bladder opening, blocking it. The round knob of tissue plugs the opening like a ball stuck in a hole, hence the analogous ball valve.

"You have a few choices," Dr. L. said. "You can try and live with it. Or we can put you on drugs and see if that helps. Or we can do a minimally invasive procedure and get rid of the growth."

Obviously I couldn't live with it, or I wouldn't have come to him. Being a good American, I opted for the pharmaceuticals. If a drug might help me, why would I undergo a procedure, however "minimally" invasive?

Dr. L. filled out two prescriptions, one for Proscar, to slow prostate enlargement, and another for Flomax, to relax the muscles in my bladder neck.

"There is one potential side effect," the doctor said as he scribbled away with his Mont Blanc. "You may experience retrograde ejaculation."

Retrograde. I had heard this word applied to planets in astrology. I knew, for instance, that when Mercury is in retrograde, human communications are known to break down, and even cars, computers, and telephones sometimes malfunction. My breakdown would be of a more personal nature. I would not be able to "come" anymore. Well, I would still "come," technically speaking, but with no substantial result. With my bladder-neck muscles chemically subdued and unable to contract at the proper moment, my semen had a choice: make the long, arduous journey through a thin tube and out the tip of my penis, or take a shortcut into my open, airy, hospitable bladder. Now, what was my semen more likely to do?

My prescriptions tucked into my wallet, I stepped out of the doctor's office and into the light of a sunny day. (Why is it that bad news so often comes on lovely days?) I was feeling sorry for myself. But I had nothing to complain about, really. Except for this one problem, I was, and am, in excellent health. I'd always taken good care of myself and even swam competitively in local meets. In my last race, I'd finished second out of 150 competitors, some of them dedicated athletes in their twenties with bodies out of a Bill Blass underwear ad. They'd sent me home with a trophy, a seductively curved chunk of beveled glass with the words "SECOND PLACE MALE" etched into it, its unintentional mockery not lost on my wife. And I still look young. I have all my espresso-colored curls, yet to turn gray (though a spitefully pigmentless shaft occasionally springs up from an eyebrow). So far I've managed to hold on to my youth, to cling to it, the way a shipwrecked sailor clings to a floating hatch cover in a drowning sea.

Before leaving Dr. L's office that day, I hadn't felt forty, much less forty-eight. Now I felt closer to sixty. At the very least—and on the false assumption that men live to be a hundred on average—I had to consider myself middle-aged. In the history books the Middle Ages are often referred to as the Dark Ages, and now I began to see why. Buried deep within the brightness of this sunny day was a darkness I had only just started to detect, a sense of life as an elevator plunging toward decay and death. My life was more than half over. And with this understanding came an even less welcome one: that the thus far completed half had been the half with all the fun stuff— idealism, vigor, sexual stamina, an agile and flexible mind, a beautiful body free of unwanted growths and obstructions and able to come normally. Only I hadn't known it; I hadn't known how magnificently young I had been. My youth had been like a beautiful city you ignore because you happen to live there. In a few apt words, I'd pissed it away.

And now we come to that delicate portion of my story wherein I must tell you about my orgasms. Yes, I must. I said I once peed like an angel. Well, I used to come like the devil. I've seen enough porno movies to know the difference between a squirt and a spurt, and, trust me, I spurted. Back in those innocent days when hand jobs were about all a young lover could reasonably expect, a girlfriend of mine once remarked (on witnessing this spectacle for the first time), "Wow, it's like a fountain!" And it was: my very own Old Faithful.

Now all that would be lost. Ah, youth. Mine had been spent—and spent and spent! And now the bill had come due. I thought of that chilling scene in Saul Bellow's novel *Mr. Sammler's Planet*, where, as the old professor delivers his lecture at Columbia, a student heckler shouts out from the back row, "Why do you listen to this effete old shit? What has he got to tell you? His balls are dry. He's dead. *He can't come!*"

There I was, Mr. Sammler, walking down Park Avenue in the sunshine of a bright spring afternoon, the tulips ablaze in the esplanades. I noticed something different about the women sharing the sidewalk with me, those good-looking Park Avenue women with their trim business suits and their regal, stiff bearings. I'd always been attracted to them, to the delicate air of competence and perfume they exuded. They reminded me of Madame Glover, my junior high school French teacher, who wore miniskirts and sat on her desk with her panty-hosed legs crossed, rendering me, front row center, the happiest twelve-year-old on earth. Now my eyes were drawn to the Park Avenue women only out of habit, the way one still flicks on a light switch after the power has gone out. Though in the sixteen years of our marriage I've been as monogamous as a barnyard goose, still, I've felt entitled to my fantasies. But for my fantasies to work, there has to be the possibility, however remote, of them really happening. With my sexual arsenal about to be converted to a kid's cap gun, what was the point of even daydreaming? Why slip away down mental dark alleys with theoretical conquests if only to experience my own fleshy mortification there?

That evening I didn't tell my wife anything. I didn't want to upset her. Besides, I had a sneaking suspicion that she wouldn't have been all that upset, which would have upset *me*. I wanted her to care about my growing older and, more specifically, about my endangered ejaculations. But the plain fact, ladies and gentlemen, is that the only people who really give a damn about men's ejaculations are men. And though we are pleased to equate our climaxes with hurricanes, typhoons, geysers, et cetera, they are more like what happens when you slam down a telephone receiver: on your end it sounds like a big deal, but on the other end there's just a *click*. Most women would just as soon have their male lovers shoot blanks.[1] For one thing it's a lot less messy; for another it greatly decreases the risk of unwanted pregnancy. (Long ago my wife and I decided against having children.)

So I said nothing and took my first dose of the drugs, following which I performed a rudimentary test and found, to my relief, that nothing had changed.

Alas, the test was premature. The drugs took a week or so to kick in. Six days later, sure enough, like the planet Mercury, my ejaculations went retrograde. It wasn't, I learned, just a matter of nothing coming out, but a distinct change in the quality of the experience, a loss of what some men describe as "pumping action." One still achieves a "climax", but it's a climax in quotation marks, with an asterisk. It's like a hearty meal eaten with a head cold, or the colors of a flower garden on a cloudy day. The first time it happened, I grew instantly, tearfully nostalgic for my old orgasms, as Charles Foster Kane grew nostalgic for his sled. I felt sad. I felt sorry for myself.

I stopped taking the drugs.

Over the next six months, faced with a Hobbesian choice between orgasms and urinating, I went on and off the drugs several times. Peeing, and the sleep that went with it, usually won out. Then the drugs stopped working. I'd grown immune to their effects. Or, as my next urologist, whom I'll call Dr. K., put it, I had "failed" the drugs (not the drugs had failed me, but *I* had failed *them*).

I'd started seeing Dr. K., hoping there might still be some solution short of a "procedure," and because I still remembered the way Dr. L. hadn't shaken my hand, and that hideous necktie of his, and the fact that he never looked me in the eye. A man who'll shove his finger in your rectum but won't look you in the eye can't be trusted.

Dr. K.'s office was in the Village, in itself a reason to like him. He was a Spaniard, with a Spaniard's graceful manner and reactionary taste in furniture: a gilded rococo desk and matching chairs. His charms notwithstanding, the best that Dr. K. had to offer me was a procedure called "photoselective vaporization of the prostate."

"PVP" uses a laser to "vaporize" unwanted tissue. This was the latest in a bubbling alphabet soup of "minimally invasive" procedures for treating BPH that included TUNA, TUMT, TURP, ILC, and WIT. Of them all, PVP was the latest and least ugly. An outpatient procedure, it took less than an hour and more often than not sent one home catheter free, a tantalizing prospect.

So far Dr. K. had performed all of ten PVPs, less than a month's worth. Considering some of the possible complications (including the dreaded retrograde ejaculations), I was reluctant to let him target my prostate with his phaser. Instead, I brought my business to Dr. R., who was young and eager to rise to the top of his specialty, with a gleam in his eye and the hint of a smile on his lips. All of this I deduced from a photograph on his website. My encounter with the actual person only reinforced this opinion. Not only did Dr. R. shake my hand, he did so eagerly and asked me where I'd bought my shirt. (Now *that's* what I call bedside manner.) In his examining room, when I instantly assumed the position, he threw up his hands and said, "Whoa, what, no foreplay?" I knew then that I'd found the urologist for me.

Dr. R. did some tests, all of which I'd submitted to before, but he administered them with far more humanity. The results left no room for doubt: I needed a procedure.

7:37 A.M. The sun is up, blazing to the east. Through the window the Henry Hudson Bridge, connecting the western Bronx to the northern tip of Manhattan, gleams with the light of a new day. A torrent of traffic flows, streams, rushes, roars over the blue iron rainbow, headed for the city.

Yesterday morning, while looking at myself in the bathroom mirror, I saw something strange. At first I couldn't tell exactly what it was, but it had something to do with my lips. I thought of John Singer Sargent's famous definition of a portrait as a painting that has "something wrong with the mouth." But as I kept staring, I saw something wrong with my eyes, too, and with my jaw, and my nose, and my chin, and my forehead.

Then it hit me: I looked older. It was no longer a young man's face that greeted me in the bathroom mirror each morning. This was a middle-aged man's face—a youngish middle-aged man, true, but definitely middle aged. My face had caught up with my prostate. And yet there was something not altogether unpleasant about this. There was even a sense of relief. For years I'd been holding back age like the Dutch boy with his finger in the dyke (a urological image if ever there was one). I had been working so grimly at staying young, at being the age I felt I *should* be that, paradoxically, I had worn myself to a frazzle. Call it the Dorian Gray effect; only in my case I'd kept the outside young at the expense of the inside—which suddenly, while I wasn't looking, slipped into middle age.

In a few hours Dr. R. will vaporize my errant prostate tissue, and along with it (I hope) whatever remains of my desire to cling to youth. There's something bracing about surgery, even the least invasive sort. Like slugging whisky or smoking a cigarette or digging a ditch, it puts one's priorities in perspective. My priority now is to grow old—gracefully, I hope, but nevertheless to grow old; to trade in my boyish dreams and narcissistic desires for the dreams of a healthy, happy, humble, middle-aged man.

Am I looking forward to this procedure? No. But I don't dread it, either. And I look forward to getting it over with, and trust that it will go well.

But it's not just a part of my prostate that I'll be shedding. It's the *puer aeternus*: my boyish self-image, my unquenchable sexual vanity and desire, all those tired old fantasies, the flotsam and jetsam of my libidinous youth. Good riddance. I am a boy no more. I am a man. The Man from Stanboul.[2]

NOTES

1. When this essay was originally published I received quite a few indignant letters from women readers saying, on the contrary, that they were thoroughly invested in their lovers' ejaculations, that the quality thereof contributed greatly to their own level of sexual gratification. As much as I hate to be wrong, I was heartened to hear it.

2. The procedure succeeded.

P. and I

alfway across the George Washington Bridge, he shouts. The car lights are on, the defroster exhales, wipers thwack ineffectually at the frost he's been too impatient to scrape off the windshield. National Public Radio fills the car with wars, genocides, floods, earthquakes, fires, famines, and terrorist attacks, but that's not why he shouts.

Nor does he shout because, a mile ahead of him on the Interstate, a tractor trailer has jackknifed, and he'll be stuck here for the next forty minutes, and arrive late to the university where, at eight in the morning, he teaches freshmen composition to a classroom full of students who want to be there no more than he.

These are all perfectly sound reasons for shouting, but they are not why he shouts. Nor does the sound that he makes shape itself into any sort of oath. He is not shouting out of rage, anger, fear, grief, pain, frustration, distress, or hysteria. He shouts with joy, with happiness, and what exhales from his mouth to cloud the already cloudy windshield is his term of endearment for his wife.

At six-thirty on a frosty winter morning, stuck in traffic on the upper level of the George Washington Bridge, he is shouting with joy for his wife, who lies snoring in bed with no idea, none, that her husband shouts for her like this almost every morning on his way to work.

1.

With hindsight, I saw it coming. As I watched her roll off in a friend's SUV on that balmy Saturday morning in March (her belongings having preceded her the day before), I felt, under my tears, as if I'd been rehearsing the moment for months. Friends said what they usually say under such circumstances: What happened? You got along so well.

And it's true: we did. So the question is a fair one. Why did our marriage end?

2.

When we met in the early 90s, marriage was the farthest thing from both of our minds. We both belonged to a consortium of actors, directors, and playwrights known as Drama Project, about which we'd joke that it produced more marriages than plays. We shared a double bill of one-act plays at the theater at St. Peter's Church, at the Citicorp Center in Manhattan. Both our plays had gerundic titles. Hers was called "Jazzing," mine "Playin'." The two plays made a perfect pair, and for a long time so did we.

I remember our first date. I invited her on a picnic. A blustery April day. I wanted to share it with someone, preferably of the opposite sex, but not the type I'd been dating since coming off a broken six-month engagement—actresses, mostly, for whom sex had formed the core of our interest in each other. I wasn't looking for sex or flirtation or titillation; I just wanted someone to share a balmy afternoon with. I ran down a mental list of all the women I knew. Her name rose to the top of the list.

Not that P. wasn't attractive; she was pretty, though she seemed not to care about her looks. She wore a raggedy man's bombardier jacket, baggy drawstring pants, and tennis sneakers, clothes with everything to do with comfort and nothing to do with attracting men. Nor had she made any effort to cover the gray in the hair, or to fix her crooked front teeth, the legacy of a Long Island dentist more intent on his golf swing than on gum disease. Of all the women I knew back then, she was the least flirtatious.

We met in Prospect Park, at the botanic garden. We spread out a blanket in the shade of a Caucasian Wingnut tree. I'd brought figs, olives, a chunk of feta cheese, a bottle of wine. She brought a baguette and a salami. As we ate, seeds drifted down from the tree branches over our heads. We discovered our shared love of things Italian, including bitter greens, anchovies, and *gelato nocciola*.

We spent the whole day there in the botanic garden, until a park warden came by and threatened to summon us for public drinking.

3.

We didn't fall in love, exactly. Fall is the wrong verb. It didn't feel like falling. It was more like stepping into a warm bath or a pair of old, fur-lined carpet slippers. There was nothing abrupt or momentous about it, nothing to upset my bachelor's equilibrium. It was as if I'd been driving along a familiar stretch of road when I happened to notice this other road veering off at a gentle angle, one I'd never noticed before, running not quite parallel to the one I'd spent my life on, so I couldn't resist taking it.

Two weeks after out first date, faced with a long Memorial Day weekend, I phoned and asked if she would spend it with me on Block Island. An audacious request, considering we'd had only one date, and except for a perfunctory goodnight peck had yet to so much as kiss each other. She said yes. We rode the train to Montauk and took the ferry through a storm, huddled among seasick passengers.

All weekend it poured. We spent the whole time in the lounge of the Surf Hotel, where we threw ourselves into the task of assembling a giant jigsaw puzzle of a double-decker cheeseburger. By the time we had finished, it was a quarter to midnight and our hunger for the genuine article sent us reeling into the rain. At that hour, except for a pizza parlor, nothing was open. While sitting across from P. in that dreary midnight pizza parlor, watching her bite into a soggy slice with those crooked front teeth, I said to myself, here's someone I could spend the rest of my days with. Or no: what I said exactly was here's a face I wouldn't mind waking up to for the next twenty or so years. That's what I said.

That night P. and I slept together for the very first time. Again there was nothing momentous about it, just a feeling of ease and comfort, as if we'd done it so many times before, as if we'd known each other, in every sense of that phrase, for years. I felt at home in her arms, like I'd come back to them after a long absence. Grateful.

4.

We'd been together for over a year when I proposed by means of a brass novelty ring plopped into her miso soup by an obliging waiter at a Japanese restaurant. She nearly broke one of her crooked teeth, but said yes. By then we'd moved into a brownstone on the Upper West Side, so my proposal was as anti-climactic as everything else in our relationship had been so far.

I had no reason to expect her to say yes. For almost forty years she'd steered clear of marriage. She wanted nothing to do with it. She'd told me so more than once. If there was a reason to get married, it was to have children, and she didn't want children. *There but for the grace of God* summed up her views of motherhood.

In a sense she'd already been a mother, having helped raise a mentally challenged sister. Her parents, sweet people who scraped by selling odd-lot women's undergarments at flea markets, weren't entirely up to the task, so it fell to her to get her sister up and ready for school, to make her lunch, to tend to her other needs while her parents shucked odd-lot bras and girdles. Since her mother didn't drive and her father was prone to making disastrous decisions (like investing sight unseen in Florida real estate), she often had to help them, too. In that sense P. had been her parents' parent. By the time we met, her maternal instincts had been more than satisfied.

5.

I had my own reasons for not wanting to marry, among them the fact that I was my father's son—my father, who married three times. For him three had not been the charm. My parents' marriage was rocky at best, with them fighting all the time, mostly over my father's indiscretions, vicious fights that often ended with our mother breaking something, hurling an ash tray or a shoe into a mirror, or scrawling across the walls with a grease pen, actions so frightening that George and I pleaded with them to get a divorce—not an upbringing to predispose one to holy matrimony. Nor did it help to have seen my twin divorced, bitterly, along with two best friends.

So why did I propose? For the same reason I used to love mowing the grass when I was a kid, *except* when my mother told me to do it. Because it made me feel noble, it made me feel like a good guy, a hero.

As for why P. accepted, maybe she, too, couldn't resist the call to do something she had no need or obligation to do.

6.

Our plan was to elope aboard the *Queen Elizabeth 2*. We'd already sailed on her twice, with me paying our passage by sketching the passengers. I'd befriended some of the ship's officers and crew, including Staff Chief Engineer John Tomlins, who promised to pull some strings to make a marriage at sea possible.[1] A month before our planned elopement, while on a two-week shore leave, Tomlins and his teenaged son were killed in a car crash. So we ended up eloping in our apartment, with two friends as witnesses and an ordained gay Episcopal priest presiding. No hotel rooms for friends and relatives, no engraved invitations, no flower arrangements, no fretting over who to invite, where to hold the reception, whether to serve poached salmon with dill sauce or prime rib *au jus*. A convenient marriage, a no-fuss nuptial. I didn't even bother with a tuxedo, just one of my silk caricaturist's vests under a dark suit. After the ceremony, we repaired to the corner Italian restaurant, had dinner, and went back home to bed.

The next morning I phoned my parents.

"Dat'sa *nice*," my mother said, her thick accent oozing innuendo. My father, on the other hand, was impressed. "Eloped, eh, did you?" He poured on the Oxford don. "What a good idea! Now why didn't I think of that?"

7.

We both felt that our love was not only real, but inevitable—so inevitable it didn't require pomp or circumstance to proclaim or justify or ratify itself. We were soul mates, two compatible natures married in spirit long before we met in person. *That* was the big deal; to have made a bigger deal of it would have suggested a lack of conviction, a questioning of faith.

In a way, P. and I were like George and me. When you grow up a twin you don't need to proclaim your "twindom." It's ineluctable: no ceremony or ritual can make or break it. Like the smell of wood smoke or the shape of a maple leaf, it just *is*.

That's how I felt about P. Nothing had put us together, and nothing would tear us apart.

8.

When I shouted out her name on the George Washington Bridge, P. and I had been married fifteen years. Statistically, that already made ours a strong marriage. By then we'd made three homes together, the last in the Bronx, overlooking the waterway dividing that borough from Manhattan.

On the whole we'd been happy, our married existence filled with good friends, paintings, books, and artistic ambitions. P. had gone to culinary school and started a literary magazine. I painted and wrote and got my graduate degree. Up there in the Bronx we lived luxuriously. Surrounded by trees and water, we kept a pair of field glasses in the living room and used them to monitor the activities of egrets and herons patrolling the far shore. From where we lived we'd walk to Wave Hill, a public garden established on the merged grounds of two Hudson River estates, where I'd paint, and she'd write, or we'd sit together drinking cappuccinos on a terrace overlooking the Palisades. Sometimes our work schedules had us going there at different times. I'd be heading home with my canvas tote bag full of painting supplies when, down the woodsy road, I'd see her heading my way, and my heart would swell with pleasure and pride. Here was this lovely woman, my wife, walking toward me. The wind tousled the trees, scattering red and gold autumn leaves across the road. As we drew near we'd pretend not to notice each other, eyes fixed dead ahead, trying not to grin as we passed. After a dozen more steps we'd turn and run to each other.

We didn't have much money, but we lived stylishly, throwing parties to which all our faithful Manhattan friends arrived by car and train, sumptuous events at which P. displayed her culinary skills, and I my latest paintings. Once every other year at least we went to Europe, taking short-term rentals in Rome, Amalfi, Paris, Venice . . . In Venice our apartment was in the Dorsoduro, three blocks from the Guggenheim. I'd leave early in the mornings with my watercolor paints and block, and set myself up at a cafe table, and work through two waiters' shifts with strangers stopping by, saying *Complimenti!* and wishing me *Buon lavoro!* and *Coraggio!* At three o'clock I'd come home to a feast prepared from items P. had bought at the *mercato: insalata di cicoria, frit-*

tata, acciughe, coppa, grana padana . . . I'd uncork the wine. Before lunch I'd unveil my latest painting and accept her verdict. Then we'd toast and eat and drink and make love and nap with the shutters drawn and the sounds of church bells and children playing and doves cooing carrying further and clearer than they did back home.

9.

I've tried to forget the fights, but whenever I remind P. of those days, she remembers them for me. "You don't *remember*?" she'll say, for instance, of our first trip to Rome. "We nearly broke up then. I came this close (gestures) to leaving you." No, I say; I don't remember. But I do. I'd caught a flu, and felt miserable, and wanted to go home. It was January and unseasonably cold. I couldn't warm myself anywhere. The floors of our hotel room were paved with ice. In the bar across the street the patrons huddled in winter coats while an electric heater warmed the barista's feet. It was our first time in Rome together. P. had studied there, in a school near the Forum. She'd so looked forward to our loving the city together. But I couldn't love the fountains, the Pantheon, the Coliseum, the shop windows, the Forum's crumbling relics; I felt too rotten. So we fought: I remember now. On the Spanish Steps and along the Via Condotti and in front of the *Bocca della Verità*, in all the places where I might have wooed her; instead, I blew my nose and coughed and sniffed and grumbled. God, was I miserable! She deserved better, and expected more. Cold or no cold, I owed it to her. Our togetherness in Rome or anywhere was a luxury, but I treated it like an annoyance, as if our trip to Rome were the cause of the common cold. I took it out on Rome, and in taking it out on Rome I took it out on P., since she loved the city, since she identified with and considered it a part of her. She had wanted me to play Gregory Peck to her Audrey Hepburn. Instead, I was grumpy Humphrey Bogart in *Sabrina*.

10.

We fought at home, too. I won't deny it, though it shames me now to think of it. I remember one of our fights. We were headed down to Little Italy to join a group speaking conversational Italian. The group met in a *pastisseria*. I was teaching freshmen composition at a university in New Jersey and hating it. I mentioned the topic of my latest assignment, explaining how most of my students had been confounded by it, wondering how they could have found my elegantly articulated instructions so baffling.

"All I asked them to do," I said while driving us down the West Side Highway, "was summarize a passage of 'The Yellow Wallpaper' from the husband's point of view. Now does that sound so confusing? Does it?"

As she always did when about to side against me, P. paused briefly before responding. "Honestly?" she said.

"Yeah. Honestly."

"I think you may have confused them."

"How?"

"You could have given them a little more information."

"More information about *what*? What other information could they have needed?"

"Well, you know."

"No, as a matter of fact I don't."

"Yes, you do."

"Are you saying that I should define point of view, is that what you're saying? It's not like I haven't done that, you know, like at least a dozen times."

"Maybe you didn't define it clearly."

"What do you mean? Of course I did! I made it as clear as I possibly could. Why would you assume otherwise? I'm not stupid, you know."

On Canal Street the traffic grew thick, with trucks and taxis crowding in on us as I argued my case as if at a criminal trial, cross-examining and then bullying the witness, who tried to be reasonable with me at first, then stewed, then wept, then raged, banging on the steering wheel with her fist and shouting: *I hate you, I hate you, I hate you!*—and I, as sensitive to her anger as I was oblivious to my bullying, threatened to walk out of the car right then and there if she didn't stop. She didn't; I did, slamming the door and running out into that river of blasting horns and bumper-to-bumper traffic, wading up to my chest in that stream of chrome and steel, neon signs in Chinese, and faces leaping out at me from everywhere, adding to my sense of panic and confusion. Where was I going? I didn't know, had no idea.

It was crazy. I was crazy to run out into the street like that, to leave her in the car like that, just completely crazy. When I turned around to go back to the car, having come to my senses, ready to forgive, the car was gone; it had disappeared, swept away in a blur of exhaust fumes. I spent the next hour pushing past pedestrians on crowded street corners, searching every pastry shop and cafe in Little Italy for a group of people speaking bad Italian, convinced that at last I'd gone too far, I'd really done it this time. Oh, God. What an ass I was. What a stupid, miserable ass.

At a *pastisserie* called Bella Luna (P. always did love the moon) I saw the back of her head bobbing in conversation. In spite of countless reiterations by the shop's mirrored walls, she failed to see me standing out there, out in the street with a hangdog look on my face, my eyes raw from crying. I spent another minute or two out there watching her enjoying herself, doing perfectly well without me, thank you very much.

Then I swallowed my tears and went inside and stood behind her, touching her shoulders, saying in a trembling voice (my eyes streaming, my accent superior to all others at that table), *"Mi dispiace; mi dispiace."*

11.

For me, growing up, fighting had been a way of life. My parents fought because they were so different from each other; my brother and I fought because we were so alike. We fought for our separate identities, because we had come to deplore the reflection each of us carried of the other in our mirrored faces, because the only way we could break free of the things that bound us forever was by destroying each other, by smashing the mirror.

Was it any different for P. and I? Were we not as deeply invested in our autonomies? Did we not fight, at least in part, to make it clear to ourselves and to each other that we weren't the same person? Two mirrors trying to smash each other.

12.

Despite our fights, I still loved P. as much as ever: I *adored* her, as a matter of fact. That's the word I used with myself: adored. Her humor, her quirkiness, her love of Campari and anchovies and birds and the Three Stooges and the moon, her smile (no longer crooked; her teeth had been fixed, her former dentist sued); that face that my drawing pen could snare from memory in a dozen swift lines, I knew it that well, not to mention her creativity, her industry, her ambition, her willingness to take risks, from launching a literary journal to starting a catering company. Oh, I admired her. Envied, even. She had more guts, drive, determination than I ever had. Once she set her mind to something, she'd never give up or let go.

13.

Marriage is a dichotomy. Not because the two lovers are necessarily at odds, but because each lover, separately, is his or her own dichotomy. A marriage can be only as harmonious as the lives that combine to make it.

Time does its damage, too. People change, so they say, but what really happens is that we become ever more who and what we always were. Over time the allowances we make for others in the name of marriage, the subtle mechanisms by which we contrive to ignore our irreconcilable differences, break down, until all that remains is the binding force of inertia.

If once upon a time I'd been a hero to P. (as in those days when as a boy I'd volunteered to mow the grass), that time passed. Our marriage had always been unnecessary. But after sixteen years it had become both unnecessary and routine, a habit that only one of us could not imagine breaking. We went on with our lives, sharing them. But also, more and more, we kept to ourselves. I went into my studio, she to her office. We'd spend whole days apart, at different ends of the apartment, bumping into each other only on the way to the kitchen for a cup of tea (she) or espresso (me). We had stopped making love. A residue of too many fights littered our bed, fouled the sheets. The one thing we did together regularly was eat. P. still did most of the cooking. By then she'd come to think of the kitchen as hers, and resented my messing around in there.

She still cooked for me. What did I do for her? Not much. She didn't want my help, never wanted it, really. She wasn't used to being helped by those she loved. She'd always helped *them*. If I forced my help on her, she'd get angry. When her computer went screwy and I tried to fix it, she'd go nuts. It was like getting between a dog and its bone. She couldn't bear my touching her computer or the books on her bookshelves (we kept our books on separate shelves), or giving her financial advice (we kept separate bank accounts, too). Nor did she appreciate my trying to teach her things, pushing my enthusiasms on her. It frustrated me. I wanted her to need me. I felt useless to her, and out of this uselessness I manufactured all kinds of guilt. I could have done so much more for her. Why hadn't I done more? Why didn't I bring home more flowers? Give her spontaneous massages? Draw her baths? Surprise her with small, meaningful gifts and gestures? There'd been a time when I'd done so. Why did I stop? Did I sense that she didn't want my gestures anymore? That the time for gestures had passed?

14.

Once, I tried to get her to go sailing with me. We were staying at a cabin by a lake in New Jersey. Frank, the owner of the property, had a sailboat. We spent the morning, Frank and I, scrubbing the mildew from its hull and repairing the split centerboard. Then Frank showed me the ropes, of which there were a squirming dozen and of which he could only guess at the names. "Let's see now, this one here's the jib line, I think—or is it the halyard? Maybe it's the halyard. No, it must be the jib . . ." By sundown I was tacking solo back and forth across the lake, with Frank waving at me from the porch deck of his camp. Satisfied with my seamanship, I docked the boat and ran up to our cabin, where P. sat in a white wicker chair reading her Mary Higgins Clarke novel. "Come on!" I said, waving toward the dock. "Let's go sailing!"

"You know I don't sail," she said.

"Doesn't matter. I'll teach you."

"I don't want to."

"It's easy. I've been doing it by myself."

"So keep doing it. What do you need me for?"

"Please? Before the wind dies!"

Reluctantly she joined me. (I should state here that P. could not swim, but this only partially accounted for her reluctance; had I asked her to sail with me on dry land she'd have been as unwilling.) We were less than halfway across the lake when she asked to turn back. "Why?" I asked. "Please," she insisted. By then the wind had picked up. Fat gusts blew out over the water. "Just let's go to the end and back. Then I promise you'll never have to go sailing with me again." P. sat at the stern of the boat, rigid in her life vest, looking grim as she gripped the gunwale with both hands. But then as we came about, though I'd warned her to duck, the boom nearly struck her, and she cursed. From there things only got worse. The wind blew harder; the sailboat heeled hard to starboard. I was delighted; she was horrified. She begged me to make it "stop." I tacked us into the wind. As we luffed and drifted into the shallows I said, "You had to spoil it, didn't you? You've never trusted me—ever!" As I said so we ran aground, resplitting the centerboard. It broke right down the middle, into two equal halves.

15.

Do I make myself out to be a complete ass? I was *not* a complete ass, just a partial one. As a husband I had my good points. I was good for a laugh, for one thing. Like many couples we had our running gags, homespun vaudeville routines we'd perform from time to time and that had us in stitches. One had me in the kitchen replicating the opening credit sequence of the original *Star Trek* series using various culinary instruments—a whisk, a potato masher, a spatula—as substitutes for the starship *Enterprise* while I hummed the theme song, and P. attended her *crespelli* or whatever she happened to be cooking. Another gag we called "Great Composers at Home." It consisted of my conducting the *William Tell Overture* or some such symphony with a frenzy of hand gestures and my mouth doing all the instruments as an overeager Rossini himself might have conveyed his masterpiece, hot off the drafting table, to his wife in the privacy of their home. All right, so maybe you had to be there. But we laughed.

16.

Near the end our circle of friends divided, as did our interests. P. no longer wrote plays; for that matter neither did I. Except to eat and sleep, we rarely spent any time together. While she tended her dying father in a Vegas nursing home, I spent a month at a writer's colony in the Berkshires working on a novel. I should have been with her, I guess, but on the other hand I had the feeling she didn't want me there. The next time we saw each other, she told me what I already knew, or ought to have known, or would know retrospectively: that after sixteen years our marriage was through.

17.

According to my dictionary, "abandonment" has two meanings that, at first glance, seem directly opposed. On the one hand it means "to withdraw one's support or help from, especially in spite of duty, allegiance, or responsibility; to desert." On the other it means "to yield completely as to emotions; unbounded enthusiasm, a complete surrender of inhibitions."

P. and I never fully abandoned ourselves for the sake of love. She couldn't abandon herself because she had never done so, not even as a child. And I couldn't because to do so would have been to surrender the identity I'd fought so hard to preserve from my twin. Maybe if only one of us had been less afraid; if one of us had been willing and able to abandon all or part of his or her self, then maybe P. and I would still be married, and I'd probably not be writing this.

As strong as they were for each other, our enthusiasms were always limited by a passion for independence that was stronger.

18.

P. has since moved to another state far away where she lives with a man she went to high school with, a photographer, a struggling artist. *Plus ça change.* I feel no rivalry, no bitterness, not even a hint of jealousy. Since we split I've had friends come up to me and make disparaging remarks to the effect that "she was never right for you anyway"—comments meant to bolster me but that I find offensive. Why, just because she left me, should I now suddenly feel antipathy toward this person I loved for so long? In fact I still love her; in fact I will go on loving her, and to hell with anyone who doesn't think that's a good idea. Were she and her new boyfriend here with me right now,

I'd treat them to breakfast—or a drink, depending on the time of day. That's just how I'm built.

19.

Meanwhile, life goes on. It went on before with P., it goes on now without her. I write with time as my collaborator. Early fall. The leaves of trees here where I'm living have started to turn, the sky a deep blue behind their colors. From time to time I think of P. and when I do, occasionally, a small, silent cry erupts within me —not unlike the cries I used to utter while stuck in traffic on the George Washington Bridge. It's my way of connecting with her again, my way of saying—not to her, but to myself—"Love is real; it endures." And so it does. Wherever P. is, I wish her well. I truly do.

NOTE

1. Contrary to popular myth, passenger ship companies rarely engage in such proceedings.

Alone: Two Types of Solitude

And what do children do when they are left alone? They take up shells and ashes, and they build something!
—*Epictetus*

Solitude: a false councilor who nurses at both breasts the twin infants Egotism and Vanity.
—*Maxime du Camp*

y wife's departure was sudden but not, in retrospect, unplanned or without warning. Her father died, and she had recently turned fifty. Later, friends would describe these as reasons and even portents. That I was away didn't help. While she tended her dying father in a Las Vegas nursing home, I was drafting a novel at a writer's colony. When not writing or swimming in a lake across the street, I careened my Honda Civic along leafy winding Berkshire roads, blasting the same three Beatles songs over and over again on my CD player. The songs were "Ticket to Ride," "Yesterday," and "Help."

Now I'm on my own, alone.

Alone. Note how the word breaks between syllables into article and noun: a, as in one, or a single case out of the multitude; lone as in *loner*. When all else fails turn to etymology. Alone: c.1300, contraction of Old English all ana "all by oneself," from all "all, wholly" + an "one." Similar compounds found in German (allein) and Dutch (alleen). Definition: by ones self, apart from or exclusive of; single; solo; solitary; applied to a person or thing.

The word "alone" itself rings hollow, a two-syllable word where the two syllables deplete rather than fulfill or complement each other.

See: lone, lonely, single, solitary, solo, alien. Only. Exclusively. I. Am. A. Lone.
Alone: "In bad company" (Ambrose Bierce, *The Devil's Dictionary*).

I write this on the shore of another lake, Lake Sinclair, "the cleanest lake in Georgia." I've come here to fulfill a one-year visiting writer appointment at the college in Milledgeville. But I've also come here to be alone. I've rented a house right on the lake, a modest A-frame with an L-shaped loft where I work and sleep, and where my desk faces a wall of triangular windows that look directly out past some pine trees at the water.

Though I've been here less than a week, already I have my routines. I swim twice a day, across the inlet and back, three hundred strokes, at dawn and dusk. Mornings, into the sunrise; evenings, into the sunset. Afternoons, when the sun is too hot, I go out on the dock and just look at the lake.

There are neighbors here, or anyway there are other houses. But so far except for a passing water-skier I have yet to meet or even see another human soul, and I'm glad about that. I don't want company here. The lake is enough company. After thirty-two years in New York City, I've had enough society to last me the rest of my life.

Though the lake is dotted mostly with weekend cottages, through my window I see only trees and water. The distant shore is lined with pine trees, the homes there hidden. It could be a lake in Wisconsin, or in the Klondike. A geography of solitude: that's what I see from my desk. I've seen many such geographies in my time: the craggy islands of the Aegean, the frozen fiords of Norway, the sun-starved villages north of the Arctic Circle . . . But this one belongs to me; it's mine. Unlike the solitude that swept over and nearly drowned me back in New York after my wife left me, that forced solitude that took up with me like an unwanted lover, this one I have chosen for myself.

Here, at last, my solitude and I are happily wed.

Centuries divide my solitude from that of the first historical (Christian) solitary, Paul of Egypt (3rd century B.C.), who, at age sixteen, to escape the Decian persecution, fled to the Egyptian desert at Thebaid to spend the rest of his 113 years in a cave. The man to be known as Saint Paul was but the first in a phalanx of ascetics who fled the chaos and persecutions of the Roman Empire to dwell in the deserts of Egypt. These Desert Fathers were the forerunners of all monks and hermits (from the Greek *eremos*, meaning "desert" or "uninhabited," hence *eremitic* or "desert-dwelling"). The desert drew them not only for the protection it afforded with its caves, but also because it provided the perfect landscape in which to practice the skills of self-discipline as exemplified by Jesus's fasting. Living in the desert forced them to renounce worldly things, and doing so brought them closer to God. Later monks who followed them there (notably Anthony the Great) introduced more formal aspects into the hermetic lifestyle. These included prayer, chanting, and fasting. These rituals in turn developed into cenobitic monasticism (read: "communal deprivation") and flourished in what we today call monasteries.

But apart from saints and holy men, solitude has its proponents. "The wise person will flee the crowd," wrote Montaigne, "endure it if necessary, but given the choice, choose solitude. We are not sufficiently rid of vices to contend with those of others." In perhaps his most famous essay, "On Solitude," Montaigne invokes Lucretius, urging us to "purge our heart[s]" of those impurities imposed by society. "We must take the soul back and withdraw it into itself; that is the real solitude which may be enjoyed in the midst of cities and the courts of kings; but it is best enjoyed alone." In advancing the virtues of solitude, Montaigne makes no case against the company of others. He merely puts companionship in its place, arguing not just for the benefits of solitude, but for it as a necessity, an antidote to too much companionship, society as a means of avoiding or ignoring the kind of solitude that nourishes the soul, an organ fed by the act of contemplation, and for which no other form of nutrition will suffice.

But contemplation depends as much or more on deprivation as on nutrition. Like those plants that grow only in sandy soil, or those spiny fish that thrive only in the darkest ocean depths, the soul thrives not just on what feeds it, but on what it is denied. With the possible exception of Truman Capote, no soul ever thrived at a dinner party. And what are bars, nightclubs, and restaurants but places designed, often with great cunning, to draw the fires of introspection with liquor and loud noise? Add to these time-honored distractions recent electronic innovations, and even when alone today we no longer find ourselves in solitude. We zap our interior lives and put off the inevitable confrontation with ourselves. We'll go to our graves clutching

BlackBerrys and cell phones. If technology is companionship, then I say leave me alone.

Do I equate myself with Paul, or Anthony, let alone Jesus? I'm no saint, nor am I great. Yet there are places where my solitude intersects theirs, ways in which, to paraphrase Tolstoy, "all happy solitaries are solitary in the same way." First, we spend a lot of our time . . . alone. That, of course, is the primary requirement, the foundation on which all of the other attributes of asceticism are built. In his *Outline Teaching on Asceticism and Stillness in the Solitary Life,* Evagrius Ponticus (345– 399), a close observer of the Desert Fathers and one himself near the end of his life, catalogued the ascetic practices of hermits. I need only to run down Evagrius's list of recommendations for hermits to see how closely my own practices align themselves with those of Archimandrite, Athanasius, Anthony, and Augustine:

1. Keep to a Sparse and Plain Diet. Extravagant foods tempt desire. According to Evagrius, "If you have only bread, salt, or water, you can still meet the dues of hospitality." And even without these things you can still make a stranger welcome. For me, the bread is usually vacuum-wrapped packets of Fitness Bread off the shelf at Krogers, my new supermarket, thirty minutes from here by car. This bread I normally eat with peanut butter for breakfast, and for dinner with a mound of vegetables—Swiss chard or broccoli—sauteed and steamed with a dash of soy sauce over carmelized onions. I like how, no matter how impossibly high I pile them in the pan, the leafy vegetables steam down to a modest bowlfull. When in need of protein I'll add a piece of fish or a turkey leg. The rest of my hermetic diet may be summed up in three words: espresso, hot, milk.

2. With Regard to Clothes, Be Content with What Is Sufficient for the Needs of the Body. The wales on the knees of my corduroy trousers have long since been rubbed off. By now most of my cuffs and belt loops are frayed. The splendid cardigans that I bought for and then inherited from my dead papa are so badly pulled and pilled in so many places it must be hard, around the holidays, for strangers to resist hanging Christmas bulbs off of me. I am not truly poor, just too lazy to shop and indifferent to fashion. This was brought home to me one summer when, while visiting a friend in Rome, I was admonished for wearing white socks with leather sandals (to, of all places, the Spanish Steps: even Saint Anthony might have drawn a line there).

3. Do Not Have a Servant. Back in the Bronx, my cleaning lady came every three weeks. She emptied and cleaned my espresso pot, stacked my loose coins and the crumpled receipts on my dresser top, dusted, vacuumed, removed the expired food from my fridge, and generally tidied up (no windows). But since I gave her $500 to assist in her husband's battle with immigration authorities, I didn't consider this a violation. Then again Evagrius warns, "Even if you think that taking a servant would be for the servant's benefit, do not accept it." Now I have no servant, just a landlord who mows the grass.

4. Do Not Associate with Those Who Are Materially Minded and Involved in Worldly Affairs. This I find easy, since materialists don't interest me. I find them boring. Maybe this is because, materially, I haven't done that well for myself, but mostly for lack of trying. Far as I'm concerned, money is the booby prize one gets for having nothing better to do, exemplified by the financial wizards who brought us our current economic mess. For the record, I forgive their shallow greed, but not their ineptitude.

5. If You Find Yourself Growing Strongly Attached to Your Cell, Leave It. In their total withdrawal from society, early Christian monastics (known as anchorites or anchoresses) confined themselves to cells built adjacent to their churches, with the doors ceremonially bricked up and two very small windows—one facing the sanctuary and called a "squint," through which they could hear Mass and receive Holy Communion, and the other through which they would get food and pass—along with their chamber pots—spiritual wisdom to the outside world.[1] Back in the Bronx, I was fond of my apartment, with its view of the blue rainbow bridge and turbulent waters. I like it even more here. I look out at the lake and I'm happy, or anyway content. And since I'm equally fond of my work, writing, I can easily imagine staying here day after day, with no distraction other than a swim now and then, or a paddle in my aluminum canoe. I don't miss people. When the phone rings (rarely), I'm annoyed at first, and even when the caller is some-one I'm glad to hear from, after five minutes I've had enough: I want to go back to my solitude, to my sanctuary. Sometimes I have to force myself to step outside, to walk down to the dock and look at the lake and take note of the world. If I don't do so, come nightfall I'll have cabin fever, and go to bed depressed. We needn't enter social situations to get our souls crushed. A set of walls can do the trick.

6. Do Not Let Restless Desire Overcome Resolution. The Desert Fathers had a word for it: *acedia* (or accedie): in the narrow sense, indolence, sloth, laziness. Not a moral condition, but a psychological one, a bane to monks, hermits, and solitaries through history, exposing them to sinful thought and action. Acedia isn't willful sloth, but a turpitude that endangers the best of intentions. When, weakened by listlessness, a disciple of Abba Moses sought his counsel, Abba Moses replied, "Go back to your cell and pray." Acedia weakens resolve and fills men with doubt. John Cassian described this condition referred to as the "noonday devil" as a state of inertness incapable of bearing spiritual fruit. Physical labor was recommended as a remedy. Saint Paul wove baskets out of palm leaves; I paint, write, swim. Acedia plagues the novice more than it does the experienced solitary. As a child I was always bored—this in spite of having a twin brother at my disposal. I wonder now if my boredom wasn't a form of acedia, if already as a child I wasn't experiencing a dose of the "dark night of the soul," if I wasn't bedeviled. Burton's melancholy, Kierkegaard's angst, Sartre's nausea, Camus's existential revolt, Mersault's alienation, my child-hood fevers of boredom: are these not all acedia by different names? Whatever drives us out of ourselves (out of our cells), and away from integrity—that's acedia. It is the antithesis of discipline, its cure.

7. Do Not Hanker After Fine Foods and Deceitful Pleasures. "Eating with others," writes Evagrius, "carries the danger of being offered fine foods that provoke desire. Such invitations should be declined." Here in Milledgeville there are approximately three decent restau-rants: one Japanese, one Italian, and a bar. So far I have been to the bar and the Italian place. I dislike eating in restaurants. As indifferent as I am to fine foods, I am obsessed with the quality (or lack thereof) of my surroundings. Thus I detest most restaurants, with their forced chic and volume as a substitute for mirth. I hate canned music of all kinds, and resent even more that to avoid it I must pay the premium exacted by restaurants that don't offer it. (Do the rascals who shuck sound systems give kickbacks to establishments that agree to riddle their ceilings with loudspeakers?) Dim lighting annoys me, as do waiters who reach over your meal to pour your wine or replenish your ice water, and busboys hovering vulture-like over waning meals. The "pleasures" of fine dining rarely seduce me.

8. Provide Yourself with Such Work for Your Hands as Can Be Done, if Possible, Both during the Day and Night, So As Not to Burden Anyone. Plaiting reed baskets was the preferred occupation of the Desert Fathers, the busy work that best fit Evagrius's criteria. I plait essays and stories out of words and sentences. Is it not the same? In their time the Desert Fathers would entrust some disciple or agent to take their baskets into town to sell them at the marketplace, and return with provisions of flour, salt, and other humble staples procured with the proceeds. My marketplace is more amorphous, as are my proceeds. The baskets I weave from words get sold mainly to small press publishers and even smaller literary journals for equally diminutive reimbursement. My paintings also sell at prices modest to a fault. This, too, would have suited Evagrius, who tells hermits not to haggle: "When buying or selling you can hardly avoid sin. So in either case be sure to lose a little in the transaction." Done.

Have I made my solitude too appealing? But let me not kid you or myself by pretending there's nothing nasty about it, especially the kind imposed against one's wishes. When unwanted, solitude can be frightening. Two years have passed since, yet I still wake up some mornings filled with the shaky memory of how it felt to learn that my wife was no longer my wife. Friends worried about me—with reason. Asked, "How are you?" I told the truth, that I felt as if I'd had my right leg amputated without the benefit of anesthesia. I cried. Alone in the shower with the lights turned off, my tears mingled with public water. I kept saying to myself, "She's gone," but how can a verb, any verb, do justice to a negation? She simply and emphatically *wasn't*. Before

I worked up the resolve to toss it down the garbage chute, the left-over acorn squash from the last meal she'd cooked for us grew a furry mantle of mold. I lived automatically, a robot attending obligations while contemplating bleak alternatives. My Bronx apartment was by the Henry Hudson Bridge: from my window, a stunning blue rainbow of steel from which others had met their ends. I'd see the blue police boats at night combing the agitated waters with searchlights. What "alone" means at its worst: no damn bloody good reason to live. One may take cold comfort in the musings of Montaigne or Voltaire ("The happiest of lives is a busy solitude.") or Picasso ("Without great solitude, no serious work is possible.") or Goethe ("One can be nurtured in society; one is inspired only in solitude"). Such musings aside, we who spend most of our days alone know that whatever else our solitude makes us, we are bloody wretches, too. Aristotle hit closer to home when he said, "He who is unable to live in society, or who has no need because he is sufficient unto himself, is either a beast or a god." John Billings, too, hit the nail on the head when he said, "Solitude is a good place to visit, but a poor place to stay."

No matter how often and convincingly I tell myself that I have chosen my "new" solitude to replace and obliterate the one forced on me by fate, the fact is that I chose only its location and other trimmings: the dock, the lake, the canoe. The solitude is in me, put there partly by a wife who did not want to be a wife anymore. It is nothing to brag about. I fell into it as one falls into a ditch. And let us not lose sight of that nose-picking wretch, of the last time we changed the bedclothes, of beans eaten cold from a can, of towels redolent of bordellos, of used socks rerolled and replaced in the dresser drawer, of the secret fingernail clipping repository behind the couch, of the caged, frightened beast with his back to the sweating wall. Nor should we dismiss those sublime moments when, padding in socks and sweatpants from room to room, we are amazed by just how many rooms there are, and how emptily they yawn—as if no one lives there, not even he who pads there. Like the proverbial tree, with no audience to bear witness to our lives, we neither flourish nor fall. Only to the extent that we touch others do we live in the strictest sense of that term, in the sense that we enjoy life to its fullest; otherwise we—along with the inspirations, revelations, and inventions arrived at in solitude—merely *exist*.

Perhaps in reading these words you complete the circuit of my life. But one way or another, to be lived a life must be shared.

Before ending this essay, I must invoke one more solitary, the greatest of all, and without a doubt the most wretched, the prototypical Noble Savage and Beautiful Loser: Diogenes of Sinope, who made it his life's goal to "deface" societal mores and customs, rolling his bathtub/home along the streets of Athens and barking at people like a dog. Diogenes who, it was said, forswore all material comforts, who on seeing a peasant boy drink water from the hollow of his hands, smashed the wooden bowl that was his only possession. Having heard that Socrates defined man as a "featherless biped," he stormed Plato's academy, grasping a plucked chicken, and proclaimed, "Behold man!" When Alexander came upon him gazing attentively down on a pile of human bones, the founder of Cynicism explained, "I'm looking at the bones of your father but cannot tell them from those of a slave." When a stranger rebuked him for masturbating into the Agora, he replied, "Ah—if only I could ease my hunger as readily by rubbing my belly!"

I evoke Diogenes here to show that the solitary wretch and the prophet may be one and the same. No less a figure than Alexander thought so. Legend has it that Alexander, thrilled to meet the fabled Diogenes, asked if he might do the philosopher a favor. "Yes," naked Diogenes replied. "Stand out of my sunlight!" Diogenes made a virtue of his "doggish" behavior; indeed, the word *cynic* derives from the Greek *kynikos*, the adjectival form of *kyon*: "dog." Diogenes maintained that those who lived artificially—that is, according to the standards of a society based on hypocrisy—would do well to study the living habits of dogs. True (he pointed out), dogs are not especially contemplative, but neither do they engage in small talk or covetousness. Nor are they petty. Like the dogs he emulated, Diogenes barked at suspect mankind, and in so doing exposed society as a regressive farce. In Diogenes, solitary wretch and holy prophet were perfectly wedded: saint as bum.

Wretched or saintly, my solitude brings me a step closer to eternity. In this we solitudes are all prophets. The societal outlines that limit others blur, turn porous. In solitude the useless ego dissolves, opening us up to the infinite. Birds sing louder, the sun shines brighter, every thunderstorm turns us into King Lear wandering the desolate heath in Act 3 of his play. A spider web speaks volumes. Solitude is poetry; companionship prose. "One does not find solitude," Margaret Duras wrote, "one creates it. Solitude is created alone. I have created it."

Here, by this lake in Georgia, so have I.

NOTE

1. The word "hermetic," by the way, meaning "completely sealed," doesn't share the same root as "hermit." It comes from the Greek *Hermes*, the god of science and art, who was equated by alchemists with the Egyptian god Thoth, inventor of airtight glass tubes and possessed of a magical ability to seal treasure chests to prevent people from accessing their contents. "Hermit," on the other hand, comes to us from the Old French *heremite* by way of Medieval Latin *herēmīta* by way of Late Latin *erēmīta*, probably from the Greek *erēmiā* (desert), or from erēmos: solitary.

The Swimming Pool

Normally I like to walk to the pool. It's less than two miles, mostly through the woods, and I like seeing the sky snared by tree branches overhead while feeling hard pavement under my feet. But the weather these past two weeks of September has been rainy, and though now the clouds have parted, and the day has turned sunny and bright, at nine o'clock this morning through the fog I couldn't see the blue bridge outside my window, and the weather report said showers, so I drove.

I like swimming in the rain. I also prefer to swim in the morning, when it's cool and quiet. I get up at six or seven, spend a few hours at the computer, and then, when my brain starts to get blurry, put my body to work. Even in August, at the height of the season, usually no one is at the pool before noon.

It's not that I don't like people; I do. But for me swimming has always been a private experience. When I swim, it's as if the water and I are having a private conversation, or engaging in that other type of intercourse, something not to be shared with spectators.

I park my car on the edge of the small paved road that leads to an enclave of well-to-do homes named for the stream that courses mainly underground[1] between them. Once upon a time the pool belonged to one of these homes, the biggest of them, a Hudson River gothic with carved stone gargoyles guarding its mansard roof. Twenty years ago the aging couple who owned it decided the upkeep was too much, so they cut a deal with the community, who formed a private pool club, which now accepts outsiders.

There are no posted hours. A combination lock lets me in whenever I choose. I can swim at six in the morning, or at midnight. With my gear in a bag slung over my shoulder, I give the hasp a jerk, let the chain fall, and let myself in.

It's an old-fashioned, cement pool: no glittering blue ceramic tiles, no fancy mosaics or aqua bottom, just rough concrete poured sometime during Prohibition, with two holes and a streak of rust where there used to be a diving board. Though cordoned off by a chain-link fence topped with spools of barbed wire, you can barely see the fence, the ivy has grown so thick, as have the hedges and trees, including the mulberry tree swinging high overhead, a tree whose small, hairy fruits plop into the water from June through July with a patter like rain: berries that, bleached by the chlorinated water, turn white as grubs. The earthworms that come out at night to drink the chlorinated water turn the same sickly white after they die and drown; they look like tapeworms at the bottom of the pool. I've seen all types of dead things in that water, from mice trapped in the filter baskets to a drowned raccoon floating with its mask facedown over the deep end. I don't mind. Dead things are part of life. I skim them out with the long-handled strainer and toss their corpses into the garbage pail. One must learn to live with the dead.

But I like anything natural that has to do with the water, that tries to turn the pool into a pond. Where I grew up, in Connecticut, I always swam in lakes and ponds. I swam with fish and snakes and snapping turtles; with algae, weeds, and silt; with the waste products of woodland creatures, of deer, birds, skunks, possum, ducks, and geese. Not once did I ever think of germs. I took it for granted that I was as foreign to the water as anything, more, that nothing dirtier than me had swum in it. And maybe it was this attitude that spared me, but I never got an ear, eye, or throat infection. Never.

Once, a family of mallards took up residence in our pool, a mother and her six ducklings. Jorn, president of the pool club, said he'd have to get rid of them. Some members protested. Those ducks had every bit as much right to be there as we did, we said. Ours was not the majority view. For a few weeks we all swam together, the ducks and I: or we swam around each other, with them quacking up a storm. The local paper sent a photographer; the ducklings made page one. Mothers brought their children to see. "Look!" they said, pointing through the chain links. But the lifeguard who had to scrape the ducks' droppings off the pavement complained. And then there was the health inspector. Eventually the six ducklings disappeared one by one, snatched by hawks, or waddling off to be preyed upon by raccoons, cats, and dogs. With them all gone, their mother flew away.

But just now there are no ducks or people. I'm alone. I look at the water. A beautiful pale green, like the glass infrared filters my papa used in his inventions. A tattered blanket of gray mist hangs over it. Late in the season, when few use the pool, the chlorine levels are kept low. The water tastes cool and sweet, like mint candy.

I get a chair from the shed and sit to untie my shoes. My swimsuit is already on. I yank off my shirt, climb out of and fold my pants, snap on my silicone bathing cap (necessary to keep the hair out of my eyes), take up my goggles, and walk to the shallow-end ladder.

I prefer not to jump in. I prefer to enter calmly, to remain in harmony with this peaceful morning, and save the splashing for my swim. I don't like violence of any kind: violent movements, violent sounds, violent emotions. I hate movies where the plots are made of gunfire and explosions. I don't care for violent sports, for football or hockey or even basketball. I'm not drawn to bodies colliding any more than I am to highway accidents. I even disapprove of children who scream when they play. To the parents of such children I'm tempted to say, Why do you let your child scream that way? Why must he or she play so violently? Why not teach him or her that pleasure need not be so *loud?* I'm tempted, but of course I don't; I know better. Those parents would see me as a bitter man who hates children, or worse, a misanthrope intent on eliminating all forms of human pleasure. But discipline and pleasure are not mutually exclusive. On the contrary, they're linked. Without discipline there can be no deep or lasting pleasure. Maybe I feel this way because as a child I wasn't sufficiently disciplined, and now as an adult I'm forced to make up with grim determination for that which my parents failed to give me.

Anyway, I don't jump into the pool.

Another reason I don't jump: because when one jumps into a body of cold water, the body goes into shock, the heart beats wildly, partly in response to the shock, but also as a way of trying to maintain the body temperature by pumping blood to the extremities. One becomes breathless, which is no way to start a long swim. And I always swim a mile. That's forty-four laps, or eighty-eight lengths.

Nonswimmers ask me, When you swim, don't you ever worry that you might have a heart attack? Being almost forty-seven, the thought has crossed my mind. But it doesn't worry me. In fact I know no swimmers who think of heart attacks. On Labor Day weekend, my friend O, who just turned seventy, swam across the Hudson River with me, a distance of well over a mile through treacherous currents and the wakes of big barges. A heart attack was the last thing on either of our minds. Swimmers don't think of *drowning*, they think about *swimming*. I think of the water and my body's attitude toward it, of my hand entering in front of me, of twisting my head just as the fingers break the surface, of thrusting, kicking, the next breath, and the next, and so on. Or I think of nothing to do with swimming, some problem in need of solving, that agent who has my manuscript: Why hasn't she read it yet? When will she read it? Why is she taking so long? That student whose work I critiqued too harshly last week: Did I break her spirit? Will she return to class? Of a heart—not my own heart, but my father-in-law's—which needs a new valve, and of my wife's decision to fly to Las Vegas and stay there through his recovery, which could take weeks. These are my thoughts when swimming laps. I drown *in them*.

But I try not to let my mind wander. If I do, I forget what lap I'm on, and then must think back to the last certain lap, and start over. Those are the rules. I made them up and I can break them, I guess, but I don't. It's part of the discipline that unlocks pleasure. So I limit my thoughts, restrict them to subjects suggested by the numbers one through eighty-eight.

I step down the ladder.

There's always that first shock of the toe tasting the water's coolness. People who aren't swimmers should know this: that unless kept at 89.6 degrees or warmer, all water feels cool to the touch. Even at 89 degrees, if the air is warmer, the water feels relatively cold. And on a very hot day, with the sun beating down and our skin temperature reaching the nineties, that first touch of water can indeed be shocking. But once immersed and moving, the shock wears off; the water "heats up" and even starts to feel unpleasantly warm. For this reason I dislike swimming in indoor pools, where those in charge invariably keep the water temperature at a balmy 82 degrees at the behest of the old farts who constantly complain, whatever its temperature, that the water's too cold. These are not swimmers. These are people who get into the water and do nothing. They stand in the shallows jabbering, or do a languid backstroke, or do water aerobics—next to speed walking the silliest exercise on earth. Or they do what they are pleased to call swimming. The strokes people come up with! Had I not seen them with my naked eyes I'd deny their existence. Lame dog paddles and limp sidestrokes that barely get them to the other side of the pool, strokes that take back with one arm what they give with the other, that negate each other so the swimmer ends up swimming in place, or worse, backward: I've *seen* it. I've seen people who look as though they're going to drown at any moment: in fact, what they do is closer to drowning than to swimming, and it's only by some miracle that they survive. Once, I had the odd pleasure of watching an elderly woman spend close to an hour getting from one end of a small pool to the other, waving the water away in a gesture that seemed to say with each stroke, *To hell with you*, while dragging her legs behind her like the corpse of a murder victim. I'd already finished my swim and was mesmerized both by exhaustion and by the sight of this creature making her tortuous way across the pool, fascinated by whatever force it was that kept her afloat against the laws of physics, and by her perseverance, which never flagged, and which I felt could have kept her swimming like that forever, until doomsday. It was a strange mix of emotions. On the one hand I admired her: she was dogged and determined and exemplified the human imperative to push onward against overwhelming odds. On the other hand she disgusted me. She was an eyesore, a travesty, a disgrace. I resented having to share my pool with her. When I swim, if I must share a pool, let me share it with mermaids and dolphins, or their human equivalents, not with some waterlogged, wheezing old hag.

But nonswimmers are of no concern to me here, now. Here and now I don't have to worry about old hags or noisy children, or any of all of the unpleasant categories in between. Here and now it's just me and the water, my water, my liquid lover.

(It is as a jealous and possessive lover that I insult an old woman whose only crime against humanity is that of swimming ungracefully. But possessive lovers know neither guilt nor shame.)

I climb in. I put one leg down, then the other. Another mistake nonswimmers make: they think too much about getting into the water; they psyche themselves out. They sit with their legs dangling and the hot sun baking their shoulders, convincing themselves that when they get hot enough they'll go in, but really they're just stalling, delaying the inevitable. When all bets are off, they plunge, scream, and splutter, crying, "Oh my God, it's *so cold!*" No way to get in the water.

A few weeks ago I encountered someone, a young woman, in this very predicament. Jamie, her name. She sat there dangling her feet, waiting for the hot sun to inspire her. I said to her, "Jamie, may I give you a piece of advice? When you contemplate an action you know you're going to take, then the thought process itself becomes a substitute for action, and is, therefore, self-defeating.

"Here is my advice," I continued. "Climb into the shallow water and stand there. Take a deep breath, and then release it. Then take another deep breath, hold it for a moment, and then let it out in a big, long sigh, *Ahhhh*—as if you're experiencing an extremely pleasant form of release, I won't say which form; I'll leave that to your imagination." (Jamie is fourteen, and though I'm told that young people today are precocious in matters of sex, still, I was not about to enter *those* waters.) "While letting out the sigh," I went on, "don't jump but let yourself glide, ever so gently, into the water, like so—." I demonstrated for her, then stood up again. "The point is to be as relaxed as possible, to not let your muscles tense up, to disarm that mechanism in your body that prepares it for a shock, that says Beware: danger! and turns every cell into a soldier on full alert, ready for battle. You need to disarm that mechanism, what psychologists call the fight-or-flight instinct, to say to yourself, This is nothing, or better still, This is so peaceful and lovely! And go in with that attitude. Try it!"

Jamie tried it. She took two deep breaths and, sighing, let herself slip into the water. Afterward I said, "Well?"

"It worked!" she said.

"There. See?"

I felt good about that. It's not often that I talk to young people, and less often that they listen. At rare moments like this I wish I had children.

Now it's my turn. I wade in up to my belly, then put on and adjust my goggles. I take a deep breath, then another. Ahhhh! And I'm in.

As my ritual, I swim gently to the other side, not wetting my head yet, my strokes tentative, even a bit feeble. Then I swim back, still slowly, this time putting my face in the water. When I reach the other side, then and only then will I start swimming in earnest.

When I was five or six years old, my papa would take me and George, my brother, to a swimming hole at the edge of the town under a railway trestle where other fathers brought their children to

fish and swim. My brother and I would already have jumped into the
muddy water, from which I'd look up and see my father, by then already in his fifties (our mother was his third and final wife) going in
ever so slowly, rubbing handfuls of brown water over his skinny arms
and his gray, shallow chest, making painful noises—like he was being
tortured. Meanwhile, around me, other fathers dove and splashed.

I'd yell, "Jump, Papa, jump!"

Only he wouldn't; he couldn't, he said. He was *too old.* That was his
excuse. Too old: those words tolled in my head like a cracked bell, like
a death knell.

Please, Papa!

But it was no use; I could never get my father to jump. I think of
that now, crossing back to the shallow end of the pool, and feel a sudden wave of sympathy for my papa (three years dead) who swam long
before I did, doing his sidestroke/scissorkick well into his eighties,
spouting like a porpoise with each stroke, making hardly a splash, he
swam so peacefully. But he wouldn't jump. And now I, too, refuse to
jump. How like Papa I've become!

But I'm no gentle swimmer. I like to swim fast, very fast, fast as I
can, zipping through the water like a torpedo. One last adjustment to
my goggles and I'm off, counting, *three-four, three-four* with each stroke,
exhaling on the *four.* Swimming is all about breathing, about knowing
when to breathe, about moving just the right amount of air in and out
of your lungs to give the blood in your muscles exactly what it needs,
not a drop more or less. Even experienced swimmers know that, with
the slightest alteration of their stroke, they can become breathless,
how easily they can be thrown off their timing, how when only a fraction out of sync, they find themselves gasping. On the other hand,
once learned, the science of breathing becomes second nature: the
body turns into a well-lubricated breathing machine. The arms attach
themselves to the lungs like the rods that connect cylinder to wheels
on a locomotive. I chug through the water . . .

I've always been attracted to water. I was born midway through February, an Aquarius, but I don't think that has anything to do with
it. I think man's love for water is in his body, which is—what's the
figure?—75 percent water? In *Ulysses* there is that beautiful passage
where Bloom, returning from the tap where he has filled an iron kettle,

broods on a question posed for him by the anonymous, omniscient narrator, namely: "What in water did Bloom, waterlover, drawer of water, watercarrier returning to the range, admire?"

Its universality: its democratic equality and constancy to its nature in seeking its own level; its vastness in the ocean of Mercator's projection: its unplumbed profundity in the Sumdam trench of the Pacific exceeding 8,000 fathoms; the relentlessness of its waves and surface particles visiting in turn all points of its seaboard: the independence of its units: the variability of states of sea: its hydrostatic quiescence in calm: its hydrokinetic turgidity in neap and spring tides; its subsidence after devastation: its sterility in the cirumpolar icecaps, arctic and antarctic . . .

The passage goes on for another full page. It's interesting to note that among the four Aristotelian elements (air, earth, fire, water), only water can lay claim to any verb or adjective you toss at it (including *toss*). Water which—according to Hesse—"flows to fill whatever form it finds," that *rushes, rolls, folds, drips, spins, glides, bends, leaps, sprays, gushes*—that can be *wet, cold, cloudy, clear, blue, black, green, white, gray, hot, sticky, sharp, pellucid, translucent, limpid, soft, hard, muddy, murky, dense, thin, heavy, light, frozen, stiff, thrilling, cunning, playful*—but this is too easy. There's no shortage of watery nouns either: *sea, lake, river, pond, estuary, delta, port, harbor, creek, marsh, drink, shower, rain, snow, slush, frost, hail, humidity, bucket, bath, toilet, sink, well, fountain* . . . What's not already watery in the world can almost always be made so: witness a *wet smirk* or a *watery glance*, a plot *soaked in sentiment, waves of sadness, a storm of controversy,* or (my) *cloudy destiny.* Applied to air or rocks, *delight* and *terror* make no sense, but add water and you get a fountain, or a typhoon. Like a fool, water rushes in. Unlike one, it rushes out, too. Like James Bond, water always survives. In many ways it is the perfect contemporary hero: a fearless, hedonistic sensualist: the spy with [ice] water in his veins, Neptune with a license to kill. But water is both hero and heroine, the fair damsel, also the *femme fatale* who murders her paramours, who drowns them in their own reflections, then on to the next. Call *me* a fool, but even knowing this I can't seem to keep my arms from her. No love fills me like hers; there is no other body I'd rather touch, my flesh an excuse for hers. Water is my desire, my dream. I come from water, and given my druthers will go back to water. I'll die on the bottom of a lake somewhere, where the grass carp will feed off the algae that sprout from my skull sockets, where no one will find me but the *vodoni*, the Water Master, with his trident and green hair, when he returns in the Spring to tidy up his watery basement.

Eleven-twelve, eleven-twelve, eleven-twelve. The numbers roll through my head like waves, they swim alongside me like bright, tropical fish, colored by synesthesia, the *eleven-twelve* fish striped black and mauve; the *thirteen-fourteen* fish brown and yellow, and so on. But there are other games to keep me from losing count. For numbers one through eighty-eight I have mastered association. You give me a number, I'll spit back an association. Go on! Five: my age for my first trip to New York City with my father. I remember the Empire State Building lit up at night and ocean liners lined up at their berths, black hulls and massive red funnels. We stayed at the Hotel Paris on West 96th Street. There was a pool in the basement. I'm told I almost drowned there. There was no lifeguard on duty and my papa wasn't paying attention (probably flirting with some woman). Thirteen: my turn to watch someone drown. We'd gone swimming at the town reservoir, my friend Chris and I, when these two boys in a fishing boat saw us, black boys who'd come probably from Danbury or Norwalk to fish. Seeing us swim they decided to give it a try. It didn't dawn on them, apparently, that swimming was a learned skill. I watched as they flailed and cried for help; I thought they were joking, at first. Then one of the two boys went under and failed to reappear. By the time I got there I was out of breath. I dove deep, but all I saw was darkness and bubbles, black bubbles. An hour later as Chris and I and the other boy watched, men in black scuba suits pulled the boy's body onto the embankment. The dead boy's face was a strange purple color, like an eggplant. Later at the police station the town medical examiner—nicknamed "Dr. Numbnuts" for his habit of prodding our testicles during routine examinations—pointed his prodding finger at me, said it was all my fault. You'll have to live with this for the rest of your life, he said. Nineteen: the first two digits of the century in which I was born and in which I have lived four-fifths of my life. Also the year I started college and art school, late since I took two years off to travel and earn money driving a furniture truck. That was the first year when, looking into the medicine chest mirror of my dormitory bathroom, I concluded I was going bald (N.B. I still have all my hair). You will note that, for the purpose of the exercise, the associations need not be memorable or even noteworthy; in fact, the more trivial the better. Twenty-one: my first major hangover. For my birthday my dorm mates fixed me a batch of gin and tonics, and when the gin and tonics ran out they switched to rum and Cokes. I woke up with a Henna-headed coed lying on the floor next to me and no idea how she got there. I *crawled* to the bathroom and threw up. *Twenty-two, twenty-three* . . . Twenty-four: James Dean was my hero. I wanted to be just like him, to groan and writhe in Technicolor across a CinemaScope screen; I failed because I wasn't as good-looking, or as good an actor, and because I lived to be . . . *Twenty-five* . . . *Twenty-six* . . . *twenty-seven* . . . *twenty-eight* . . . Water flows through this life of mine, a stream of moments, an ocean of memories, a pool of dreams, thoughts, desires. I'm never as alive as I am here, now, swimming. The past doesn't stop me; I swim through it. Neither does the future bother me. My worries sink to the bottom of the pool where they don't touch me anymore. I forget that my papa is dead, that my mother and I argue, that my brother is far away and that when we see each other we are happy for a time but then we also fight, or revert to the nasty teasing we engaged in when we were younger, those relics of our unhappy childhoods. I forget the small betrayals of my body, the tinnitus that howls in my right ear night and day, a silver needle of sound threaded through my brain, the peptic ulcer that gnaws at my duodenum, a prostate the size of an orange that wakes me up twenty times to pee at night. I forget the Twin Towers, and the fact that it is now officially dangerous to utter the words *lovely day*. I forget that I have no career to speak of (unless you call pushing this pen around for no income a *career*), that my phone rarely rings, and that, however much I crave company, I'm also bored to tears by most people, who for their part think I'm too intense. I forget that woman from Sweden, I won't tell you her name, the full-bosomed (some would say buxom; not me) blonde with whom I kept up a correspondence: long, intimate letters that for me were lovemaking and confession, with her my mistress and my priest. Then her letters stopped. There followed a postcard: *I'm sorry, Peter, but this cannot go on*. It couldn't. I learned later that she'd had a baby, that our "affair of letters" had been her last grasp at romance, and doomed from the start. I felt used. This feeling, too, water—the universal solvent—dissolves.

I even forget that time in Montreal, alone up there following the death of my swimming coach, a close friend who never did approve of my glide, when I stood next to a sidewalk café, watching this woman—another blonde (why, when I've always preferred brunettes?) circle the rim of her white wine glass with the tip of her index finger, producing a noise which in pitch almost perfectly replicated my tinnitus—what the French call "teaching a glass to sing." I stood watching her, forgetting myself, unaware of any unsavory or weird intention on my part, until a waiter, a strapping black fellow with dreadlocks down to his shoulders, called out to me. *Que faites-vous?*

Excusez moi? Vous parlez avec moi? (My French was lousy; still is.)

Que faites-vous?

Oh, I said. *J'attend mon ami.* (I'm waiting for a friend: a lie; I'd never been more alone in my life.)

You wait for a friend? He spoke English now, with a roughness in his voice and a glare in his eyes. I felt like a private at boot camp being stared-down by his drill sergeant.

Oui. J'attend mon ami.

I am having complaints of you.

Pardonnez-mois?

My customers they complain. The ladies they say that you stare at them.

Moi?

Oui, vous: vous, vous, monsieur!

But I haven't done anything!

You stare and they think that you are strange and I think so too. Go away—*attendez* some other place.

Yes, all right, but—

Enough. Go now or I call an *agent*.

I walked to a nearby park and sat on a bench beside a man who read his latest poem to me. I couldn't tell if the poem was any good. While he read it to me I thought to myself, *Fine . . . fine . . . fine . . .* Canada had been a mistake; I should have gone to Europe, to Italy, or France, to some little town with medieval towers of stone. I could have brought my writing or my paints. I should have gone somewhere with water, where I could swim; where no one would suspect me of anything. But it was too late, there was no turning back.

Forty-seven, forty-eight, forty-nine . . .

Over these and other dead memories my body swims back and forth, back and forth, a lawnmower mowing a watery lawn. Did I mention that water is the fundamental precondition of all life? That everything from gold to vegetables derives from the Cosmic Juice? That the world as we know it has, according to at least one myth, sprung from a seed brought up from the bottom of the primordial ocean by the Earth Diver, that "water gives life to ten thousand things and does not strive? It flows in places men reject and so is like the Tao" (Lao-Tzu), that Plato's water atoms are *icosahedra*, that is, shaped like garnets, that water is the Johnny Boy of liquids ("What are you rebelling against?" "What've ya got?") its molecules crooked, bent at 104 degrees, which may explain why, as they say, water has memory: it holds memories in its crooks.

Sixty-three, sixty-four . . .

A slate-blue cloud drifts over the pool. I hear the winding pule and realize the smoke is from a gasoline engine. A lawnmower has started in the neighbor's yard. I suck carbon monoxide, cough, gasp, and curse, my oaths packaged in bubbles. I see them floating up to the surface to explode as cartoon balloons, animating my animosity. When the smoke clears, I've reached lap number sixty-six, as in "Get Your Kicks On," as in Nelson Riddle's keyboard-tickling piano theme, sure to preoccupy me now for at least the next two laps, my body no longer a locomotive, but a baby-blue '64 Corvette, plying a watery thoroughfare linking troubled lives and dramatic episodes, Martin Milner at the wheel.

And really, if you think about it, what I've been saying all along is that this pool is a sort of roadway (I think of John Cheever's astonishing story "The Swimmer," of Needy Merrill making his way across a trail of pools and cocktails linking memories and loss) . . .

Seventy-one, seventy-two . . .

On the antique oak music stand that serves as a copyholder, I keep a postcard sent to me a few years ago by a man I used to see as my therapist. The card shows a man diving off a column into a pool of green water, and comes from a fresco in the Tomb of the Diver in Paestum. And though he never said as much, I suspect that Fred sent the card to me for the following reasons: a) because I'm a fan of Etruscan art, b) because I'm an avid swimmer, and c) because *Le Plongeur* (what the French call him) bears an uncanny resemblance to me. Anyway it's how I like to picture myself, and how I often feel, here, alone at the swimming pool. As I churn through my final laps (*eighty-five, eighty-six* . . .) a heady sense of divinity washes over me, a sense that I might live eternally under God's grace, like Adam before the expulsion, that He has chosen me, one of his left-handed creatures (of all people) to dwell forever in his Kingdom. All I have to do is swim, and keep swimming. Forever.

Eighty-seven . . . eighty-eight.

I stand, pull off my goggles, wipe away the soreness they have left on my face with a handful of water. As I climb the ladder my legs quiver slightly. I feel a fresh tautness in my muscles, as if someone has turned a screw in there, or jolted them with electricity. I peel off my bathing cap, stand under the shower nozzle, my feet planted in a ring of ivy. As the water sluices down my face, neck, and shoulders I feel light-headed with a sense of accomplishment and relief. I've done my laps; I've waded through the underground stream of memory and association; I've mucked out its Augean stable, rinsed it out in the pool's mint-green water. The fog has lifted; the air is clear. The world looks fresher, gentler, clearer now. I'm not bothered by it. In fact, it seems a rather benign place, a decent place, even a kind place.

Sometimes, when I've done my laps, I let myself do something I seldom do, lie back in the water, dead-man's float, looking up at an impeccably blue sky, seeing it wreathed by tree branches. I imagine myself in a pool in the middle of an Amazonian rainforest, alone, alone, so terribly, so blissfully, so perfectly alone.

NOTE

1. Like Acheron, woeful river of the underworld.

sightline books

The Iowa Series in Literary Nonfiction